Translation and History

This concise and accessible textbook is a comprehensive introduction to the key historical aspects of translation. Six chapters cover essential concepts in researching and writing the history of translation and translation as history.

Theo Hermans presents and explains fundamental issues and questions in a clear and lively style. He includes numerous examples and case studies and offers suggestions for further reading. Four of the six chapters take their cue from ideas about historiography that are alive among professional historians. They pay attention to the role of narrative, to the emergence of transnational, transcultural, global and entangled history, and to particular fields such as the history of concepts and memory studies. Other topics include microhistory, actor–network theory and book history.

With an emphasis on methodology, how to do research in translation history and how to write it up, this is an essential text for all courses on translation history and will be of interest to anyone working in translation theory and methodology.

Theo Hermans is Emeritus Professor at the Centre for Translation Studies, University College London (UCL), and the author of, among other titles, *Translation in Systems* (1999, reissued as a Routledge Translation Classic in 2019) and *The Conference of the Tongues* (2007).

'Theo Hermans has written the book we need in the wake of the historiographic boom in Translation Studies and the translational turn in the humanities. Drawing deeply on teaching and research experience, this textbook avoids all pedagogical pedantism and simplified manual-like instructions for research. Instead, it provides inspiration for future researchers to ask decisive questions about the field: how is translation history even possible, what translations can teach us about history, and what historiography has to offer translation research.'

Lavinia Heller, *Johannes Gutenberg-Universität Mainz, Germany*

'A fascinating study of the significant role played by translation in history, particularly in relation to narrative and memory. The book makes a new and innovative contribution to the disciplines of both history and translation studies and provides an invaluable source of material for postgraduate students and established researchers alike.'

Judith Inggs, *University of the Witwatersrand, South Africa*

Translation and History

A Textbook

Theo Hermans

 Routledge
Taylor & Francis Group

LONDON AND NEW YORK

Cover image: Getty Images

First published 2022
by Routledge
4 Park Square, Milton Park, Abingdon, Oxon OX14 4RN

and by Routledge
605 Third Avenue, New York, NY 10158

Routledge is an imprint of the Taylor & Francis Group, an informa business

British Library Cataloguing-in-Publication Data
A catalogue record for this book is available from the British Library

Library of Congress Cataloging-in-Publication Data
Names: Hermans, Theo, author.
Title: Translation and history : a textbook / Theo Hermans.
Description: Abingdon, Oxon ; New York : Routledge, 2022. |
Includes bibliographical references and index.
Identifiers: LCCN 2022002428 | ISBN 9781138036970 (hardback) |
ISBN 9781138036987 (paperback) | ISBN 9781315178134 (ebook)
Subjects: LCSH: Translating and interpreting–History. |
Translating and interpreting–Research–Methodology. | LCGFT: Textbooks.
Classification: LCC P306 .H44 2022 | DDC 418/.0209–dc23/eng/20220217
LC record available at https://lccn.loc.gov/2022002428

ISBN: 978-1-138-03697-0 (hbk)
ISBN: 978-1-138-03698-7 (pbk)
ISBN: 978-1-315-17813-4 (ebk)

DOI: 10.4324/9781315178134

Typeset in Bembo
by Newgen Publishing UK

Contents

Preface   vii

Acknowledgements   xi

1 Stories and Histories   1
Three Stories from the End of the World 1
Narrative 7
Narrativism: Hayden White 11
After White: Pushing On, Pushing Back 17

2 Translation History   26
Key Issues 27
Cutting Up the Cake 33
Dynamics of Change 38
Discourses about Translation 43

3 Questions of Scale   53
Microhistories 54
Scaling Up 60
Entanglements 65
The Whole World? 69
Big Data 71

4 Concepts   79
Concepts and Conceptual History 80
Reinhart Koselleck and Quentin Skinner 83
Transnational Conceptual History 86
Translation and Travelling Concepts 90

5 Memory   100
Memory Studies 101
Transcultural Memory 104
Memory and Translation 108

6   Translation as History   115

Layers of Time 116
Reading for Traces 120
Translation as Intervention: A Model 124
Translation as Intervention: Illustrations 128

Conclusion   139

Bibliography   141
Index   157

Preface

The past lives inside us. It is there in the form of private memories and in the historical knowledge we have acquired, individually and collectively. Its remnants are all around us in the form of pictures, recordings, books, statues, objects in museums and other sites of public or collective memory. It is growing with every moment that passes but also selectively remembered and forgotten. We cannot think of ourselves without simultaneously dredging up a version of our past history.

History is about the past. It can refer to the past as such, to our understanding of the past, or to an account based on that understanding. Historiography means the production of written accounts based on our understanding of the past.

History writing and the study of history deal with the past but are anchored in the present. This is partly because all we have to make sense of the past are our contemporary ideas and concepts, and partly because the primary data for historical study are those traces from the past that are still with us today, whether in the form of memories, of existing knowledge or of material items such as documents or other objects. We look at the past from where we are standing now.

The present book is concerned with the relation between translation and history. It discusses basic ideas and methodological issues regarding the study of that relation. This means several things. There is, of course, the study of the history of translation. There is also the study of translations as part of history; that is, the study of translations as nested in their historical environment and interacting with that environment and its history. Finally, there are ideas, principles and insights that have been debated among professional historians and are of use to historians of translation.

Why engage in the study of translation history in the first place? For a number of reasons, such as the following:

- The present has grown out of the past. To understand why things are the way they are, we must understand how they have come to be this way. Translation today is the product of its history.
- Translation was done differently and thought about differently in the past. Delving into the past reveals practices, ideas, conditions, presuppositions

and motivations markedly different from those in our contemporary world. Recognising that richness adds to the complexity and depth of our understanding of translation.

- Because it is different, the past is also a treasure trove of the unexpected. Rummaging through it and being surprised by its diversity is not just exciting, it expands our vision by taking us out of our comfort zone.
- The past has the potential to irritate the present. The fact that translation was done differently and thought about differently in the past makes us query things we might otherwise take for granted. It makes us realise that our present practices and concepts are contingent, tied to our world, and open to challenge and change.
- This works the other way round as well. Our contemporary concepts and vocabularies may fall short of doing justice to the uniqueness of past phenomena, making us reflect critically on the conceptual tools we use to tackle that which lies beyond our immediate horizon.
- Engaging with past ideas and practices makes us better at assessing problems and devising solutions in the present, if only because the benefit of hindsight allows us to appreciate the outcomes of past actions. A great deal of historical study is concerned with unintended consequences.
- Because histories of translation and interpreting have so far been researched only patchily, there is a vast field of studies lying wide open, clamouring for attention.

This last point should not be taken as belittling the substantial amount of work that has been done on aspects of translation history. We now have several national and some supra-national histories of translation, along with a specialised journal (*Chronotopos*, set up in 2019) and a vast array of large and small case studies. There has been theoretical reflection in the last couple of decades and a spate of recent books (Andrea Rizzi, Birgit Lang and Anthony Pym, *What is Translation History? A Trust-Based Approach*, 2019; Carmen África Vidal Claramonte, *La traducción y la(s) historia(s)*, 2018; and especially Julia Richter, *Translationshistoriographie*, 2020). Much of the currently available material is listed in the comprehensive *Routledge Handbook of Translation History* edited by Christopher Rundle (2022).

What we have not had until now is a book that speaks to students and covers the essentials. Among these essentials I count what professional historians have had to say about their subject. Several translation scholars, including Paul Bandia, Anne Malena and Judy Wakabayashi, have stressed the need to listen to historians, but, apart from forays into microhistory and memory studies, these suggestions have had only modest uptake among translation historians. In the present book, four of the six chapters are organised around the ideas and preoccupations of historians.

What can historians offer students of translation? Four things: sustained theoretical and philosophical reflection on the nature of history and of historical knowledge; reflection on specific kinds and types of history, such as memory studies or the history of concepts; methodological reflection on researching and writing history; and superb practical applications of historical acumen.

It is true that, traditionally, historians often overlooked translation, took it for granted, or repeated common platitudes about translation as transparently equivalent to a foreign original or as forever inferior. Today this is no longer the case. The transnational, transcultural and global turns of recent decades have helped historians discover languages and translation. As the coming chapters will show, historians are now independently making observations about translation that sometimes closely resemble those made by translation scholars.

This convergence suggests that students of translation have something to offer historians as well. They can show that, more often than not, translation is a complex matter. They can highlight aspects of history neglected or underestimated by historians. They can demonstrate that virtually any slice of history harbours a translingual dimension. Above all, they can bring to historical research their refined sense of the cross-lingual and cross-cultural.

The present book speaks primarily to Masters and research students in translation studies. Junior researchers or anyone new to translation history may also find something in it. The aim was not to write a research monograph or a research manual but a textbook setting out key ideas and developments and offering methodological guidance. Inevitably, the book reflects my own background and limitations. The perspective remains mostly European, perhaps even Anglophone. It is not just that the book is in English; I have also been attached for many years to a London-based academic institution whose library favours English-language resources. Although I have tried to counteract this bias, I cannot fathom whether I have done enough.

Finally, a word about the structure of the book.

Chapter 1 is about the basics. It starts with a case study on which to hang a range of ideas about the difference between the historical record as it survives in the archive and the stories historians tell about the material they come across. The focus is on Hayden White's narrativist approach to historiography.

Chapter 2 is about the obvious. It addresses the history of translation, covering such questions as periodisation and choosing which geographical space to write a translation history of. It also seeks to discover what makes the practice of translation change over time and how we can approach historical discourses about translation.

Chapters 3, 4 and 5 deal with particular kinds of history and therefore, like Chapter 1, take their cue from historians. The different fields surveyed have all turned decisively towards the transcultural in recent decades and stumbled on translation along the way.

Chapter 3 is about scale, from microhistory to transnational and world history, with a few words about *histoire croisée* (or entangled history) and actor–network theory. Globalisation and advanced computing power warrant some brief comments about working with big data.

Chapter 4 deals with concepts and the history of concepts. It considers the founding fathers of modern conceptual history, Reinhart Koselleck and

Quentin Skinner, and goes on to explore the transcultural turn in conceptual history.

Chapter 5 is about memory, or the past brought back into the present. Like other forms of historical study, memory studies have followed a trajectory from the national to the transnational, and they have been particularly innovative in devising new terms to capture the transmission of memory in the contemporary world.

Chapter 6 is about translation as part of history. It discusses the temporal layers contained in translations and offers suggestions for reading translations in their historical context, eventually shifting attention to the context itself and the place of translation within it.

Each chapter comes with suggestions for further reading.

I have decided not to devote a separate chapter to book history. Book-historical insights are dispersed throughout the other chapters in references to the physical appearance of individual books and to material aspects of their production and distribution. A separate chapter would have made for repetition and reduplication.

Acknowledgements

I am grateful to the Boston Library Consortium and the Boston University School of Theology Library for permission to reproduce parts of *Gospel Jon Ecamanaci* (1886).

Thanks are due to Geraldine Brodie, Mona Baker, Lawrence Wong Wang-chi and Christopher Rundle for critical comments on the initial idea for this book, even though the end product has turned out very different from the project's starting point.

Thanks also to Dorota Gołuch, Lucelle Pardoe and He Sui for their perceptive comments on the three stories from the end of the world.

Finally, my thanks to Tomasz Rozmyslowicz, Julia Richter, Stefanie Kremmel, Larisa Schippel and the participants in the 2021 Vienna Summer School 'Doing Translation History' for their questions and suggestions when I presented versions of some chapters to them.

1   Stories and Histories

Three Stories from the End of the World

Let's begin with three stories, three historical stories, three histories.

The scene is the southernmost tip of the American continent, a collection of islands known as Tierra del Fuego. The capital of Tierra del Fuego is Ushuaia, situated on the Beagle Channel, a waterway that connects the Atlantic with the Pacific Ocean some three hundred kilometres south of the Magellan Strait. Farther south there is the desolate Cape Horn, followed by a stretch of stormy ocean and then the white vastness of Antarctica. Because the road network that covers the American continent ends at the Beagle Channel, Ushuaia prides itself on being the city at the end of the world. The end of the world is not a time but a place.

The three stories that follow concern the Anglican missionary Thomas Bridges (c. 1842–98), who spent most of his life in the area. The native people who used to live along the shores of the Beagle Channel and on the islands as far south as Cape Horn were the Yámana – or Yahgans, as Bridges called them. They were nomadic hunter-gatherers who built only temporary shelters and used canoes to move from island to island. Bridges learnt their language, set up a mission among them where several previous attempts had failed and eventually, in the 1880s, with the help of indigenous converts, translated parts of the Bible into Yámana. Here is the story of this translation and the events surrounding it.

The first story

In 1856, aged just fourteen, Thomas Bridges travelled from England to the Falkland Islands (also known as the Malvinas, to the east of Tierra del Fuego). The Patagonian Missionary Society ran a mission station there and persuaded some Yámana from Tierra del Fuego to spend longer or shorter periods at the station. Bridges initially learnt the language from them, one of the very few outsiders ever to gain any fluency in it. In return he taught the Yámana to read and write English, using a phonetic script. He became

DOI: 10.4324/9781315178134-1

an excellent linguist. When, in October 1866, a visiting chaplain conducted a service attended by thirteen Yámana, Bridges was able to act as interpreter (Bull 1867, 48). Around this time, he also started work on a grammar and a dictionary of the language.

Bridges briefly returned to England in 1868–9 to be ordained. Soon afterwards, the mission at Ushuaia was established and this became his new home. In 1872, a first group of thirty-six Yámana were baptised at Ushuaia. In a letter dated 11 March 1872 and published in the *South American Missionary Magazine*, to which he contributed regularly, Bridges mentioned that his plan to translate one of the Gospels had made little progress due to his still imperfect grasp of the language, its 'poverty and peculiar construction', and the amount of daily toil required to keep the new settlement going (T. Bridges 1872, 98). He felt 'unable to make a satisfactory translation in which you are tied by words', but a paraphrase seemed feasible (T. Bridges 1872, 99). A year later, he reported another challenge: the Yámana had no inkling of the kind of world portrayed in the Bible, so that, explaining one story to them, 'I should have to explain who a publican was, what the taxes were for, and the necessity of persons paying, and for others to receive taxes'; with regard to another story, he had to 'tell them who Caesar was, and how one country had subjugated others, and how it became necessary to obey foreign governors, and submit to foreign taxation, which the Jews so rebelled against' (T. Bridges 1873, 28). In 1875, he still had not made a start due to a lack of time to study the language 'and many difficulties' (T. Bridges 1875, 220).

By the close of the decade he was more confident, reporting 'good progress in a deepening knowledge' of the language, which he now also recognised as 'unique, and wonderfully erected', concluding that 'I feel I must spend my time on the language in completing dictionary and grammar, and then in translating portions of God's Word' (T. Bridges 1879, 103). The grammar was never completed but the dictionary, which ran to over 32,000 entries, was eventually, after many tribulations, published in 1933.

From the end of 1879 through to March 1881, Bridges was in England again, partly for health reasons and partly to see his first translation, the Gospel of Luke, into print. He wrote his second translation, the Acts of the Apostles, during the outward voyage across the Atlantic; it appeared in print in 1883. A third translation, the Gospel of John, followed in 1886. All three translations, each printed in 500 copies, employed the phonetic script he had been using to teach the Yámana to write. All three are slight little books of around 100 pages that fit into the palm of one's hand. Their title pages do not mention a translator. Most remarkably, they offer only plain text, without any introductory material or explanatory notes. In view of the difficulties Bridges reported in conveying the Biblical world to people wholly unfamiliar with it, the question arises: why are the translations as bare as they are and feature neither introductions nor annotations?

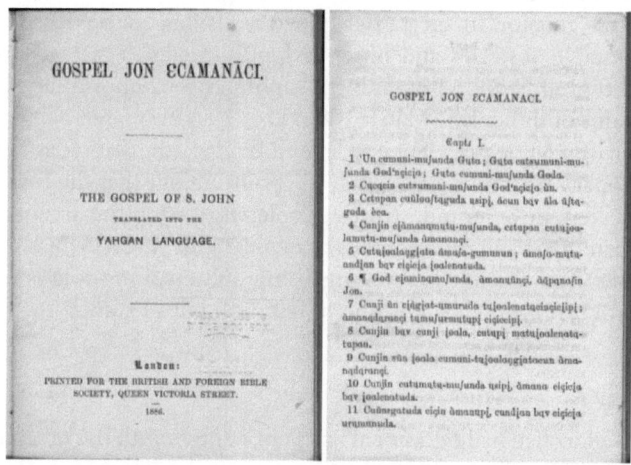

Illustrations 1 and 2 Title page and opening verses of Thomas Bridges' Yámana translation of the Gospel of John, 1886. (Reproduction courtesy of Boston University School of Theology Library and Boston Library Consortium.)

The answer lies in the institutional context supporting Bridges' efforts. The books were published in London by the British and Foreign Bible Society, which possessed both the financial means and the technical equipment to print a wide range of scripts. Because, from its foundation in 1802, the Society catered for different Protestant denominations and missionary organisations, it adopted the principle that all Bible translations into foreign languages had to appear without doctrinal and therefore potentially divisive notes or comments (Mak 2015). When missionaries objected that without explanatory glosses the Bible remained incomprehensible to their audiences, the Society, keen to secure its fundraising base among all Protestant persuasions in Britain, advised that oral explication could be provided locally. This may explain the small, eminently portable format of Bridges' translations. In the texts themselves, Bridges appears to have tried to gloss the Biblical world in terms the Yámana could recognise. A short passage (Luke 1:1–13), which Bridges on one occasion back-translated into English, affords a glimpse of his technique. Where the Authorised Version – almost certainly Bridges' point of departure – mentions 'incense', Bridges has 'oil' or 'sweet oil', with 'the altar of incense' becoming 'the place (structure) where the oil was burned'. In a similar vein, 'angel' is rendered as 'messenger' and 'priest' as 'appointed teacher' (Ellis 1884, 48–9).

When Bridges returned to Ushuaia from England with his translation of Luke's Gospel, he reported that the natives were pleased to see their language in print for the first time (Marsh 1883, 130). In missionary circles his work earned extravagant praise. The *Narrative of the Origin and Progress of the South American Mission* spoke of the mission in Tierra del Fuego as having succeeded despite 'almost insurmountable obstacles' and 'bitter disappointments', a case of 'Divine promises abundantly fulfilled, […] of faith triumphing over impossibilities, and removing mountains of difficulty' (Marsh 1883, 116–7). A year later, one patron of the South American Missionary Society lauded Bridges' translation as 'one of the greatest missionary triumphs ever achieved', pointing out that the formerly depraved Yámana were now 'an industrious people engaged in the arts of agriculture, and performing many of the duties of civilized life' (SAMS 1884, 59).

The overlap between the mission's evangelising and civilising role is at the heart of the second story, which is not one of triumph but of ruin.

The second story

While European sailors had had occasional brief encounters with the inhabitants of Tierra del Fuego since around 1600, the first extended contact took place in 1830 when the crew of the Beagle captured four natives and took them back to England. Two years later, the Beagle returned to Tierra del Fuego with the three surviving natives on board as well as, famously, Charles Darwin, then aged twenty-three. Darwin's description of the Fuegians he met in what became subsequently known as the Beagle Channel was uncomplimentary. Believing them (wrongly) to be cannibals, he spoke of them as 'savages of the lowest grade' and 'stunted miserable wretches', although he also recognised that they were fully adjusted to the harsh climate and did not appear to be decreasing in number (Darwin 1989, 172, 179, 181). In later years Darwin continued to take an interest in Tierra del Fuego. He contacted Thomas Bridges in 1860 for his book on the expression of emotions in humans and animals, and he patronised the South American Missionary Society.

In the course of the 1860s, as his command of the language improved, Bridges began to write ethnographic accounts of the Yámana, describing them as morally degraded but fiercely egalitarian: no one told anyone else what to do (T. Bridges 1866). As the Ushuaia settlement took shape, he reported the health of the people as being generally good. He also made efforts to get them accustomed to wearing clothes as well as to regular labour and a sedentary lifestyle, and he spoke with them about the concept of owning land (T. Bridges 1870a, 41; 1870b, 131). He regularly thanked well-wishers in Britain for the clothes they sent (T. Bridges 1873, 29; 1884a, 33–4; 1884b, 222). He was obviously unaware that the clothes and other European items might carry germs and diseases deadly to the people of Tierra del Fuego.

By the time Bridges was having his translations printed, the Yámana population was in rapid decline. In June 1884, Bridges conducted a census which recorded a population of only about 1,000, less than half, he noted, of what it had been twelve years earlier and under a third of what it had been thirty years back (T. Bridges 1884b, 223; 1885, 289). In early 1886, Bridges estimated that there were about 400 Yámana left (Hyades 1886, 202–4). On the eve of the First

World War, the population was estimated at around 100 (Cooper 1917, 74). The Yámana ceased to exist as a people. What had caused the tragedy?

A first epidemic in 1863–4 appears to have left some 500 dead, but by the end of the decade Bridges reported that few deaths were occurring (A. Chapman 2010, 481; T. Bridges 1870a, 41). In the early 1880s, however, tuberculosis and then measles decimated the Yámana. Bridges registered the high mortality but denied it was due to the presence of outsiders and the clothes they brought (T. Bridges 1882), just as a few years earlier the bishop of the Falklands did not think 'the Fuegians suffer in health through increased civilization' (as Bartholomew Sullivan reported to Darwin in 1874; Burckhardt and Secord 2015, 108). The French doctor Paul Hyades (1847–1919), who had accompanied a French scientific expedition to Tierra del Fuego in 1882–3 and tended the sick at Ushuaia during that period, thought differently. He reckoned that the changed lifestyle of the Yámana and their contact with whites had left them defenceless against epidemics, especially since Argentina had now established an administrative presence in Ushuaia (Hyades 1884; 1885a; 1885b).

The episode in question occurred in September 1884. Following a territorial agreement with Chile, the Argentine navy sent four ships to Ushuaia to set up a subprefecture there. A ceremony was held to assert sovereign rights and hoist the national flag. In true colonial fashion, Thomas Bridges pledged loyalty to the Argentine state on behalf of the indigenous people at the mission station (L. Bridges 2019, 126–7), even though the symbolism of the raising of the flag and the very idea of national sovereignty must have passed them by. The subprefecture was staffed by about thirty men and their officers, a dramatic increase in the number of whites compared with the handful of missionaries until then (Hyades 1886). Six months later, Bridges reported that the Yámana population had declined by half in less than a year (Hyades 1885b, 463). For the Yámana, the arrival of the whites meant the end of their world. Nevertheless, in Britain, the anthropologist J.G. Garson, writing in a leading journal in 1886, still argued that the mortality among the indigenous people was due to '[t]he great scarcity of food, the toil with which it is procured, the severity of the climate, and their very inefficient protection from the elements, both in clothing and shelter' (Garson 1886, 146), ignoring the fact that the Yámana had been living in the area for several thousand years.

The third and last of Thomas Bridges' translations also appeared in print in 1886. Yet, in this same year, he resigned his position as a missionary and turned to farming instead. Why? This is the subject of the third story, which is about personal choice and responsibility.

The third story

Thomas Bridges' decision, as a young man of not yet twenty, to learn the Yámana language did not find favour everywhere. The visiting chaplain for whom Bridges interpreted a church service in 1866 appreciated the effort but opined that 'the sooner English was substituted for Fuegian the better' (Bull

1867, 48–9). In the same vein, Bartholomew Sullivan, Darwin's main informant about Tierra del Fuego over the years, noted in 1874 that native children picked up English very fast and that, since different indigenous groups spoke distinct languages, English would be a convenient common medium to replace the local tongues (Burckhardt and Secord 2015, 108). Yet Bridges persisted, perfecting his own command of Yámana and teaching his Yámana converts English. As it turned out, he taught them the wrong metropolitan language, for, after Chile and Argentina divided Tierra del Fuego between them, Spanish quickly became dominant. With the increasing number of white settlers in the area, the native languages (not only Yámana but also Shelknam, or Ona, and Kawésqar, or Alacaluf) would probably have been pushed into oblivion even if their speakers had not been physically destroyed.

In writing down the Yámana language for his dictionary and grammar, and in teaching the Yámana English, Bridges employed a phonetic script that had been created shortly before by Alexander Ellis. Because Ellis had developed his system with reference to the sounds of English, Bridges modified it with symbols of his own devising to represent the sounds of Yámana. His Bible translations used this modified script. Ellis was anything but pleased with Bridges' 'self-invented symbols' and said as much in his Presidential address to the Philological Society in London in May 1882, using the occasion to comment that the apparent complexity of the Yámana language was actually 'a mark of inferiority' (because 'it harasses thought, and prevents proper generalisation') and, even more crudely, that a 30,000-word dictionary was rather 'a wealth of language for a naked bar-barous tribe now only 3,000 strong!' (Ellis 1884, 33, 35).

The dictionary took Bridges decades to compile. Today it stands – more than his Bible translations – as his lasting legacy, a monument to a now vanished tongue. It also testifies to his commitment to the Yámana. His view of them was obviously shaped by his missionary faith, and paternalistic: he found himself 'painfully impressed of the wretchedness of these people, owing solely to their own folly and wickedness, which necessarily arises from their ignorance of God', and he relished the prospect of 'evangelizing and civilizing this destitute, degraded, but well inclined and naturally pliant and tractable people' (T. Bridges 1869, 11; 1872, 29). The link between conver-sion and civilisation was also apparent in newly baptised Yámana being given English names. Upon receiving baptism, Bridges' main linguistic informant and co-translator, Sesoienges (or Sisanianjiz), was called John Marsh (Marsh 1883, 126).

Yet his concern for the wellbeing of the Yámana was genuine enough, espe-cially during the devastating epidemics of the early 1880s, as the French doctor Paul Hyades testified. He was also fully aware of white farmers, seal hunters and adventurers encroaching on Tierra del Fuego in ever growing numbers. At the end of 1883, a group of natives from further north turned up in Ushuaia because their clanspeople were being gunned down by whites (Hyades 1886, 203). In 1881, eleven natives (not Yámana but Kawésqar) were captured and exhibited as ethnological specimens in several European cities including Paris and Berlin. Only four survived, and Bridges took care of them on their return to Tierra del Fuego (Manouvrier 1881; A. Chapman 2010, 492–502).

The mortality among the Yámana and the certainty of the coming invasion of Tierra del Fuego by white settlers convinced Bridges of the need to find an alternative to protect the remaining natives. He resigned from the mission and, in July 1886, travelled to Buenos Aires and then on to England, returning within a year with building materials for a farm. His resignation as a churchman appeared in the *South American Missionary Magazine* of 1 January 1887 (T. Bridges 1887, 7–8). The Argentine government had granted him land rights to an *estancia* of some 200 square kilometres about eighty kilometres east of Ushuaia. There he was able to employ natives as farm labourers, sometimes more than sixty at a time (L. Bridges 2019, 139–43, 151). It seemed to him the best way to support the indigenous population whose downfall he had almost certainly helped initiate but could not have foreseen and sought to alleviate as best he could once the full scale of the tragedy sank in.

Narrative

The historical cake can be cut up in many ways. We can focus on a large or a small geographical space. We can zoom in on a single person or object, or survey groups of people active in broad domains such as the economy, politics, religion, science, art. We can trace abstract entities like ideas and concepts. We can approach things from the perspective of those at the top of social hierarchies or from the standpoint of those below them. We can consider a cross-section at a particular moment or take in longer temporal stretches, the so-called *longue durée*. There will be more about some of these choices later in this book.

The rest of the present chapter is concerned, first, with the basic building blocks of narrative, then with the influential views of the American historian Hayden White on what it actually means to shape a slice of the past as a historical account, and, finally, with developments since Hayden White, including attempts to push his views as far as they will go and ongoing resistance to them.

First, then, narrative. What all histories have in common is that they tell a story. This is because history involves change, and an account of change inevitably involves narrative. Even if we think of a snapshot of the past at a certain moment, or of an analysis of a certain fixed state of affairs in the past, these are fragile islands of stability in a sea of ongoing change. A cross-section, too, incorporates change because what is there at a certain time was not always like that and will not remain forever. In this way, change insinuates itself into even the most static historical account. And an account of change takes the form of a story: first there was this, and then this led to that. All historians tell stories.

Another word for story is 'narrative'. As it happens, narrativism has been the most important trend in historiography in the last half-century or so. This is not because some historians suddenly realised that, like their colleagues before them, they had been telling stories all along. Much more is at stake. Grasping this 'much more' is fundamental for everything that follows in this book. Let's therefore inspect it more closely. We should begin with an explanation of what constitutes a narrative (or a story or narrative account – I will use the terms interchangeably). The three historical narratives from the end of the world will help us. They will also form a bridge to the 'much more' that comes under the heading of narrativism.

Simply put, a narrative is a semiotic construct (a text, a film, a perform-ance) containing elements whose interaction in a structured sequence effects a meaningful change. This is a basic, non-technical definition, but it contains all we need to grasp some of the key ingredients of narratives, including histor-ical narratives. For the sake of convenience, and because most of the narratives produced by historians appear in the form of written texts, I will take verbal (rather than, say, audiovisual) narratives as the default.

1. Narratives have a *beginning* and an *end*. This matters for historical narratives because history itself has no beginning (except, perhaps, in the Big Bang) and ends only with the present moment. Narrative beginnings and endings have to be picked. The first Thomas Bridges story began with his arrival in the Falkland Islands in 1856 but then harked back to 1802, and it ended with the publication of his dictionary in 1933. The second story started around 1600 and ended with the extinction of the Yámana as a people around the First World War. The third story opened with Bridges' decision to learn Yámana sometime after 1856 and closed in 1886 when he became a farmer. In each case, the start and end points were chosen based on the story to be told. They were not given in advance.

2. The elements contained in a narrative comprise *characters* (agents, participants) and *events* (actions, occurrences) located in time and space. These make up the basic 'who', 'what', 'when' and 'where' of stories. Fictional narratives can contain whatever characters and events an author dreams up. Historical narratives must draw on the surviving documen-tary record. However, as the three stories from the end of the world show, the same set of records can give rise to different narratives, depending on which characters and events are included, excluded or foregrounded. In other words, there is a degree of *selectivity* involved, governed by the the-matic line that the story wants to develop. Here are some of the things that could have been included in one of the Thomas Bridges stories but were left out:

    •   In 1865–7, Bridges' superior took four young Yámana (two aged around 20, one around 11 and the youngest around 7) from the mission station in the Falklands on a tour of England, showing them off as already half-civilised Christians to raise funds for the mission. The 11-year-old, Sesoienges (or Sisanianjiz), later became Bridges' main linguistic informant (A. Chapman 2010, 420–1, 465, 480).

    •   Bridges also appears to have donated the skulls and bones of deceased natives to ethnological collections in English museums. J.G. Garson

(1886, 147), for instance, reported that the Museum of the Royal College of Surgeons of England possessed eleven skulls, seven of them presented by Bridges.

- We don't know who Bridges' parents were. He was abandoned as a baby and found, allegedly, on a bridge in Bristol (which may explain the surname he later took). Co-incidentally, the French doctor Paul Hyades, who tended the sick in Ushuaia in 1882–3, was a found-ling, too.

3. The interaction among elements of the narrative takes the form of a structured sequence that brings about a meaningful change. The events, that is, are ordered temporally (first this, then that) and connected in some meaningful way. The short term for this structured meaningful sequence is *plot*, and *emplotment* means arranging the story elements into an intelligible story line, a sequence that makes sense (Somers 1994, 616–7; 2001, 360–1). Plot and emplotment are crucial to the understanding of narrative.

A century ago, the novelist E.M. Forster reckoned that the difference between (a) 'The king died and then the queen died' and (b) 'The king died and then the queen died of grief' was that (b) had a plot, a meaningful connection between the two events that was lacking in (a). Narratologists, however, have pointed out that readers are likely to assume that even in (a) the two events are connected and that the king's death contributed to, or maybe even caused, the queen's death (S. Chapman 1978, 45–6; Rimmon-Kenan 1983, 17). In other words, even when the exact nature of the connection between the two events remains unstated, readers will probably infer a meaningful link, as they also do in 'He felt the cold and closed the window', where we readily assume that the person closed the window *because* he felt the cold. If we cannot establish a meaningful link, we will probably conclude that we are dealing with a series of isolated utterances – a chronicle, perhaps, but not a narrative.

If we connect the events in sentences like 'The king died and then the queen died' and 'He felt the cold and closed the window', it is important to realise that we ourselves, as recipients, are making the connection and, most likely, are also ascribing to the person telling the tale the intention to have us connect the events. Although strictly speaking the sentences only indi-cate a sequential order of events, not a causal or other motivating link, the later event becomes more intelligible to us when we take the earlier event into account. And this is precisely where the power of narrative, and of his-torical narrative, lies. Because it is emplotted or perceived as emplotted, i.e., forming a meaningful sequence, historical narrative provides an explication of the past. By implicitly or explicitly linking events and occurrences in meaningful ways, the historical narrative yields insight into the past and, in so doing, makes it intelligible (Lemon 2001, 109–23).

The way that historians emplot their narratives is constrained by the documentary record but not dictated by it. As already suggested, different narratives can be construed from the same set of records. The record may contain its own narratives – as in the explanation Thomas Bridges provided for turning from missionary work to farming – but these embedded narratives are part of the historian's object of study. The historian's narrative comes with a plot line of its own, reflecting his or her *interpretation* of the primary material. The plot line tells us how, in the historian's view, we can understand a series of actions and events as a sequence that makes sense. This is why Louis Mink describes narrative as a cognitive instrument and as 'a primary and irreducible form of human comprehension' (2001, 213, 214).

Two footnotes are in order here. First, while plot binds a narrative together into a sequence that makes sense, the question of whether, how, in what respect or to whom a sequence 'makes sense' will depend on genre expectations, on conventions of reading and textual organisation, and therefore on the cultural environment of both writers and readers. In cross-cultural contexts, these issues are invariably problematic.

Second, there is a certain asymmetry between the documentary record and the historian's account. On the one hand, the record that the past leaves behind is often fragmented and always less than what actually happened in the past. On the other, the historical account, because it is an interpretation, gives us something necessarily different from, and conceivably more than, the documentary record.

4. Stories don't tell themselves. Someone is doing the telling, which means there is always a teller in a tale. One reason why this matters is that the teller necessarily takes up a certain position with regard to the story being told. In its barest form, the use of the past tense locates the teller at some point in time after the events, thus enabling hindsight. Even a simple sentence like 'The Thirty Years War began in 1618' contains three temporal moments: (1) the beginning of the war in 1618, (2) its end thirty years later, and (3) the moment sometime after 1648 at which the statement evoking both the beginning and end of the war is made (as Arthur Danto explains in Domańska 1998, 177). The fact that historians can present their accounts of the past with the benefit of hindsight is of prime importance because it allows them to assess the unintended consequences of the actions of historical agents. Today's historian describing Thomas Bridges' activities in Ushuaia around 1870 knows, as Bridges himself could not, how calamitous the mission would turn out to be for the Yámana fifteen years later. Hindsight enables the historian to connect the dots afterwards – that is, to read certain events as anticipating or prefiguring later events in ways inaccessible to those living at the time of the earlier events. Cueing a narrative in this way reveals the teller's handiwork (White 2013, 41–3).

In stories told by means of words (rather than, say, images), the choice of words carries value judgements. They can be explicit, as in the third Thomas Bridges story when Alexander Ellis reckoned 'even more crudely' that Bridges had compiled a large dictionary of a very small language. They can also remain implicit. The brutal contrast, in the second Bridges story, between the missionaries bringing 'civilisation' and the Yámana dying is left to speak for itself. Or the judgements may be ambiguous and open to interpretation. The mention, in the second Bridges story, that Darwin wrongly believed the Yámana to be cannibals not only evokes different temporal moments (Darwin's believing this, and the subsequent correction), but it could also be read as at least partly excusing Darwin's uncharacteristically crass view of the Yámana.

In the case of stories told by means of words, the words that reach a recipient who reads or hears the story are uttered by a voice we attribute to a *narrator*. The author of a text and its narrator are not necessarily the same. Fiction writers, for instance, have been ingenious in inventing all manner of narrators as part of their storytelling. Leo Tolstoy's story 'Kholstomer' fields both an omniscient narrator and a horse talking in the first person singular. Historians tend not to use fancy constructions of this kind, which is why, in historical accounts, the author and narrator are routinely conflated. Yet it may be useful to keep them separate. The three Thomas Bridges stories dramatise this point. Whereas the first story celebrates Bridges' missionary achievement, the second story, narrated from a different point of view, highlights what the first narrator failed to see or say, namely, that the mission also hastened the downfall of a whole people, while the third story, from yet another standpoint, seeks to home in on Bridges' personal choices and sense of responsibility. Each subsequent story can act as a corrective to the one before it and thus defines a different position for its narrator.

For the sake of clarity, let me add here that, as regards all three stories from the end of the world, I am their author, while I also tried to be three different narrators. I discovered Thomas Bridges after reading about him in his son's autobiography (Lucas Bridges, *Uttermost Part of the Earth*, 1947, re-issued in 2019). Having done some further reading online and in London libraries, it seemed to me that the material was intriguing enough to permit different approaches – one fairly naïve or institutional account casting the Bible translation as a success story, one adopting a perspective that might be called postcolonial, and one focused on ethical aspects. Let me also add that I have been talking about Bridges' translations into Yámana without knowing this language. Who says you need languages to speak about translation?

Narrativism: Hayden White

If the historian's narrative embodies his or her interpretation of the past, it follows that alternative interpretations will give rise to different narratives. A particular historical narrative is then only one story; it is neither the whole story nor the only possible story. In this sense, the interest in narrative among historians militates against the idea that the historical account can be an objective, complete or transparent representation of the past. Where does that leave the question of the historical truth? We will come to this question, but let's stay with narrative for now.

'History is a subject primarily concerned with the crafting of narratives', Dipesh Chakrabarty has noted (2000, 98). In the 1960s and '70s, in a move subsequently labelled the linguistic turn in historiography, the 'crafting' of historical narratives became a hot issue. The main figure in this development was the American historian Hayden White (1928–2018). He argued that writing history had rather more in common with writing fiction than many historians imagined or were prepared to admit. For White, 'The conjuring up of the past requires art as well as information' (2005, 149). His views proved to be controversial but also highly influential.

Before White: Barthes

That writing history involved an element of fictionalising was already clear in the early nineteenth century. In 1821, for instance, the German statesman, linguist and translator Wilhelm von Humboldt delivered a lecture on historiography to the Berlin Academy of Sciences (where Friedrich Schleiermacher had spoken on different methods of translating a few years earlier). Von Humboldt stressed that, to arrive at a historical account, the documentary record was necessary but insufficient. It needed to be supplemented, stitched together, by the historian, who provided connections and a sense of direction that were not there in the record itself. This, for Humboldt, was a creative process akin to artistic creation (Humboldt 1967). In a similar vein, the Belgian historian Henri Pirenne noted in the early twentieth century that '[h]istory is a story, nothing more and nothing less', adding that this story 'cannot be told without the admixture of explanatory and speculative elements' (as quoted in Dray 1954, 24).

An incisive contribution came from the French critic Roland Barthes in 1967 in a short essay translated into English as 'The Discourse of History'. Barthes noted that a story – indeed any utterance – always derives from a speaker. Speakers can make their presence explicit (as in 'I believe Bridges was in Ushuaia in July 1873') or they can cover their tracks and erase all signs of themselves as speakers (as in 'Bridges was in Ushuaia in July 1873'). When this latter kind of withdrawal happens in historical writing, it is as if the history is telling itself. The nineteenth-century French historian Fustel de Coulanges used to tell his students: 'It is not me who is speaking to you, it is history itself speaking through me' ('ce n'est pas moi qui vous parle; c'est l'histoire qui vous parle par ma bouche'; Monod 1897, 138–9).

Presenting a story as if it is telling itself creates what Barthes called a 'referential illusion', an impression of objectivity (1981, 11). Barthes showed, in other words, that 'objectivity' is a construction: it gives the appearance of letting the facts speak for themselves, but it can do this only because the speaker has gone into hiding. The 'facts' that such a discourse refers to are not simply occurrences or entities in the real world. They have been selected and they are presented in a certain light. Rather, a seemingly objective discourse brings about a 'reality effect', the impression that the words match external referents (Barthes 1981, 17). This 'reality effect' has also been called the transparency effect (Kansteiner

1993, 275), making us imagine language as a transparent window on factual reality.

Barthes pointed out that what he called the 'referential illusion' and the 'reality effect' applied to historical fiction as well as to historiography. Suddenly, then, literature, fiction and writing history were yoked together in a manner that made many historians uncomfortable. Looking at Barthes' point through a translation lens, however, it is not hard to grasp at all. What he described as the 'referential illusion' is similar to what happens in illusionist (in Jiří Levý's terms) or domesticating (in Lawrence Venuti's terms) translations, which make us believe we are reading the original. We know they can do this only because the translator has created an illusion of transparency by making his or her presence (as the one who selected the words we are reading) as inconspicuous as possible. Just as Fustel de Coulanges imagined history speaking through him, the seventeenth-century French translator Nicolas Perrot d'Ablancourt, a self-consciously 'domesticating' translator, said of his translation of the Greek historian Thucydides that it showed Thucydides himself had become French (1972, 202).

Historical narratives as artefacts

If Barthes sowed the seeds of the idea, Hayden White and others brought in the harvest. During an interview in 1993, and speaking of historians, White observed that 'anyone who writes a narrative is fictionalizing' (Domańska 1998, 28). The reason is that constructing a narrative on the basis of historical evidence requires, as a minimum, the evidence to be organised in a certain way. This narrative organisation is not there as such in the documentary record. As White's colleague Frank Ankersmit put it in the same series of interviews: 'Telling the past, or even one's own past, is unavoidably a violation of that past in order to effect such a narrative organization of the past – an organization that is not intrinsic to the past itself' (Domańska 1998, 78). Ankersmit here echoed a much quoted remark by White (from the 1974 essay 'The Historical Text as Literary Artefact') to the effect that historical narratives 'tailor' the data to the requirements of the story form, as a result of which historical narratives are 'verbal fictions, the contents of which are as much *invented* as *found*' (White 1978, 82; his emphasis).

This is a strong claim, which has its basis in the idea that the historian's narrative reflects an *interpretation* of the past. The decisive statement in this respect occurs in White's 1972–3 essay 'Interpretation in History'. Because the historian's account interprets the historical record, White argues, historiography simultaneously falls short of and exceeds the historical record:

> On the one hand, there are always more facts in the record than the historian can possibly include in his narrative representation of a given segment of the historical process. And so the historian must 'interpret' his data by excluding certain facts from his account as irrelevant to his narrative

purpose. On the other hand, in his efforts to reconstruct 'what happened' in any given period of history, the historian inevitably must include in his narrative an account of some event or complex of events for which the facts that would permit a plausible explanation of its occurrence are lacking. And this means that the historian must 'interpret' his materials by filling in the gaps in his information on inferential or speculative grounds.

(White 1978, 51)

On the one hand, the kind of story the historian wants to tell leads to some elements being foregrounded while others are omitted or pushed into the background. This is what Margaret Somers (we shall meet her again) calls 'selective appropriation'. Since the documentary record cannot be reproduced as it stands, the historian picks those things that fit the story he or she wants to tell, leaving other things unused. On the other hand, weaving the verbal fabric means that, as Humboldt and Pirenne already saw, the historian supplies links, inferences, explanations and guesses over and above what the record contains. Because the world itself is not storied, the historian's narrative is superimposed on it. Events happen in the world, but the historical narrative transforms them into elements of a story. As a linguistic construct, moreover, the historical account is crafted, which necessarily involves artistry, the use of rhetorical figures and tropes, and hence a degree of fictionalisation.

What about the truth?

But surely things in the past happened as they did and not otherwise? Will any interpretation do? Can we bend the facts to suit the story, tailor evidence to fit a plot line? What about the malign fantasies of conspiracy theorists, creationists, climate change or Holocaust deniers? Is it not the task of the historian to describe the past 'as it actually was' (*wie es eigentlich gewesen*), to quote the famous phrase of the nineteenth-century historian Leopold von Ranke (1824, vi)?

The reality of the past is not in doubt, and the material evidence, the historical record, must be respected, as White states emphatically (2005, 148). However, he also points out that the historian's narrative is not so much about *what* occurred as about what those occurrences *mean* (White 1986, 487). These meanings can vary across constituencies. Moreover, the meaning-making that the historian engages in is itself located in a certain time and place, just as individual historians operate within social, institutional and intellectual networks in which certain ideas may be taken for granted and others contested (Prakash 1990, 383–4).

Other historians have provided additional answers. Dipesh Chakrabarty demands of historians that they accept 'shared rational and evidentiary rules' and that their narratives allow for 'a rationally defensible point of view or position from which to tell the story' (2000, 98, 99). There may not be global agreement about exactly what 'rational' means, but being taken seriously by fellow professionals seems like a good starting point.

While the individual statements that historians make must obviously conform to the available evidence, the narrative arc that the historian creates on the basis of this evidence is of a different order. The historian's account offers an *interpretation* of the past (White 1986, 487). As interpretations, these accounts do not definitively wrap up the past; on the contrary, they open up prospects on the past (White 1989, 25). The truth of a historical account cannot be checked by confronting this account with the reality of the past, because the 'reality' of the past does not reveal itself except in the accounts that historians propose. All we have are different accounts embodying different interpretations. We therefore compare different accounts and interpretations. Historians write their histories in the knowledge that there are other histories and interpretations, and they position their own work in relation to these existing accounts.

Several historians have elaborated the idea that historical accounts, and the interpretations nestling in them, are *proposals* to view the past in a certain way (Lemon 2001, 122–3; Ankersmit 1983; 2017, 39–40). Depending on their outlook, historians perceive certain continuities between historical events and they articulate those lines of continuity they see as best fitting the available evidence. Thinking of historical narratives as proposals has some interesting consequences.

- Proposals may be wise or unwise, appropriate or inappropriate, responsible or irresponsible, but they cannot be true or false.
- Historians write with an eye not only to the available evidence but also to their prospective readers, especially the historians among them. The significance of a proposal to view the past in this or that way lies in how plausible or convincing fellow historians will judge it to be.
- Proposals allow for alternatives. In most cases, the individual historian enters a field in which various interpretations and types of interpretation are circulating already, and so each new proposal has to demonstrate its surplus value in relation to available or likely alternatives.
- Seeing historical narratives and interpretations as proposals helps us understand why the subjectless, seemingly objective discourse that Roland Barthes analysed as creating a 'referential illusion' is so insidious. It suggests that the language used is transparent, that it provides a direct and unproblematic window on the world to which it refers, and that it gives the only possible true account of that world.

Applied White: Venuti

In his early work, Hayden White wrote at length about the deep-seated conceptual structures he discerned in the work of some major historians. He saw tropes such as metaphor, metonymy or irony not as discourse features but as conceptual lenses with which to interpret the world. In the same way, he distinguished four major modes of emplotment: romance, tragedy, comedy and satire – where the terms do not designate standard literary genres but archetypal plot structures (White 1973, 8–9; 1978, 60, 121–34).

For instance, we can view a particular slice of history as a story of someone (or something, such as a nation or some other entity) contending with obstacles but finally winning through and realising his or her (or its) full potential. This would be the mode of *romance*. Think of Thomas Bridges publishing his Yámana gospels after many tribulations; or of what Antoine Berman (1990) calls a 'great translation': previous translations have all been defective but then one comes along that gets everything right. If we read the world in terms of relations of cause and effect, one thing leading to another until some basic truth is revealed, the plot structure might be that of *tragedy*. Bridges' attempt to convert the Yámana was bundled with his civilising mission which resulted in the destruction of the Yámana. Successive failures to translate something to one's satisfaction may lead to the conclusion that it is in the nature of translation to fail. We can also view the world as containing opposing forces which nevertheless leave room for coming together and reconciliation, resulting in a *comic* plot. Translation can reach those on the other side of a linguistic divide; successive translations can open up entire fields of previously inaccessible knowledge. Or perhaps we see human endeavours to control the world as ultimately futile, which would foster an ironic point of view and be the way of *satire*. For Barbara Cassin's *Dictionary of Untranslatables* (2014), the 'untranslatable' is that which we keep on translating despite never getting it right. Or we might sneer at Neoclassical translations that seek to improve on allegedly deficient originals but also wonder if our smugness is perhaps misplaced?

White argued that these archetypal structures make the historian's account recognisable as being a narrative of a certain type and that this helps their acceptability. He also admitted (1986, 487) that they are culturally specific, which suggests that different cultures may favour different plot types.

In his later writings, White did not follow up on the idea of archetypal plot structures. I give it some attention here because it is, to my knowledge, the only aspect of White's work that has found a direct echo in translation studies, in two essays by Lawrence Venuti.

In the conclusion to an essay on retranslation, Venuti (2004, 34–6) takes a somewhat unusual approach in that he treats as historiographical not what historians say about translation, but actual retranslations and the prefaces that accompany them. A retranslation may advertise itself as superior to one or more predecessors in avoiding their alleged errors and shortcomings. The plot being enacted in such a move is that of *romance*, and it is the most common stance in retranslations. As an example of a *satiric* narrative, Venuti mentions Vladimir Nabokov's retranslation of Pushkin's *Eugene Onegin*, in which Nabokov slates all earlier translations while admitting that his own also falls short since the ideal translation does not exist. A *comedic* plot may be discerned in retranslations that pride themselves on reaching hitherto excluded readerships, such as the Penguin Classics that were made specifically for a non-elite mass audience.

In another, more polemical essay, Venuti (2005, 812–5) attacks a piece by Anthony Pym on the 1992 Olympic Games in Barcelona, more particularly Pym's account of the language policies in favour of Catalan adopted by the Catalan authorities during these Games (Pym 2000, 211–9). Venuti characterises that account as *satirical* because Pym had spoken rather airily of the large amount of effort and money the Catalan government had spent on securing what turned out, in Pym's estimation, to be only a modest place for Catalan at the Games. Venuti offers an alternative story, one emplotted as *romance*, in which the Catalan authorities, mindful of the decades of suppression of Catalan under the Franco dictatorship (1939–75), were cast as writing a successful chapter in the long struggle for the survival of their language. Setting Pym alongside Venuti, we have one event, two plots, two distinct evaluative stances and two very different takes on the historical evidence. Pym's sarcasm had been directed at what he viewed as the disproportionate material cost of gaining an elusive symbolic benefit. Venuti retraced an extended history of conflict to argue that the political prize – Catalan displayed on the global stage – was worth the effort. Where Pym's argument was transactional (the outcome failed to match the input), Venuti's was ideological (a story of resurgence and self-affirmation).

The point about attending to Venuti's application of White is not to quibble about it or to hold it up as an example. Rather, it makes us realise that the narratives we construe on the basis of historical data will inevitably have a certain plot structure, and therefore a certain form. This form is meaningful in itself, and we may as well be aware of it. As Judy Wakabayashi has noted (2019a, 24–5), especially insidious are accounts of translation history that present themselves as narratives of 'progress' or 'improvement' by depicting modern translations as somehow better than past translations. These are typically narratives in the mode of *romance*.

After White: Pushing On, Pushing Back

Socio-narrative and translation

White regarded narrative not as some superficial device enabling us to encode sets of events into stories but as rooted in the human need to make sense of the world and give meaning to it. Narrative, for him, was universal. Other historians, such as David Carr (2001, 198–9), agreed. This universal quality of narrative was picked up by a number of researchers in other fields, including the sociologist Margaret Somers and the psychologist Jerome Bruner, for whom narrative was fundamental for the way we construe our personal identity and the world around us. Their work, in turn, informed Mona Baker's *Translation and Conflict* (2006), still the major application of narrative theory to the world of translation and a book that has inspired several other scholars.

The socio-narrative approach incorporates the basic concepts of narrative reviewed above but is particularly interested in different kinds of narrative. It distinguishes between personal narratives, the stories individuals tell themselves about themselves, and socially shared narratives, which cover the entire range from local incrowd narratives to all manner of institutional narratives and, ultimately, the so-called metanarratives about 'the march of civilisation' and other such grand ideas.

Two concepts make the socio-narrative approach especially serviceable for the study of translation and its history: framing and renarration. The basic idea is that texts, spoken or written, partake in the construction of narratives by acting on and interacting with existing narratives. When they are translated, they find themselves in an environment that contains a different web of existing narratives. 'Framing' refers to the way they present themselves in this new environment and 'renarration' indicates the negotiation with surrounding narratives at the receiving end. Put simply, translation means retelling a text in new surroundings.

Here is a brief illustration, taken from a 2015 article by Serena Bassi on the Italian journalist Roberto Saviano in English translation (Bassi 2015). Saviano had shot to fame in Italy in 2006 with the non-fiction book *Gomorrah*, in which he analysed the business deals of a major Italian crime syndicate. He received death threats and needed police protection but also became a celebrity. When the book appeared in English translation in 2008, both its marketing and the press reviews consistently linked Saviano to Salman Rushdie, the concept of free speech and what was then known as the 'war on terror'. The connection was that Rushdie, too, had needed police protection after the publication of his novel *The Satanic Verses* in 1988 had provoked a *fatwa* against him by the Ayatollah Khomeini. He became an icon of free speech in the face of what Western media portrayed as Islamic extremism, the same extremism that was responsible for the attacks known as 9/11, which in turn had led the then US President to declare a 'war on terror'.

The point of Bassi's study is that the English translation of Saviano's book retells the Italian story, but it has become a very different story because it is packaged differently. Note the multiple narrative layers that are involved. There is Saviano's first-person account of his own experience. In Italy, this account fitted into a wider narrative of individuals facing up to organised crime. The English translation was framed by an unrelated and much larger narrative, which lent Saviano's story a symbolic value it never had in its Italian version (the frame also had an ideological aspect in that, implicitly and insidiously, it associated Islamism with organised crime). In turn, there is Bassi's narrative construction of the way these various narratives interlink, and finally my own narrative summary and interpretation of Bassi's work. We live in a web of narratives.

Pushing on and pushing back

Among historians, White's observations on the element of fabulation in historical writing proved influential but also unsettling. Some, like Alun Munslow, pushed the idea of narrative as far as it would go in postmodernist directions, stressing the gap between, on the one hand, a past that is unrecoverable and, on the other, histories as textual constructs that can evoke but not recreate the past. Here, to give a taste, is a quick sampling of Munslow's claims and pronouncements (all from Munslow 2017).

- 'The past is the time before now and a history is our narrative about it' (2017, 485). While this is plain enough, for Munslow the nature of history is that of a 'fictive construed narrative description of the past' (481).
- The need to work with attested data remains undiminished but interpreting the data and shaping them into a narrative are activities of a different order. Hence, 'the reality of the past is always subject to the narrative techniques chosen by historians to render what they take to be its "history"' (480). Because a narrative is 'authored', it contains the features of every narrative, namely voice, focalisation, order, duration, frequency, agency, argument, emplotment and tropes (475). Writing history amounts to a 'transfiguration' of the past (485). Three things follow from this:
  - first, there is no isomorphism between the past and its history (487); that is, the verbal account which the historian gives of the past does not mirror or replicate the past;
  - second, 'the meaning and explicatory worth of a history is never more than the efficacy of the authorial artifice which controls the selecting, shaping, forming and ordering of the empirical content of the history' (477), which puts the emphasis on the historian's storytelling skill, and
  - third, 'the belief that the historian is objective, dispassionate, detached and indifferent is plainly nonsensical' (478), which sums up the matter polemically.
- As an addendum, Munslow notes that all history writing is ironical in that it says several things at the same time: it speaks about the past while transfiguring it, but it also interacts with what other historians are saying about the past (478).

Other historians pushed back. The Chinese historian Xin Chen, for instance, who helped introduce Hayden White's work to China, notes that Chinese historians generally value empirical research and archival sources more than theoretical speculation (Chen 2019, 551). Both Martha Cheung (2012) and Judy Wakabayashi (2012) had earlier written in a similar vein about the insistence of many historians in China and Japan (respectively) that their aim remained that of establishing the objective truth about verifiable facts. For these historians, primary sources and any comments about them are to be kept separate.

It would be wrong, as Wakabayashi points out (2012, 183), to dismiss this insistence on facts, objectivity and truth. Indeed, there may be several ways to engage with it. In one chapter of his *Futures Past* (published originally in German in 1979), Reinhart Koselleck lists the basics of all historical method: recognising the authority of the sources, checking their authenticity and reliability, and applying the rules of textual exegesis to establish their meaning (1985, 152–3). But, he goes on, the further we stray into the past, the patchier its remnants, and the more we approach our own time, the more bewildering the excess of sources, making guesswork and selection unavoidable. In addition, the questions historians ask stem from their own contemporary perspective; they may, for example, concern long-term processes of which people at the time cannot have been aware. The historian's questions – 'the primacy of theory' in Koselleck's terms (1985, 155) – give meaning to the sources. In this sense, the historical account surpasses the sources because it follows its own trajectory. 'Sources protect us from error', Koselleck observes, 'but they never tell us what we should say' (1985, 155). He therefore urges historians to have 'the courage to form hypotheses' (ibid.) about what they reckon actually happened. Although Koselleck is not speaking here about narrativity, his dual emphasis on respect for the sources together with the courage to form hypotheses keeps archives and speculation apart but still under the same roof and talking to each other. (We will meet Koselleck again in Chapter 4.)

Pushing-Hands

There may be another way to address the tension between fact-based history and the relativist inclinations of Hayden White-style narrativism. This is the pushing-hands approach proposed by Martha Cheung (2012; Robinson 2016, 19–33), which has the added distinction of being the only distinct approach to historical study as such and to translation history in particular to have been put forward by a translation researcher.

The background to this approach lies in *tuishou* or 'pushing-hands', a Chinese martial arts form with philosophical roots in the idea of the inter-play of opposites, such as *yin* and *yang*. The pushing-hands principle is not to oppose an incoming force directly but to engage with it and then displace it by a combination of yielding and redirecting. As a practice, *tuishou* involves both harmonious movement and combat, unison as well as opposition, a non-confrontational engagement that is nevertheless firm and prepared, if necessary, to resist an opponent. The key statement in Cheung's essay applies to translation and reads as follows:

> For scholars in translation studies, the pushing-hands approach provides a fruitful model of engagement with translation history and historical research on translation. It allows them to think of past and present in a relation of interdependence, with past events informing the present and present perspectives illuminating the past, the two alternately pushing and yielding. Other positions and perspectives that are often regarded as existing in a state of tension can also be brought together in a harmonious coexistence of opposites: theory and practice, primary and secondary, East and West, macrohistory and microhistory, universalism and localism, to name just a few of the binaries characterizing the contemporary scholarly mindset.
>
> (Cheung 2012, 162)

To illustrate how this 'model of engagement' could be applied, Cheung offered several examples drawn from her own research on Chinese translation history. I'll briefly set out two.

• Her interest in the evolution of ideas about translation in China brought her up against the prevailing account, which presented this evolution as a linear development, a narrative of progress (Cheung 2012, 163). Her response was not to offer a counter-narrative but to go for a different type of presentation. She opted for an anthology of primary texts, with a fragmented narrative and various kinds of annotations that allowed different voices and viewpoints to emerge, including discussion of how past issues might be rephrased in modern terms or how modern terminology might struggle to capture past practices. Without directly confronting the notion of a linear development, she sought to unhinge it by refracting it. (We will return to this anthology in the next chapter.)

• Chinese translations of Buddhist sutras have a long history, which, considered from a Western perspective, seems comparable to the history of Bible translation. Similarities can indeed be noted. For instance, in both cases the discourse about translating revolves around the most appropriate ways to convey the source text. In pushing-hands terms, this is a matter of yielding. But this is followed by deflecting and displacing the opponent's incoming force. In contrast with Bible texts, sutras were often unstable as source texts: some were translated from memory, the surviving texts show significant variations and often no clear origin, and in some cases it remains uncertain what language a translation was made from. These differences could be taken further and used, in turn, to question some of the assumptions informing Bible translation.

Cheung stressed that her pushing-hands idea was not a theory or a method but a form of engagement that was non-confrontational and dialogic but also firm. Its main technique is to undo threatening binaries by shifting the ground. This could be one way of negotiating the apparent opposition between the search for an objective historical truth on the one hand and the narrative insistence on the relativity of perspectives on the other.

Further Reading

Baker, Mona. 2006. *Translation and Conflict. A Narrative Account*. London & New York: Routledge.
This is the major application of narrative theory to the study of translation. It takes the particular approach known as socio-narrative and is interested primarily in the role of narrative in situations of conflict. Its lucid exposition and numerous examples make it a very profitable read.

Roberts, Geoffrey, ed. 2001. *The History and Narrative Reader*. London & New York: Routledge.

The 26 essays in this collection span the period from the 1960s to the 1990s and were written by and for historians. The book is structured around debates about narrative as a mode of explanation, the ontological nature of narrative, the connection between narrative and historical truth and the linguistic turn. There are key essays by the likes of Louis Mink, Hayden White, David Carr, Lawrence Stone and Margaret Somers.

White, Hayden. 1978. *Tropics of Discourse. Essays in Cultural Criticism.* Baltimore & London: Johns Hopkins University Press.
A collection of White's early essays, originally written between 1966 and 1976, including incisive pieces such as 'The Burden of History', 'Interpretation in History', 'The Historical Text as Literary Artefact' (this essay is also in *The History and Narrative Reader*) and 'The Fictions of Factual Representation'. White's careful phrasing does not always make for easy reading, but it is worth persisting.

Bibliography

Ankersmit, Frank. 1983. *Narrative Logic. A Semantic Analysis of the Historian's Language.* The Hague: Martinus Nijhoff.

Ankersmit, Frank. 2017. "A Dialogue with Jouni-Matti Kuukkanen." *Journal of the Philosophy of History* 11: 38–58.

Baker, Mona. 2006. *Translation and Conflict. A Narrative Account.* London & New York: Routledge.

Barthes, Roland. 1981. "The Discourse of History." Translated by Stephen Bann. *Comparative Criticism* 3: 7–20. Original, French, 1967.

Bassi, Serena. 2015. "Italy's Salman Rushdie. The Renarration of 'Roberto Saviano' in English for the Post-9/11 Cultural Market." *Translation Studies* 8: 48–62.

Berman, Antoine. 1990. "La retraduction comme espace de la traduction." *Palimpsestes* 4: 1–7.

Bridges, Lucas. 2019. *Uttermost Part of the Earth. Tierra del Fuego's Indians and Settlers. A Personal Story* [1947]. Ushuaia: Südpol.

Bridges, Thomas. 1866. "Manners and Customs of the Firelanders." *A Voice for South America* 13: 201–14.

Bridges, Thomas. 1869. "The Southern or Fuegian Mission." *The South American Missionary Magazine* 3: 10–4.

Bridges, Thomas. 1870a. "The Fuegian or Southern Mission." *The South American Missionary Magazine* 4: 39–43.

Bridges, Thomas. 1870b. "The Fuegian or Southern Mission." *The South American Missionary Magazine* 4: 127–37.

Bridges, Thomas. 1872. Letter, 11 March 1872. *The South American Missionary Magazine* 6: 98–101.

Bridges, Thomas. 1873. Undated letter. *The South American Missionary Magazine* 7: 27–30.

Bridges, Thomas. 1875. "Southern Mission. Ushuwia." *The South American Missionary Magazine* 9: 214–21.

Bridges, Thomas. 1879. Letter, 1 January 1979. *The South American Missionary Magazine* 13: 102–5.

Bridges, Thomas. 1881. *Gospl Lyc Ecamanāci. The Gospel of S. Luke Translated into the Yahgan Language.* London: British and Foreign Bible Society.

Bridges, Thomas. 1882. Letter, 5 January 1882. *The South American Missionary Magazine* 16: 101–5.

Bridges, Thomas. 1883. *Aposl'ndian Ūstāgų. The Acts of the Apostles Translated into the Yahgan Language*. London: British and Foreign Bible Society.

Bridges, Thomas. 1884a. Letter, 24 October 1883. *The South American Missionary Magazine* 18: 30–4.

Bridges, Thomas. 1884b. Letter, 20 June 1884. *The South American Missionary Magazine* 18: 222–4.

Bridges, Thomas. 1885. "The Yahgans of Tierra del Fuego." *The Journal of the Anthropological Institute of Great Britain and Ireland* 14: 288–9.

Bridges, Thomas. 1886. *Gospel Jon Ecamanāci. The Gospel of S. John Translated into the Yahgan Language*. London: British and Foreign Bible Society.

Bridges, Thomas. 1887. "Tierra del Fuego. Past, Present, and Future." *The South American Missionary Magazine* 21: 7–8.

Bridges, Thomas. 1987. *Yámana-English. A Dictionary of the Speech of Tierra del Fuego*. Edited by Ferdinand Hestermann and Martin Gusinde [1933]. Buenos Aires: Zagier y Urruty Publicaciones.

Bull, Charles. 1867. "Journal of a visit [...] to Keppel Island, by the colonial chaplain of the Falkland Islands, October, 1866." *The South American Missionary Magazine* 1: 47–9.

Burckhardt, Frederick, and James Secord, eds. 2015. *The Correspondence of Charles Darwin*. Volume 22. Cambridge: Cambridge University Press.

Carr, David. 2001. "Getting the Story Straight. Narrative and Historical Knowledge" [1994]. In *The History and Narrative Reader*, edited by Geoffrey Roberts, 197–208. London & New York: Routledge.

Cassin, Barbara, ed. 2014. *Dictionary of Untranslatables. A Philosophical Lexicon*. Translated by Steven Rendall et al. Princeton & Oxford: Princeton University Press.

Chakrabarty, Dipesh. 2000. *Provincializing Europe. Postcolonial Thought and Historical Difference*. Princeton & Oxford: Princeton University Press.

Chapman, Anne. 2010. *European Encounters with the Yámana People of Cape Horn, Before and After Darwin*. Cambridge: Cambridge University Press.

Chapman, Seymour. 1978. *Story and Discourse. Narrative Structure in Fiction and Film*. Ithaca & London: Cornell University Press.

Chen, Xin. 2019. "The Reception of Hayden White in China (1987–2018)" in "Globalizing Hayden White." Edited by Ewa Domańska and María Inés La Greca. *Rethinking History* 23: 546–53.

Cheung, Martha. 2012. "The Mediated Nature of Knowledge and the Pushing-Hands Approach to Research on Translation History." *Translation Studies* 5: 156–71.

Cooper, John. 1917. *Analytical and Critical Bibliography of the Tribes of Tierra del Fuego and Adjacent Territory*. Washington: Bureau of American Ethnology, Smithsonian Institution.

Darwin, Charles. 1989. *Voyage of the Beagle* [1839]. Edited by Janet Browne and Michael Neve. London: Penguin.

Domańska, Ewa. 1998. *Encounters. Philosophy of History after Postmodernism*. Charlottesville & London: University Press of Virginia.

Dray, W.H. 1954. "Explanatory Narrative in History." *The Philosophical Quarterly* 4: 15–27.

Ellis, Alexander. 1884. "Eleventh Annual Address of the President to the Philological Society, Delivered at the Anniversary Meeting, Friday, 19th May, 1882." *Transactions of the Philological Society*, 1–148.

Garson, J.G. 1886. "On the Inhabitants of Tierra del Fuego." *The Journal of the Anthropological Institute of Great Britain and Ireland* 15: 141–60.

Humboldt, Wilhelm von. 1967. "On the Historian's Task." [1821; translator unknown]. *History and Theory* 6: 57–71.

Hyades, Paul. 1884. "Sur les Fuégiens." *Bulletins de la Société anthropologique de Paris* 7: 616–20.

Hyades, Paul. 1885a. "Sur l'état actuel des Fuégiens de l'archipel du cap Horn." *Bulletins de la Société anthropologique de Paris* 8: 200–9.

Hyades, Paul. 1885b. "La rougeole chez les Fuégiens." *Bulletins de la Société anthropologique de Paris* 8: 462–3.

Hyades, Paul. 1886. "Les épidémies chez les Fuégiens." *Bulletins de la Société anthropologique de Paris* (2nd series) 1: 202–5.

Kansteiner, W. 1993. "Hayden White's Critique of the Writing of History." *History and Theory* 32: 273–96.

Koselleck, Reinhart. 1985. *Futures Past. On the Semantics of Historical Time*. Translated by Keith Tribe. Cambridge (Mass.): MIT Press.

Lemon, M.C. 2001. "The Structure of Narrative [1995]." In *The History and Narrative Reader*, edited by Geoffrey Roberts, 107–29. London & New York: Routledge.

Levý, Jiří. 2011. *The Art of Translation* [1963]. Edited by Zuzana Jettmarová. Translated by Patrick Corness. Amsterdam & Philadelphia: John Benjamins.

Mak, Kam Wah (George). 2015. "To add or not to add? The British and Foreign Bible Society's Defence of the 'Without Note or Comment' Principle in Late Qing China." *Journal of the Royal Asiatic Society* 25: 329–54.

Manouvrier, L. 1881. "Sur les Fuégiens du Jardin d'acclimatation." *Bulletins de la Société anthropologique de Paris* 4: 760–74.

Marsh, John William. 1883. *Narrative of the Origin and Progress of the South American Mission*. London: South American Missionary Society.

Mink, Louis. 2001. "Narrative Form as a Cognitive Instrument" [1978]. In *The History and Narrative Reader*, edited by Geoffrey Roberts, 211–20. London & New York: Routledge.

Monod, Gabriel. 1897. *Portraits et souvenirs*. Paris: Calmann Lévy.

Munslow, Alun. 2017. "History, Skepticism and the Past." *Rethinking History* 21: 474–88.

Perrot d'Ablancourt, Nicolas. 1972. *Lettres et préfaces critiques*. Edited by Roger Zuber. Paris: Didier.

Prakash, Gyan. 1990. "Writing Post-Orientalist Histories of the Third World: Perspectives from Indian Historiography." *Comparative Studies in Society and History* 32: 383–408.

Pym, Anthony. 2000. *Negotiating the Frontier. Translators and Intercultures in Hispanic History*. Manchester: St Jerome.

Rimmon-Kenan, Shlomith. 1983. *Narrative Fiction. Contemporary Poetics*. London & New York: Methuen.

Roberts, Geoffrey, ed. 2001. *The History and Narrative Reader*. London & New York: Routledge.

Robinson, Douglas, ed. 2016. *The Pushing-Hands of Translation and its Theory*. London & New York: Routledge.

SAMS (South American Missionary Society). 1884. "Christian Civilization and the South American Mission." *The South American Missionary Magazine* 18: 53–67.

Somers, Margaret. 1994. "The Narrative Constitution of Identity: A Relational and Network Approach." *Theory and Society* 23: 605–49.

Somers, Margaret. 2001. "Narrativity, Narrative Identity and Social Action: Rethinking English Working-Class Formation" [1992]. In *The History and Narrative Reader*, edited by Geoffrey Roberts, 354–74. London & New York: Routledge.

Venuti, Lawrence. 2004. "Retranslations: The Creation of Value." *Bucknell Review* 47: 25–38. Reprinted in Venuti, Lawrence. 2013. *Translation Changes Everything*, 96–108. London & New York: Routledge.

Venuti, Lawrence. 2005. "Translation, History, Narrative." *Meta* 50: 800–16.

Von Ranke, Leopold. 1824. *Geschichten der romanischen und germanischen Völker*. Vol. 1. Leipzig & Berlin: G. Reimer.

Wakabayashi, Judy. 2012. "Japanese Translation Historiography: Origins, Strengths, Weaknesses and Lessons." *Translation Studies* 5: 172–88.

Wakabayashi, Judy. 2019a. "Time Matters: Conceptual and Methodological Considerations in Translation Timescapes." *Chronotopos* 1: 23–39.

White, Hayden. 1973. *Metahistory. The Historical Imagination in Nineteenth-Century Europe*. Baltimore & London: Johns Hopkins University Press.

White, Hayden. 1978. *Tropics of Discourse. Essays in Cultural Criticism*. Baltimore & London: Johns Hopkins University Press.

White, Hayden. 1986. "Historical Pluralism." *Critical Inquiry* 12: 480–93.

White, Hayden. 1989. "'Figuring the Nature of the Times Deceased': Literary Theory and Historical Writing." *The Future of Literary Theory*, edited by Ralph Cohen, 19–43. London & New York: Routledge.

White, Hayden. 2005. "Introduction: Historical Fiction, Fictional History, and Historical Reality." *Rethinking History* 9: 147–57.

White, Hayden. 2013. "History as Fulfillment." In *Philosophy of History after Hayden White*, edited by Robert Doran, 35–46. London: Bloomsbury.

2   Translation History

When I was an undergraduate student at the University of Ghent in Belgium, we had a professor of European history called Jan Dhondt. In one of his lectures, he explained how the Crusades – a now infamous series of expeditions around 1100 in which Western European Christian armies tried to take control of Muslim-occupied Jerusalem – could be traced back to the invention of a new kind of plough around 350 years earlier. It seemed quite a leap, from the humble plough to crusading armies. The argument went as follows. The ploughs used earlier, in the Roman world, were essentially pointed sticks or rods pulled through the ground, and they did little more than disturb the soil. In the eighth century or so, an iron plough with a curved blade was invented in Western Europe. It cut deeper and turned the clods of earth. This led to more plentiful harvests of crops with better nutritional value, which after a few generations led to an increase in population and eventually to a population surplus. It was this demographic surplus that Europe decanted into the Near East. The Crusades, our professor pointed out, were the first aggressive wars that Europe had been able to fight outside its borders since Roman times.

I may not remember the lecture correctly, and I doubt the theory has much purchase among medievalists today. Even on its own terms (as I remember them), the causal chain seems too simple. The better harvests resulted not only from the introduction of a new type of plough but also from the use of horseshoes, crop rotation and collars for horses and oxen, and the Crusades were conditioned by more than just population growth. No matter. The lecture stayed with me because, at the time, I was struck by the ingenuity of the reasoning: a seemingly minor technological innovation contributing to an agricultural revolution which eventually had social, political and military consequences.

Doing history is a matter of joining dots, seeing links, tracing patterns and then articulating them in the form of a narrative. As we saw in the previous chapter, a narrative assigns meaning to events by making significant connections with other events. In historical contexts, this means applying hindsight to decide on a setting (place, time), participants (agents, actors), a plot structure and an angle from which to tell the story.

The present chapter is concerned with the history of translation, in the double sense of getting a handle on how translation changes over time and of

DOI: 10.4324/9781315178134-2

understanding translation in its historical context. The first section addresses the key issues of a research project on translation history: the aim of the exercise, the research questions, the gathering of primary data and how to start building a narrative plot. The second section is about how to cut up the cake, especially as regards the difficult questions of periodisation and geographical spread. The third section considers the dynamics of change in terms of both text-centred and agent-centred models. The fourth and final section concerns the historical discourse on translation and the fact that much of this discourse is available to us in the form of anthologies.

Key Issues

Project aims

The first issue to be clarified about any research project concerns its goal. What kind of insight does the project aim to achieve about what exactly? As regards historical research involving translation, Christopher Rundle (2012; 2014) has argued that it makes a difference whether the aim is (1) to understand translation by studying a slice of its history, or (2) to understand a slice of history by studying the role of translation in it. In the first case we study historical manifestations of translation. We draw on the historical context, not for its own sake but to better understand what translation is and does. In the second case we study a historical phenomenon, and we draw on translation because it may shed a certain light on this historical phenomenon. The difference is in the disciplinary centre of gravity – translation studies or history – and in the scholarly community we are addressing with our research. Of course, disciplinary boundaries can be crossed, even though this is generally harder than it seems because different research communities have different discourses, communication circuits and points of reference.

For my own part, I take the view that the two disciplinary angles do not have to be mutually exclusive. Translation matters because it fulfils a social and cultural role. This applies to the past and to the present. To understand that role in historical configurations and processes, we need to be aware of what historians have said about them, the kind of issues they have raised and the terms in which they have done so. In this respect, Rundle is right to insist that translation historians need to learn to think more like historians. But to be able to contextualise translation we need to appreciate its historical manifestations and perceptions, and students of translation are well placed to do this. As the contextualisation of individual translations proceeds and gains in scope and depth, the larger constellation of which translation forms a part comes into view as well. At that point we slide into seeking to understand a historical constellation and the place of translation in it. Hence my belief that the two disciplinary perspectives are complementary. I will return to this point towards the end of Chapter 6.

The present chapter is concerned with the history of translation. As will become clear, even if the focus of one's research is translation rather than the slice of history into which it fits, the motives for translating and the effects of translation always exceed translation.

That leaves the question of which scholarly community a researcher wants to address, historians or students of translation. The answer depends on whether someone is prepared to make him- or herself sufficiently familiar with the relevant discipline to be taken seriously by its practitioners. Crossing disciplinary lines requires considerable effort, but it can be done, and there are scholars who are regarded highly by both historians and students of translation (Peter Burke, Hilary Footitt, Lydia Liu, Vicente Rafael, to name but a few).

Research questions

Every research project hinges on a research question. The present book is not a research manual, so we can be brief about the basic criteria a research question has to meet. It must take the form of a real question with a question mark at the end, it must be capable of a rational, evidence-based answer that is not self-evident, and it must address an issue of some intellectual or social significance. Beyond this, a research question helps to keep a research project manageable. It restricts the project's scope (time, location, genre, environment, key actors) and provides a focus of attention, a filter which retains some things while setting aside others as marginal or irrelevant. When correlated with an appropriate methodology, it enables project planning and management.

Research questions don't come out of thin air. They require a certain familiarity with a field of study and with existing research on it. When, on the basis of this initial familiarity, a research question has singled out the kind of things that will be of interest and why, researchers are in a position to distinguish between what they are looking *for* from what they are looking *at*. They may be looking *at* a certain historical phenomenon (period, genre, figure, network, institution, text, practice, process and whatnot) but within this scenario they are looking *for* those elements or aspects that will enable them to answer their research question. This is the crucial filter the research question puts in place. It permits the researcher to negotiate inventories with a sense of purpose.

Gathering primary data

Finding primary data remains problematic in the case of translations, as indeed many researchers have pointed out (Poupaud, Pym, and Torres Simón 2009; J. Richter 2020, 70–82). This is because translation is an ill-defined category and translations have often been held in low esteem.

Bibliographies would seem the obvious places to start, but most general bibliographies were not designed with translation in mind. In the standard national bibliographies, for instance, translations tend to remain invisible as a category (Zhou and Sun 2017, 105, 107). The largest bibliographical database currently available is WorldCat, a union catalogue said to contain almost 500 million abbreviated bibliographical records of items held in libraries worldwide, with an indication of which library holds which item, and links to electronic copies when available. It is searchable by keywords, title and author. Searching by 'author' will also throw up translators, but only if their names appear on the title page.

Bibliographies need careful handling. They may look impressive and even objective, but not only are they invariably deficient in one respect or another, they are also, as Julia Richter notes (2020, 70), deeply subjective because they reflect the compiler's selection criteria as well as personal decisions in cases of doubt.

Archives are no different. They are not neutral storehouses: someone decided what was worth keeping, how the holdings were to be organised and catalogued, and what kind of search terms would unlock the material. Like standard bibliographies, archives are not usually geared to translation (Adamo 2006, 92). Even if they house materials relevant to translation, these may be catalogued under different headings. For instance, the Harry Ransom Center for the Humanities at the University of Austin, Texas, has rich holdings on major American translators but 'translation' is not among its subject categories, as Jeremy Munday found when he went there (Munday 2014, 71). If locating even major translators is hard, digging up minor translators is harder still, not to mention interpreters. Perhaps the invisibility of translators in the archives says something about the public perception of the value of translation more generally (Israel and Frenz 2019; Kujamäki and Footitt 2016, 61; J. Richter 2020, 152–3).

Often, then, translation researchers need to start with specialised bibliographies on subjects other than translation. For instance, the online database on the French Book Trade in Enlightenment Europe (FBTEE),[1] initiated in 2012, maps the trade of a Swiss publishing house between 1769 and 1794. It is narrowly focused and translations are of only minor significance, but it may still be of interest because the publisher had Europe-wide trade links. The site also showcases sophisticated visualisation tools and is worth a visit for this reason alone.

Closer to the world of translation are transcultural databases like that on the Perso-Indica website,[2] which explores Persian works on Indian learned traditions between roughly 1200 and 1850. Because over half of these works are translations, its various indexes have ample space for translators and their products. The site covers only a limited number of works, under 200, but gives detailed information when the sources allow.

There are also online databases that have translation as their main focus. They are as yet few and far between, but their number is growing.

Best known, though fading fast, is UNESCO's Index Translationum,[3] which began in printed form in 1932, became available as an online database for the years 1979 up to around 2010, but then stalled for financial reasons and is no longer being updated. As a database searchable in several ways (names, dates, titles, languages) it should have been the ideal tool for translation historians.

However, the online version covers a mere 30 years, and even within this time span its quality remains very uneven.

By contrast, the Renaissance Cultural Crossroads Catalogue,[4] an online searchable database geared to Early Modern translation in the British Isles, is a model of its kind. It lists all translations, whatever the subject, printed in England, Scotland and Ireland between 1473 (when the first English book was printed) and 1640, plus translations into English printed elsewhere during this period. It is a tool of limited size – a good 6,000 records – intended for specialists, but it offers a shining example of what a database sensitive to translation history might look like. For instance, the search category 'intermediate language' throws up indirect translations, whether these are identified as such in the title or not (French and Latin, it turns out, are the most common intermediate languages). Just as valuable are the descriptions of liminary materials and the sometimes extensive additional notes.

The amount of information made available in a database like this can serve as a reminder that compiling these resources requires funding, commitment and teamwork, as advanced knowledge of translation, history and book history has to be brought together with bibliographical and web design skills into a managed project.

This also goes, in a different way, for another type of online reference work that is rapidly growing: lexicons of translators. The model here is the lexicon of Swedish translators,[5] with currently some 500 entries (in Swedish) comprising not only translators but also institutions, prizes, concepts, book series and the like, plus a detailed bibliographical apparatus (including translations published in periodicals) with cross-references. The lexicon is geared to literary and humanities translation but has obvious potential to expand. It has already inspired similar initiatives in Germany and the Netherlands.[6]

Still under construction, but conceived on a larger scale, is the Digital Library and Bibliography for Literature in Translation (DLBT) at the University of Vienna.[7] It gives access to translations and reception documents, in some cases linking to digitised versions of the actual texts. This is an online library still in its infancy, but with the ambition to be much more in the future.

Websites like these are promising, and no doubt similar initiatives are being taken in various parts of the world. But research projects in translation history tend to be specific, and they are rarely served in full by any one bibliography or database. In practice, therefore, researchers have to be pragmatic and determined, while keeping in mind the purpose the bibliographical data are meant to serve.

Consider, for instance, how an experienced researcher like Michaela Wolf went about collecting bibliographical data for her comprehensive study of translation and interpreting in the multiethnic and multilingual Habsburg monarchy in the period from 1848 to 1918 (Wolf 2012; 2015b). Gathering quantitative data regarding printed translations across these languages would be impossible, so Wolf restricted her searches to translations of a single genre (literature) into a single language (German). Even that proved to be far from simple, as bibliographies of translations into German even from some languages spoken within the Habsburg state simply did not exist. Wolf still checked bibliographies for over a dozen source languages (2012, 238–46; 2015b, 150–5) and found that they varied hugely in quality and in their selection criteria (they differed, for example, in what they counted as literature; some included translations in periodicals or anthologies, others did not). The statistics produced on this basis (2012, 247–62; 2015b, 155–67) could obviously not be exact, but – and this is the saving grace – they were indicative of trends, and that was all that mattered in the context of the study. Having to decide next on a case study to put some concrete flesh on this skeleton picture, Wolf picked translations from Italian into German because these were the best documented (a pragmatic reason). But even then, although she had at her disposal an excellent bibliography, she still scoured the catalogues of ten libraries in six cities, checked other bibliographies and monographs, and leafed through half a dozen periodicals. This enabled her to extend the existing bibliography, good as it was, by about 30 percent (2012, 281–2; 2015b, 179).

Assembling a picture

A research project does not begin with a random collection of data followed by a search for possible explanations of the data. It begins with curiosity, due diligence and an initial hunch that leads to a research question. The data collection is guided by the parameters of the question and by the tentative answers that the researcher has in mind. This is why research is not a two-stage process of first data collection then explanation. The data collection is already an informed, controlled exercise.

For the history of translation, it has become standard to list a series of forensic questions derived from classical rhetoric: *who* translated *what, where, when, how, why, for whom* and *with what effect* (Kittel 1988, 160; Pym 1998, 5; Burke 2007, 11; D'hulst 2014, 28–41). Questions of this type are common among historians as well (Froeyman 2009, 119). They will always be addressed selectively, with a project's guiding research question acting as a searchlight.

The answers to the majority of the standard questions are fact based. They supply the elements (participants, events, time and place) required for the historical narrative, as we saw in the previous chapter. All the questions need to be interpreted broadly and flexibly. The *who* question includes not just scouts, agents, commissioners, editors, publishers and translators but the whole network of contacts that play a part in the long process of selecting, manufacturing and disseminating translations. It extends to policymakers, enforcers and resource providers who may be able to control what gets translated under what conditions. *What* may involve bibliographical and archival searches but also the place of individual translations in a larger body of translated works, as well as its negative foil: what was made accessible by means other than translation or left untranslated even though available? *Where* usually throws up the obvious metropolitan centres and contact zones, but niche translations may appear just about anywhere given the right conditions. *When* bears on individual translations but equally on larger trends and flows, on time lags, diffusion speeds and retranslations. *How* comes with a reminder that translators never work alone: they rely on previous practice, on contacts, informants, collaborators, dictionaries, grammars, institutions, the internet and other material and intellectual infrastructure. Archival records may allow a glimpse of the conditions, queries and decisions shaping individual translations. *For whom* may be inscribed in a translation itself, as its addressee, but more often recipients are at a further remove so that in some cases this question blends into *with what effect*, which may mean the exploration of complex and long-term repercussions – or the assessment of short-term benefit (or harm) or of paths opened (or blocked).

The question *why* is of a different order. It invites a speculative answer and involves the recognition of stakes and interests and the attribution of motives, and hence narrative emplotment. Of course, translators and other participants may volunteer information about why they did certain things, but the researcher would do well not to take these claims at face value.

Looking for a key?

The *why* question just mentioned goes much further than might appear. Asking *for whom* a translation was made is one thing, asking *why* someone did what they did, or what they were doing it all *for*, is altogether different. What made someone request, commission, produce, print, distribute, lend, borrow or buy a translation? What made them undertake this rather than some other course of action? What did they hope to achieve by it? What benefit did they expect to derive from it? In short: what were they doing it *for*?

In her book *Translationshistoriographie* (2020), Julia Richter provides an eminently useful answer to this question. First, however, she points out that many translators and other actors, including translation scholars, will respond to the *what for?* question with statements that reflect the idealised self-image of translation. According to this self-image, translation removes comprehension barriers, builds bridges and promotes mutual understanding. In the same vein, translators are cast as selfless mediators and translations as transparent panes of glass or faithful copies. Julia Richter's advice is to be wary of images like these. Translators and those around them may indeed be altruistic and keen to foster intercultural harmony, but they are just as likely to be led by completely different motives (2020, 138–42).

Writing translation history requires a combination of the factors beloved of TV detectives investigating a crime: motive, means and opportunity. Working these factors into a story is a process of emplotment.

As for means and opportunity, these terms are shorthand for the social, material and intellectual conditioning of translation at a certain juncture. This conditioning may be constraining as well as enabling. Enabling conditions would be, for example, the presence of a metropolitan centre with multilingual resources and good communication networks, or simply the availability of someone with relevant expertise and sufficient time and goodwill. Constraining conditions might include such things as censorship, a xenophobic ideology, frequent power cuts or a shortage of candles.

The most likely motive for any act of translation is self-interest, whether on the part of the translator or of others involved in the process. It can take the form of personal or collective gain in one form or another, or simply of self-preservation. The gain may be material, social, intellectual or affective. Material gain includes payment in money or in kind (in 1660, the Dutch poet Joost van den Vondel received 180 bottles of wine for his translation of Virgil, roughly one bottle for every 70 lines of verse). Social gain may mean the prospect of access to new circles or an increase in the number of useful contacts, or a desire to be valued by a church, a nation, a political regime, a group of friends. Intellectual gain might include the hope for greater knowledge of a subject or a better understanding of a language or of a particular work (some philosophers translated Heidegger in order to improve their grasp of his ideas; J. Richter 2020, 157–8). Affective gain would comprise admiration, the desire to be valued that was just mentioned, or the satisfaction of knowing one is doing the right thing (as with, say, volunteering to interpret in the community or for an NGO, or wanting to disseminate Holocaust testimonies by translating them).

Julia Richter (2020, 152–62) describes these different types of motive, in terms derived from Pierre Bourdieu, as the wish to accumulate different kinds of capital: cultural capital (embodied in the form of knowledge and skills), social capital (prestige, contacts) and economic capital (payment, material profit). She also makes it clear that these categories are to be viewed flexibly. For example, in 1869 the Habsburg monarchy decided to publish all national laws simultaneously in all the commonly used languages of the empire. Richter reads this decision as stemming from the regime's desire to accumulate social capital, because it envisaged the equal treatment of all ethnic groups within the monarchy and this was expected to strengthen their sense of shared belonging (J. Richter 2020, 160–1; Wolf 2012, 155; 2015b, 89).

But Julia Richter also warns (2020, 151) against the common methodological fallacy of working back from effects to motives or intentions. Translators intend certain effects with their translations and there is something that drives them, but while we may be able to observe effects, we cannot observe intentions or motivations. In other words, the fact that a translation achieves a certain effect does not mean it was the translator's intention to achieve that effect; the outcome of a process is not necessarily the intended outcome. We therefore cannot simply infer motives or intentions from effects. Indeed, as noted before, the study of history often involves the study of unintended consequences.

Cutting Up the Cake

The basic premise is that translating is not usually done for its own sake. It serves a purpose in particular contexts, be they diplomacy, politics, commerce, conversion, healthcare, warfare, finance, entertainment, jurisdiction, know-ledge transmission, public administration or whatever. Because translation rou-tinely caters for these other domains, it slots into their history. In other words, translation is not an autonomous but a largely heteronomous and diversified field. While it can develop a momentum of its own and thus stimulate or even engender change elsewhere, it normally falls in with the requirements of the fields it serves. As a result, the periodisation and geographical delimitation of translation history is mostly culture-specific.

Historical studies of translation therefore tend to follow the broad divisions of time and space made in political and cultural history. There is also the prag-matic consideration that history writing requires material evidence. In the absence of such evidence – in the case of oral traditions or where sources have been lost or destroyed – only limited guesswork is possible. This explains why historical surveys of translation in Africa (Nama 1993; Bandia 2005, 2009) or the Americas (Bastin 2009; Delisle 2009; Venuti 2009) have little or nothing to say about the centuries before European contact. For the period since then, they all apply the political division into first a colonial era followed by a period of national independence reaching into the present. By contrast, surveys of translation in India, China the Middle East and Europe are able to cover about 2,500 years or more and tend to combine political and cultural subdivisions. A summary survey of translation on the Indian subcontinent, for example, highlights well over a thousand years of Buddhist translation before addressing Moghul and then colonial rule, followed finally by the modern period of inde-pendent states (Krishnamurthy 2009).

Ideally, perhaps, the periodisation of translation should be based on changes in translation itself. This has been tried, but it has not worked. A notorious example is George Steiner's *After Babel*, which divided Western thinking on translation into four successive periods: the first covering almost two thousand years, the second a little over a hundred, and the third and fourth less than fifty, with the added snag that these last two were supposed to overlap (G. Steiner 1975, 236–8). This does not mean that a translation-specific periodisation is impossible. As a rule, however, gear changes in translation are correlated with social, political and cultural changes.

Periodisation

Most case studies in translation history are on a relatively small scale, both time-wise and in the geographical reach and domain of activity they cover. They tend to take conventional divisions into periods and areas for granted. This is no doubt convenient, but it may also leave them hostage to convention. It can even be misleading insofar as the standard period divisions may evoke stereo-types, exaggerate internal uniformity or suggest sharp breaks from one period to another. A more general review of the options may therefore be useful. Judy Wakabayashi (2019a, 28–31) has provided a handy overview of different pos-sible bases for periodisation.

Least useful because entirely conventional are forms of continuous dating in terms of centuries, decades or years. They simply mark the flow of time. Not a great deal changed when the clock indicated the start of the year 2000.

Non-continuous forms of periodisation are all culture-specific in the sense of being restricted in time, space and scope. Their usefulness for a translation history project depends on the project's research focus, but Wakabayashi's listing may also generate ideas by drawing attention to alternative options. At the very least, it stands as a reminder that the choice of a temporal framework should be a conscious decision.

- Broad divisions such as ancient, medieval, early modern and modern are common in Europe, but, as Wakabayashi points out (2019a, 29), they are also unstable and ambiguous. Nevertheless, to the extent that the Industrial Revolution made itself felt globally, the 'modern era' is often seen as beginning somewhere in the nineteenth century.
- Dynasties, reigns and eras (such as 'the Ming dynasty' or 'the Victorian era') connote dominant political and cultural constellations. More exclusively cultural are period concepts like Renaissance or Enlightenment. Often these terms carry an evaluative load (renaissance means rebirth, the Arabic *nahda* means reawakening), which is even stronger in the 'Golden Age' claimed by different national cultures for different periods. A concept like 'the Age of Discovery' betrays an obvious bias (who discovered whom?). Less value-laden are period divisions based on changes in the use of languages, scripts or genres.
- Often periodisation is based on national history. This may create anomalies when the modern state is projected back into a time when it did not yet exist or covered a different territory. Political and economic events, wars, conquests, migration and colonisation tend to act as markers of historical change in this context.
- Technological change can have a vast cultural impact – think of the invention and spread of paper, of print and digital technologies – especially in combination with other factors such as literacy and the circulation of material goods.
- Generations are not culture-specific in themselves, but sometimes groups define their collective identity in contrast to the previous generation's aesthetic, moral or other choices.

The list is not exhaustive. What matters in the choice of a type of periodisation is its relevance to a research project. The same goes for a project's spatial delimitation. In principle, any spatial entity that makes sense will do. But here, too, complications soon arise.

Geographies

The scene of translation activity may be restricted to a room, a building, a square, a village, a town, a city or a region, although there will always be roads and ramifications stretching further afield. Cosmopolitan cities where languages meet and mingle have historically been hives of translation activity.

The default entity for much translation history is a modern state. It is tempting to imagine, as the simplest scenario, a state with a single official language into which all translating is done, but such a state does not exist. Even officially monolingual countries invariably comprise minorities speaking different languages. More interesting from a translation point of view are multilingual states such as India, South Africa or Dagestan, with a range of officially recognised languages, or, historically, an entity like the Habsburg monarchy which Michaela Wolf (2012, 2015b) studied for the years 1848 to 1918, during which time it accommodated a dozen languages. Colonial conditions tend to reveal similar complexities even if local languages received no official recognition. However, as these last two cases suggest, modern states are an inadequate frame for research reaching further back in time. And these earlier times have surprises in store. Considering pre-colonial India, for instance, Harish Trivedi found a 'history of non-translation' (2006, 106) because elites were multilingual and had no need of translation; moreover, while Indian scriptures were rendered into languages like Chinese, Persian and Arabic, nothing at all was translated from those languages into an Indian language (Trivedi 2006, 103–8).

A translation history may cover an area where a particular language is spoken regardless of political boundaries. Some of the largest extant histories of translation deal with English and French, each spread across several volumes and – depending on the time frame – continents (France and Gillespie 2005–; Chevrel and Masson 2012–19). Projects of this kind come up against practical as well as conceptual issues, as illustrated by the historical dictionary of translation in Spanish-speaking America (Lafarga and Pegenaute 2013). We might have expected this large area to show a number of common historical developments, but the book's editors faced the practical problem that, with few exceptions, all the available research had been done along national lines. This precluded a comprehensive history and dictated the choice for a historical dictionary centred on individual translators and modern countries. As a result, the only article to cover the whole geographical area is that on the colonial period (roughly from 1500 till the early nineteenth century), when the modern states did not yet exist. Parallel developments across the post-independent states are for the reader to tease out.

A history may focus on a grouping of different languages spoken in a politically heterogeneous area. This is undoubtedly challenging, but there is unique historical insight to be gained because relevant commonalities need to be identified for the exercise to be meaningful. Sometimes the commonalities are fairly rough and ready. Charles Nama (1993) and Paul Bandia (2005), for example, produced brief sketches of translation in Africa on the basis of a common three-stage history comprising a precolonial, a colonial and a decolonial period.

A more nuanced picture emerges from Judy Wakabayashi's account of translation in what she describes as Sinitic Asia (2005, 19): China, Korea, Japan and

Vietnam. Despite their very different languages, the cultural history of these four nations is tied together by a string of commonalities: (1) the pervasive presence of Chinese culture, including, for much of their history, the use of Chinese characters and of Classical Chinese as the dominant form of writing by the elite, (2) frequent contacts, both friendly and unfriendly, resulting in the transmission of goods, knowledge and beliefs, and (3) the common experience of 'Eurocentric cultural colonialism' in the second half of the nineteenth century (2005, 34). Each of these commonalities requires careful handling, as nothing happened in quite the same way in all four countries. There were significant divergences, for example, in the ways Koreans, Japanese and Vietnamese negotiated Chinese characters and Chinese texts, all bearing some resemblance to translation but none reducible to it. When translation did take place (Buddhist sutras, vernacular Chinese fiction, European novels and science), the area showed a common dynamic with, again, plenty of regional variation. The comparative angle which the commonalities create allows us to see what is shared and what makes each country distinctive.

The most ambitious project in this vein traces the history of translation in Central Europe, roughly defined as the area between Germany to the west and Russia to the east, where sixteen languages are spoken (Chalvin et al. 2019). Despite cultural heterogeneity and political borders shifting over time, the project posited five commonalities pertinent to translation:

1. the written languages which subsequently grew into national languages were constituted as a result of religious translation, primarily Bible translation;
2. the movements that led to the establishment of nation states date from the eighteenth and nineteenth centuries;
3. culturally and intellectually, Central European countries took their cue from Western Europe, resulting in significantly more translations flowing from west to east than vice versa and in a relative dearth of translations among the Central European languages themselves;
4. translation shaped much of the emergence and evolution of secular literature in vernacular languages; and
5. from 1945 to 1989, the area lived through a period of Soviet dominance which put translation under severe ideological pressure (Chalvin 2011, 80; Chalvin et al. 2019, 7–8, 366–7).

These commonalities were not, of course, picked at random. They presuppose a certain familiarity with the history in question. At the same time, they serve a heuristic purpose as probes: what does the landscape look like, as a whole and in parts, when viewed through this lens? Indeed, the composition of the actual history began with a detailed questionnaire which was sent to subject specialists and solicited fixed kinds of information about each of the sixteen languages. It provided the common grid onto which both similarities and differences could subsequently be mapped. The early religious translations, for instance, revealed more or less the same pattern everywhere but different start dates, the time lag sometimes running to several hundred years.

Both the translation histories of Sinitic Asia and of Central Europe juggle convergences and divergences, holding on to a common thread despite local idiosyncracies. The main gain is in the transnational perspective enabling insight into both commonalities and singularities, each illuminating and nuancing the other.

The question arises: how much heterogeneity can a historical account bear? Would it make sense to treat, say, the history of translation in the whole of Europe as a single entity – an idea floated by the editors of the Central European volume (Chalvin et al. 2019, 369–70)? The complexities would increase exponentially: more languages, more internal divergences and time lags, fewer and more tenuous commonalities. What about a global history of translation? The key to a question like this is not whether enough commonalities to keep the whole together really exist. That would be an essentialist approach. What matters is whether a case can be made or an angle found or hypothesised, and whether the resulting account comes across as both plausible and illuminating. The likelihood is that, in a global translation history, commonalities would be explored selectively, for certain regions at certain times under certain respects, resulting in a thematically organised rather than a continuous or linear story. Just how 'global' such a survey would turn out to be remains a moot point.

Historians would probably recognise issues like these. Their work, too, ranges from microhistory to national, transnational and global history. We will return to this question of scale in the next chapter.

Dynamics of Change

Lineages

In a short and exquisitely written essay from 1935, the Argentine writer Jorge Luis Borges discussed several French, English and German translations of *The Thousand and One Nights* (Borges 2012). Its opening paragraph evokes one translator, Richard Burton, setting to work in Trieste in 1872, 'in a palace with damp statues and deficient hygienic facilities'. Burton, Borges tells us, aimed to annihilate one of his predecessors, Edward Lane, whose version had, in turn, supplanted that of Antoine Galland: 'Lane translated against Galland, Burton against Lane; to understand Burton we must understand this hostile dynasty' (2012, 92). Borges offers us simultaneously a slice of translation history and a model for its interpretation. In fact, he offers us more than that.

Borges begins with Antoine Galland, whose French version of *The Thousand and One Nights* was published in the early eighteenth century, the first to appear in Europe. It proved extremely successful, perhaps because its decorum echoed eighteenth-century tastes. A little over a hundred years later, in 1839, Edward Lane made a new translation, now into English. In his preface, he slated Galland for 'errors of the grossest description' which 'perverted' the Arabic original and ignored its style, giving a 'false character' to the whole (Lane 1839, viii). Borges qualifies Lane's version as 'highly scrupulous' and 'exceedingly erudite' but also an 'encyclopedia of evasion' (2012, 92, 94) because Lane consistently omitted anything he deemed morally objectionable. This, and the fact that Lane rendered the verses in *The Thousand and One Nights* as prose, aroused Richard Burton's wrath a few decades later. Burton slated Lane for pages 'disfigured by many childish mistakes' and for writing 'the stiff and stilted style of half a century ago when our prose was, perhaps, the worst in Europe' (1885, xii). His own style, as Borges notes, was gaudy and flamboyant, his abundant notes indulged the most diverse topics, and, as the translation was privately printed, Burton did not have to hold back on sexual matters.

Borges goes on to discuss two further versions, a French one from the turn of the nineteenth century by J.C. Mardrus, which claimed to be literal but (in Borges' tongue-in-cheek reading) breathed an Art Nouveau air, especially in the numerous interpolations of the translator's own invention, and a German one from the 1920s by Enno Littmann, which Borges describes as accurate, unflinching, lucid and monumentally dull.

Although Borges' essay is a witty literary piece and not a scholarly study, it demonstrates at least three things:

1. The 'hostile dynasties' appeal to an oppositional or agonistic principle of change, one marked by rupture and discontinuity. The new undoes the old and insists on going in another direction. Lane demolished Galland, Burton demolished Lane. The animosities in this case are stated by the actors themselves, the researcher only has to register them, and the sequence has the dynamic of a self-propelling device or, in an alternative vocabulary, an autonomous system. Although the sequence here is made up of retranslations, we can think along the same lines of styles or modes of translation more generally.

2. But continuity and variation play their part as well. Borges notes that Burton rewrote the first and last stories of *The Thousand and One Nights* and that Mardrus extended this procedure by rewriting the entire collection (2012, 99). In a similar fashion, a particular way of translating may evolve by being applied in different contexts, or by mutating and producing variants, while continuing to be recognisable as that particular way of translating. This creates lines of filiation that may rely on personal inclination such as respect for or affinity with a predecessor, or on institutional factors such as training and apprenticeship. Moreover, in the case of Mardrus continuing what Burton began, it is Borges who establishes the lineage: the prefaces that accompany Mardrus' translation (Mardrus 1903) disparage Galland but make no mention of Burton. The continuity that Borges perceives is therefore a matter of interpretation. As for Littmann, Borges uses him only as a foil: he is similar to Mardrus in standing for accuracy and completeness but different from those before him in being lifeless.

3. This lifelessness enables Borges to dramatise the historical embedding of some of Littmann's predecessors, at least in literary terms. In Burton's translation, Borges senses the language of John Donne, Shakespeare, Cyril Tourneur, Swinburne and seventeenth-century chapbooks. He reads Mardrus as breathing the air of La Fontaine's fables, of Flaubert's historical fiction and of the literature and art of the years around 1900. While these echoes may be of Borges' own invention, they make the point that translations, like other texts, are products of their time, including that time's historical – and, in this case, literary – heritage. Earlier in his essay Borges had tied Galland's language to eighteenth-century decorum and Lane's sexual inhibitions to Victorian prudery; perhaps he could also, had he wanted to, have read Littmann's matter-of-factness as being in line with the so-called New Objectivity (*Neue Sachlichkeit*) popular in 1920s Germany. This, then, suggests a third model of change as regards translations: while some set new trends, most reflect the tastes that prevail in the domains for which they cater. That also makes this third model different from the two mentioned above. Both discontinuity and continuity locate the engine of change in the relation between later and earlier translators: they portray translators as either reacting against or extending the practice of their predecessors. For this third model, however, the engine of change lies outside translation, in the various fields which marshal translations.

Borges' essay on the translators of *The Thousand and One Nights* remains a highly ironic exercise, but it provides us with some key insights into the variables of translation historiography.

1. One variable concerns the source of the connections that the historian establishes. In identifying the loathing that Lane apparently felt for Galland and Burton for Lane, Borges followed the lead offered by the translators themselves, allowing their narratives to shape his own narrative. It seems an obvious thing to do, but it comes with a risk. The narratives supplied by historical actors are part of their self-presentation and positioning. That makes it worth asking what they were trying to achieve by adopting this or that stance, what unstated agenda might inform their public posturing. The alternative to which these questions point is that of the historian's own interpretation, either because the translators did not comment on their own work or because the historian decides to ignore the comments or take them with a grain of salt. Borges perceived a connection between Mardrus and Burton despite the absence of a statement to that effect by Mardrus himself. This way of accounting for continuity or change clearly carries a risk as well. It puts the burden of explanation, of making plausible connections, squarely on the historian's shoulders. Borges, in this instance, skated rather lightly over the link he claimed to see between Mardrus and Burton.

2. We can account for change along at least two different axes. One considers the diachronic series – the succession of translations being produced in a certain genre or field. The other is interested in identifying triggers. The two axes are complementary and even overlap, and both need to be taken broadly and flexibly. The first captures change in terms of affiliations and ruptures. Just how gradual or sudden a process of change is perceived to be will depend on the scope and scale of the investigation and on the aspects the researcher wants to highlight. It is possible also to imagine different forms of continuity and discontinuity: from growth, progress, decline, diversification and adaptation to personal antagonism, the anxiety of influence and changes in material or intellectual conditions. Whatever the angle, attention is focused on the features of a series of translations and on the relative prominence of certain features at the expense of others. This approach tends to be text-based and has to balance the idea of translation as a more or less self-propelling (or self-referential) series with that of translation as imbricated in and subject to pressure from other spheres.

3. The other axis concerns the trigger of change rather than its manifestations. It tends to home in on a small number of cases and to privilege translators as decision-makers. Seen from this angle, changes in ways of translating are due to individual translators and their personal agendas or to environmental factors, from the political or intellectual climate to practical requirements, commercial pressures or working conditions. In his discussion of Lane and Burton, Borges reduced their motivation to a simple dislike of a predecessor's version, but each obviously had rather more complex reasons to translate. Lane, for example, produced his version in response to a commission, and he saw ethnographic value in *The Thousand and One Nights*, having just published a commercially very successful book about Egyptian society (Schacker-Mill 2000, 165). As Julia Richter points out, translators may have multiple reasons for translating and their motivation invariably reaches beyond translation (2020, 152–62).

4. A diachronic perspective suggests that studying isolated translations, or single pairs of original and translation, makes little sense. Every translation presupposes other translations, other translation events, other texts. What makes each translation unique is determined precisely by the relations it entertains with the discourses that precede and surround it.

Conditions and opportunities

Of course, Borges can only take us so far. Change may also be conceived in quantitative and material rather than in purely qualitative terms. In his *Science in Translation*, Scott Montgomery reminds us that papermaking was invented in China around the second century CE. The city of Samarkand, a centre of Chinese paper manufacture, was taken by Muslim armies in 704. Within a hundred years, Baghdad had a paper mill. By 1150, Muslim Spain was manufacturing paper. The availability of cheap, locally produced paper had cultural effects: better retention and distribution of manuscripts led to increased demand for scribes and texts, and hence to larger libraries, a flourishing book trade and a growth in text-based knowledge, much of it the result of increased numbers of translations (Montgomery 2000, 106, 140; Pym 2000, 80–9).

Material, quantitative and qualitative factors may interact quite closely. Norbert Bachleitner (1989; 2009, 425–9) has shown how translations, and especially translations of fiction, mushroomed in Germany in the first half of the nineteenth century. Between 1820 and 1845, the number of novels published in Germany increased threefold but the number of translated novels grew fourteenfold, meaning that the proportion of translated to original novels changed drastically. By 1850, half of all the novels printed in Germany were translations, up from just 11 percent in 1820. Various factors contributed to this development. Improved literacy created greater demand. Upstart competitive publishers drove book prices down. New technologies such as mechanised papermaking and steam-powered printing enabled faster and cheaper book production. Lending libraries could expand thanks to efficient postal and transportation services. With international copyright nonexistent, several rival translations could be dumped on the market simultaneously. As a result, translations of mostly English and French popular fiction were produced on an industrial scale in what became known as 'translation factories', where translators were paid per translated page and speed rather than quality was of prime importance. Translations were sent to the press as soon as they were delivered, with no time for revision or correction. Translators not infrequently described themselves as robots, and one translator employed four stenographers to take down his dictation (Bachleitner 1989, 27–8; 2009: 428–9).

As this example shows, material, economic and cultural factors conspired to swell the production of translations in such a spectacular fashion that translators had to devise new working methods to keep up. The picture is complex. The various contributing factors can be disentangled up to a point, but it would be futile to try and assess their relative weight. It is their coming together that matters. For the researcher, the first task consists in discerning the contributing elements and their interconnectedness. Understanding them more fully requires cross-disciplinary reading in fields like publishing history, social and economic history and the history of technology and public services.

This will also help to put translation into perspective. The translation factories are only one part of the commercial success of popular fiction as such in Germany at the time, and this success itself is part of the economic and socio-cultural history of the period. To understand translation historically, we have to go beyond translation to the interests that translation serves. For German publishers of popular fiction in the years 1820–50, competition and profit were the main drivers. Translation was merely a means to those ends.

At the same time, pointing to a complex tangle of factors working together to create the phenomenon of translation factories means offering a causal explanation of sorts. Causation is a difficult subject for historians, mainly because, unlike laboratory scientists, historians cannot conduct experiments or manipulate variables to identify causes and effects unambiguously. The conjunction of elements leading to translation factories may be understood as a 'causal process', meaning that multiple factors cause, and are caused by, each other (Froeyman 2009, 118). Narrative emplotment, as we saw in the previous chapter, structures the interaction of the various story elements in similarly complex ways, without the narrative as a whole amounting to a definite causal statement. This gives historical narratives their coherence and their explanatory power, and, indeed, as Anton Froeyman notes (2009, 121–2), narratives and causal processes have much in common.

Another way to put an episode like the German translation factories or indeed the story of paper reaching the Middle East and Europe in context is to see them in the tradition of book history. Book historians focus on the material aspects of books and the book trade. They study individual books as physical objects and as commodities, paying attention to the significance of such things as a book's format, fonts, layout, paper quality and illustrations. But they also research the production process, the distribution and the reception of books, from copyright issues to library statistics on borrowing and the scribbles left by individual readers in the margins of books they happened to be reading. Book history has much to offer students of translation because it comprises the entire spectrum from concrete detail to quantitative research and because it readily moves from individual case studies to the broader social conditioning of book production, dissemination and reception. Book historians and historians of translation share an interest in the mobility and transmission of texts across time and space and in the multiple agents and different media involved in these processes (Bachleitner 2009; Belle and Hosington 2017; Colombo 2019; Littau 2016).

Discourses about Translation

Critics who commented on the products of the German translation factories were quick to condemn the inferior quality of the translations. Their judgements, based on a traditional standard of accuracy applied to translated literary fiction, mostly ignored the conveyor-belt conditions under which the translations had been produced. This shows – quite apart from the rift between mass-market and elite culture – two speeds of development occurring simultaneously: rapid changes in the mode of production of certain types of translations and the critics' more enduring ideas about what translated fiction should look like. It also shows that the production and circulation of translations is constantly accompanied by a discourse that embodies normative as well as cognitive ideas about translation – cognitive in the sense of ideas about what translation is and does, normative in the sense of ideas about what translation should be and how it should be done.

Exactly how actual translations and discourses about translation relate to each other is hard to say. The absence of extensive or authoritative statements about translation does not necessarily suggest a lack of thought about translation. The ancient Romans, for example, translated copiously, mainly from Greek, but they never even settled on a single term for translation and their discourse on the subject is scattered across numerous brief references (Montgomery 2000, 41–2; McElduff 2013, 2). In the case of the German translation factories, the critical discourse about translation was obviously out of step with the translations rolling off the presses.

It seems reasonable to assume that the discourse about and the practice of translation are correlated, but one cannot be reduced to the other. Translation practice requires decisions in specific circumstances, while the discourse about translation is given to abstraction, idealisation and self-justification.

Despite these complexities, there is much to be said for the concept of a 'translation culture', a term introduced by Erich Prunč (2007, 330–1). It refers to the way that translation is both practised and conceptualised in a given community at a given time. It covers the whole amalgam of habitual practices and ways of translating, along with the legal, economic and other conditions that circumscribe the production and dissemination of translations, plus the expectations and value judgements that observers – including translators and critics – bring to translation. It also leaves room for disagreement and mismatches. Prunč recognises that, while a translation culture possesses a degree of self-referential autonomy and therefore a certain historical momentum of its own, it forms part of the culture surrounding it and evolves with and within this larger whole. Translation practices and discourses about translation cannot but be affected by more encompassing ideas about such things as identity, language and the common good. In this and other respects, Prunč's notion of a translation culture is similar to that of translation as a social system (Hermans 2007, 109–36).

The curse of the anthologies

Traditionally, the historical study of translation showed a bias towards literary translation and discourses on translation. As a result, many of the primary materials documenting ideas about translation over time have been made available, often in the form of anthologies. These anthologies are useful – they provide a sampling of primary texts, thematic variety and a handy overview – but they come with a major drawback. In most cases, the anthologies privilege the primary texts, which are made to speak for themselves, with minimal contextual information. This invites the danger of reading texts out of their historical context and taking the words on the page at face value.

A single example will be sufficient to make the point. Etienne Dolet's 'The Way to Translate Well from One Language to Another', published in 1540, is a very short treatise of just two pages, in French ('*La manière de bien traduire d'une langue en aultre*'). It is of historical significance because it constitutes the first theoretical treatise on translation in a European vernacular.

The treatise consists of five numbered rules for translators: (1) translators should understand the subject matter of the original and (2) be familiar with both languages involved, (3) they should not translate word for word but

(4) follow common usage and avoid loanwords, and (5) they should write in a pleasing, harmonious style (Dolet 1981).

As a statement about translation, this seems thin and trite, no more than a collection of rules of thumb to guide a novice translator. This is indeed how it is presented in introductory textbooks on translation. When its context is taken into account, however, a very different and much richer reading suggests itself, as Glyn Norton showed a generation ago (Norton 1984, 203–17; Baddeley and Debrosse 2015, 335–45).

Etienne Dolet (1509–46) was a man of considerable learning, well versed in Latin and Ancient Greek, and an admirer of the Roman orator and prose writer Cicero, several of whose works he translated into French. He wrote books in Latin on the Latin language and on ways of improving one's writing style by imitating ancient authors, especially Cicero. Books like these marked him as a so-called humanist, an intellectual with a strong interest in the ancients. Humanists formed an international 'republic of letters' through their common use of Latin, but many, including Dolet, also cultivated their native language by writing grammars and by translating, in an effort to raise the vernaculars to the level of the classical Latin they venerated as a model of perfection.

Dolet's treatise on translation fits into this context. It was to be part of a larger work, *The French Orator* ('*L'orateur français*'), envisaged as comprising nine chapters (on grammar, spelling, accents, punctuation, pronunciation, etymology, translation, rhetoric and poetics). In the event, only three were drafted (on accents, punctuation and translation). The project came to an untimely end when, in 1546, Dolet was arrested, tried for heresy and executed.

Reading Dolet's treatise against the background of humanist ideas about language and translation transforms its content. Around 1425, for example, the Italian humanist Leonardo Bruni had described translation as surpassingly difficult due to the advanced knowledge and skill required in first grasping a sophisticated foreign author's thought and then rendering the stylistic qualities of that author's discourse (Hankins 1987).

Dolet's first two points echo Bruni in stressing the need not just for some degree of familiarity with the subject matter and the relevant languages but for complete intellectual and linguistic command. This level of refinement makes the very notion of rendering word for word a sign of mental poverty (the third rule). The fourth rule applies particularly to vernacular languages still under construction, which need the classical tongues to raise themselves up. The treatise culminates in the fifth point, which celebrates the power conveyed by 'oratorical numbers', a term referring to the use of a harmonious, rhetorically effective style. Just what this means might be glimpsed from a Latin preface (published in 1569 but written over a decade earlier) by the Cambridge humanist John Christopherson, who neatly sums up the humanist view. For translation to succeed, Christopherson says,

> [...] four things seem to be required: a true explanation of sense and meaning, good latinity, harmony, and [...] perspicuity of speech [...]. The

first is usually held to be relevant of fidelity, the second for delight, the third for the judgment of the ears, the fourth for the understanding. For who will believe it if the meaning is suspect? Who will take pleasure in reading if the speech is rude and unpolished? Whose ears will not be disgusted if the discourse is badly connected and disordered? Whom will it not deter if it seems obscure and overcome by darkness?

(Binns 1990, 135–6)

Here, the four things required of good translation are stated three times, always in the same order, the third time in the form of four rhetorical questions, each containing the negative counterpart to the four positive requirements. Brief as it is, the passage offers a rhetorical description of a rhetorically informed concept of translation. Christopherson's key words – 'perspicuity', 'harmony', 'delight', 'pleasure' – echo Dolet's terms – 'dignity', 'grace', 'sweetness', 'splendour', 'eloquence'. Leonardo Bruni's 1425 treatise on translation had expounded similar ideas and used similar keywords (Hankins 1987). And it matters in this respect that the word translated as 'harmony' in the quote from Christopherson above is *numerus* in Latin, that Bruni also uses this term repeatedly (1928, 86–8; Lafarga 1996, 84–8; 'rhythm' in Hankins 1987, 221) and that it appears in Dolet as 'oratorical numbers' ('*nombres oratoires*'), the rhythmic pace and balance that gives a discourse its force and elegance. Textual echoes of this kind are the nodes that establish intellectual filiations. Dolet is not offering a few rules of thumb. He presents, in French, a concept of translation that derives straight from the high-prestige, Latin-speaking world of humanist culture.

Contextualising the historical discourse on translation guards against naïvely taking the words on the page for granted. It adds resonance to the primary documents by framing them as part of larger constellations in which authors pursue their own agendas and texts respond to each other as interventions in exchanges that may extend over many years. Just how much context does a document need? In principle, as much as possible. That could lead to entire monographs, and they do exist – examples include James DeLater's edition cum translation of the 1683 version of a Latin treatise by Pierre-Daniel Huet, with a substantial introduction and detailed notes (DeLater 2002), or Antoine Berman's book-length commentary on Walter Benjamin's famous 1923 essay, a commentary, in turn, translated from French into English by Chantal Wright with an introduction and extensive annotations (Berman 2008, 2018). More modest exercises in contextualisation have been applied to Jerome's famous letter to Pammachius (Copeland 1989) and Friedrich Schleiermacher's 1813 lecture on the different ways of translating (Hermans 2015 and 2019).

Because most anthologies are keen to present the primary texts, they minimise contextualisation and thus increase the risk of superficial readings. There are exceptions. Douglas Robinson's *Western Translation Theory from Herodotus to Nietzsche*, for instance, first published in 1997, features informative introductions to each of its 124 texts, plus explanatory footnotes on most pages, brief biographical notes on persons named in the documents, and further reading suggestions for each document (Robinson 2002).

The most thoroughly thought-through collection is probably the two-volume *Anthology of Chinese Discourse on Translation* devised and compiled by Martha Cheung (2006 and 2017). Its 110 documents, from the earliest times to 1800 and all in English translation, comprise two major Chinese translation movements, that of the Buddhist sutra translations and that of the translations of European science in the seventeenth and eighteenth centuries. Each entry is preceded by a biographical note on its author, accompanied by extensive explanatory footnotes and followed by a commentary that engages with the historical document from a modern perspective, exploring and cross-referencing its terminology, concepts and metaphors. These commentaries exemplify the pushing-hands approach mentioned in the previous chapter in that they allow the primary texts, in all their historical difference, to affect modern conceptualisations of translation while, at the same time, offering a critical assessment of the texts in their historical contexts. Key Chinese terms are marked when, depending on context, they require different renderings in English. The book comes with a full apparatus of chronologies and biographies of persons mentioned in the texts and with separate introductions to its various subdivisions. For someone new to the Chinese historical discourse on translation, these multiple access points and layers of information may be daunting, but, short of a series of in-depth studies for which a knowledge of Chinese and of Chinese history would be essential, this is probably the best one can hope for. Handling a book like this requires a modicum of effort, but no one ever said that cross-cultural historical work had to be a walk in the park.

Notes

1 http://fbtee.uws.edu.au/main/
2 www.perso-indica.net/index.faces
3 http://portal.unesco.org/culture/en/ev.php-URL_ID=7810&URL_DO=DO_TOPIC&URL_SECTION=201.html
4 www.dhi.ac.uk/rcc/index.php
5 https://litteraturbanken.se/översättarlexikon
6 www.uelex.de (in German); https://vertalerslexicon.nl (in Dutch).
7 https://dlbt.univie.ac.at/

Further Reading

Cheung, Martha, ed. 2006. *An Anthology of Chinese Discourse on Translation. Volume One. From Earliest Times to the Buddhist Project.* Manchester: St Jerome.

Cheung, Martha, ed. 2017. *An Anthology of Chinese Discourse on Translation. Volume Two. From the Late Twelfth Century to 1800.* Edited by Robert Neather. London & New York: Routledge.

Both these anthologies share the same structure. Volume One covers 82 primary texts, some no longer than a single sentence, with the Buddhist sutra translations making up the bulk. Volume Two features 28 documents, the majority from the Ming and early Qing dynasties and many dealing with the translation of European science. Both volumes are remarkable for their methodology, as they go out of their way to context-ualise the historical material. Engaging with these complex volumes calls for a more than cursory reading, but the effort pays off.

Finkelstein, David, and Alistair McCleery, eds. 2006. *The Book History Reader*. London & New York: Routledge.
This sizeable *Reader* is not concerned with translation but illustrates the rich field of book history, comprising essays and extracts by major scholars from the 1950s to the early twenty-first century. Its five sections deal with book history in general, the impact of print, questions of authorship, reading practices and the digital revolution. The editors also authored an *Introduction to Book History* (2003, 2nd ed. 2012), which follows the same structure as the *Reader*.

Rundle, Christopher, ed. 2022. *The Routledge Handbook of Translation History*. London & New York: Routledge.
A collection of essays by 33 authors, covering theoretical issues along with cross-sections and case studies. The case studies deal with Tanzania, Estonia, Soviet Russia, premodern Japan, Jewish and Christian traditions, the discourse on translation in Classical Arabic, translation under fascism and Nazism, and the history of audiovisual translation. Specific topics include translating Dante, a Finnish military interpreter, 1970s feminist transla-tion and the International Institute of Intellectual Cooperation set up by the League of Nations in 1925. Among contributions of a more conceptual or methodological kind are those on book history, travel writing, narrative theory, electronic databases and cor-pora, and national translation histories.

Wakabayashi, Judy. 2005. "Translation in the East Asian Cultural Sphere. Shared Roots, Divergent Paths?" In *Asian Translation Traditions*, edited by Eva Hung and Judy Wakabayashi, 17–65. Manchester: St Jerome.
This is a substantial and sophisticated essay that abundantly demonstrates the strengths of a supra-national, culturally based perspective on translation history. Taking in China, Japan, Korea and Vietnam, it explores both commonalities and divergences while also acknowledging the limitations and risks inherent in the approach. It is a model essay, conceptually bold and yet circumspect in its procedures and phrasing.

Bibliography

Adamo, Sergia. 2006. "Microhistory of Translation." In *Charting the Future of Translation History*, edited by Georges Bastin and Paul Bandia, 81–100. Ottawa: University of Ottawa Press.
Bachleitner, Norbert. 1989. "'Übersetzungsfabriken'. Das deutsche Übersetzungswesen in der ersten Hälfte des 19. Jahrhunderts." *Internationales Archiv für Sozialgeschichte der deutschen Literatur* 14: 1–49.
Bachleitner, Norbert. 2009. "A Proposal to Include Book History in Translation Studies. Illustrated with German Translations of Scott and Flaubert." *Arcadia* 44: 420–40.

Baddeley, Susan, and Anne Debrosse. 2015. "Dictionnaires, manuels, traités théoriques." In *Histoire des traductions en langue française. XVe et XVIe siècles 1470–1610*, edited by Véronique Duché, 291–354. Lagrasse: Verdier.

Bandia, Paul. 2005. "Esquisse d'une histoire de la traduction en Afrique." *Meta* 50: 957–71.

Bandia, Paul. 2009. "African Tradition." In *Routledge Encyclopedia of Translation Studies*, 2nd ed. Edited by Mona Baker and Gabriela Saldanha, 313–20. London & New York: Routledge.

Bastin, Georges. 2009. "Latin American Tradition." In *Routledge Encyclopedia of Translation Studies*, 2nd ed. Edited by Mona Baker and Gabriela Saldanha, 486–92. London & New York: Routledge.

Belle, Marie-Alice, and Brenda Hosington. 2017. "Translation, History and Print. A Model for the Study of Printed Translations in Early Modern Britain." *Translation Studies* 10: 2–21.

Berman, Antoine. 2008. *L'âge de la traduction. 'La tâche du traducteur' de Walter Benjamin, un commentaire*. Saint-Denis: Presses universitaires de Vincennes.

Berman, Antoine. 2018. *The Age of Translation. A Commentary on Walter Benjamin's 'The Task of the Translator'*. Translated by Chantal Wright. London & New York: Routledge.

Binns, J. W. 1990. *Intellectual Culture in Elizabethan and Jacobean England. The Latin Writings of the Age*. Leeds: Francis Cairns.

Borges, Jorge Luis. 2012. "The Translators of *The Thousand and One Nights*." [1935]. Translated by Esther Allen. In *The Translation Studies Reader*, 3rd ed. Edited by Lawrence Venuti, 92–106. London & New York: Routledge.

Bruni Aretino, Leonardo. 1928. *Humanistisch-philosophische Schriften*, edited by Hans Baron. Leipzig & Berlin: B.G. Teubner.

Burke, Peter. 2007. "Cultures of Translation in Early Modern Europe." In *Cultural Translation in Early Modern Europe*, edited by Peter Burke and Po-Chia Hsia, 7–38. Cambridge: Cambridge University Press.

Burton, Richard. 1885. *The Book of the Thousand Nights and a Night*. Volume 1. [No place:] Printed by the Burton Club for Private Subscribers Only.

Chalvin, Antoine. 2011. "Comment écrire une histoire aréale de la traduction?" In *Between Cultures and Texts. Itineraries in Translation History. Entre les cultures et les textes. Itinéraires en histoire de la traduction*, edited by A. Chalvin et al., 77–86. Frankfurt: Peter Lang.

Chalvin, Antoine, Jean-Léon Muller, Katre Talviste, and Marie Vrinat-Nikolov. 2019. *Histoire de la traduction littéraire en Europe médiane. Des origines à 1989*. Rennes: Presses universitaires de Rennes.

Cheung, Martha, ed. 2006. *An Anthology of Chinese Discourse on Translation. Volume One. From Earliest Times to the Buddhist Project*. Manchester: St Jerome.

Cheung, Martha, ed. 2017. *An Anthology of Chinese Discourse on Translation. Volume Two. From the Late Twelfth Century to 1800*. Edited by Robert Neather. London & New York: Routledge.

Chevrel, Yves, and Jean-Yves Masson, gen. eds. 2012–9. *Histoire des traductions en langue française*. 4 Vols. Paris: Verdier.

Colombo, Alice. 2019. "Intersections between Translation and Book History: Reflections and New Directions." *Comparative Critical Studies* 16: 147–60.

Copeland, Rita. 1989. "The Fortunes of *non verbum pro verbo*, or why Jerome is not a Ciceronian." In *The Medieval Translator. The Theory and Practice of Translation in the Middle Ages*, edited by Roger Ellis, 15–36. Cambridge: D.S. Brewer.

DeLater, James. 2002. *Translation Theory in the Age of Louis XIV. The 1683 De optimo genere interpretandi (On the best kind of translating) of Pierre-Daniel Huet (1630–1721)*. Manchester: St Jerome.

Delisle, Jean. 2009. "Canadian Tradition." In *Routledge Encyclopedia of Translation Studies*, 2nd ed. Edited by Mona Baker and Gabriela Saldanha, 362–9. London & New York: Routledge.

D'hulst, Lieven. 2014. *Essais d'histoire de la traduction. Avatars de Janus*. Paris: Classiques Garnier.

Dolet, Etienne. 1981. "The Way to Translate Well from One Language to Another." Translated by James Holmes. *Modern Poetry in Translation* no. 41–42: 54–56.

Finkelstein, David, and Alistair McCleery, ed. 2006. *The Book History Reader*. London & New York: Routledge.

France, Peter, and Stuart Gillespie, gen. eds. 2005–. *The Oxford History of Literary Translation in English*. 5 Vols. Oxford: Oxford University Press.

Froeyman, Anton. 2009. "Concepts of Causation in Historiography." *Historical Methods* 42: 116–28.

Hankins, James. 1987. "The New Language." In *The Humanism of Leonardo Bruni. Selected Texts*, edited by Gordon Griffiths, James Hankins and David Thompson, 197–235. Binghamton: Medieval & Renaissance Texts & Studies/The Renaissance Society of America.

Hermans, Theo. 2007. *The Conference of the Tongues*. Manchester and Kinderhook (NY): St Jerome.

Hermans, Theo. 2015. "Schleiermacher and Plato, Hermeneutics and Translation." In *Friedrich Schleiermacher and the Question of Translation*, edited by Larisa Cercel and Adriana Şerban, 77–106. Berlin & Boston: De Gruyter.

Hermans, Theo. 2019. "Schleiermacher." In *The Routledge Handbook of Translation and Philosophy*, edited by Philip Wilson and Piers Rawling, 17–33. London & New York: Routledge.

Israel, Hephzibah, and Matthias Frenz. 2019. "Translation Traces in the Archive: Unfixing Documents, Destabilising Evidence." *The Translator* 25: 335–48.

Kittel, Harald. 1988. "Kontinuität und Diskrepanzen." In *Die literarische Übersetzung. Stand und Perspektiven ihrer Erforschung*, edited by Harald Kittel, 158–79. Berlin: Erich Schmidt.

Krishnamurthy, Ramesh. 2009. "Indian Tradition." In *Routledge Encyclopedia of Translation Studies*, 2nd ed. Edited by Mona Baker and Gabriela Saldanha, 449–58. London & New York: Routledge.

Kujamäki, Pekka, and Hilary Footitt. 2016. "Military History and Translation Studies. Shifting Territories, Uneasy Borders." In *Border Crossings. Translation Studies and Other Disciplines*, edited by Yves Gambier and Luc van Doorslaer, 49–71. Amsterdam & Philadelphia: John Benjamins.

Lafarga, Francisco, ed. 1996. *El discurso sobre la traducción en la historia. Antología bilingüe*. Barcelona: EUB.

Lafarga, Francisco, and Luis Pegenaute, eds. 2013. *Diccionario histórico de la traducción en Hispanomérica*. Madrid & Frankfurt: Iberoamericana & Vervuert.

Lane, Edward. 1839. *The Thousand and One Nights, Commonly Called, in England, the Arabian Nights' Entertainment*. London: Charles Knight.

Littau, Karin. 2016. "Translation and the Materialities of Communication." *Translation Studies* 9: 82–113.

Mardrus, J.C. 1903. *Le livre des mille nuits et une nuit*. Volume 1. Paris: E. Fasquelle.

McElduff, Siobhán. 2013. *Roman Theories of Translation. Surpassing the Source*. London & New York: Routledge.

Montgomery, Scott. 2000. *Science in Translation. Movements of Knowledge through Cultures and Time*. Chicago & London: University of Chicago Press.

Munday, Jeremy. 2014. "Using Primary Sources to Produce a Microhistory of Translation and Translators: Theoretical and Methodological Concerns." *The Translator* 20: 64–80.

Nama, Charles A. 1993. "Historical, Theoretical and Terminological Perspectives of Translation in Africa." *Meta* 38: 414–25.

Norton, Glyn. 1984. *The Ideology and Language of Translation in Renaissance France and their Humanist Antecedents*. Genève: Droz.

Poupaud, Sandra, Anthony Pym, and Ester Torres Simón. 2009. "Finding Translations. On the Use of Bibliographical Databases in Translation History." *Meta* 54: 264–78.

Prunč, Erich. 2007. *Entwicklungslinien der Translationswissenschaft. Von den Asymmetrien der Sprachen zu den Asymmetrien der Macht*. Berlin: Frank & Timme.

Pym, Anthony. 1998. *Method in Translation History*. Manchester: St Jerome.

Pym, Anthony. 2000. *Negotiating the Frontier. Translators and Intercultures in Hispanic History*. Manchester: St Jerome.

Richter, Julia. 2020. *Translationshistoriographie*. Wien: nap.

Robinson, Douglas, ed. 2002. *Western Translation Theory from Herodotus to Nietzsche*. 2nd ed. Manchester: St Jerome.

Rundle, Christopher. 2012. "Translation as an Approach to History." *Translation Studies* 5: 232–40.

Rundle, Christopher. 2014. "Introduction. Theories and Methodologies of Translation History: The Value of an Interdisciplinary Approach." *The Translator* 20: 2–8.

Rundle, Christopher, ed. 2022. *The Routledge Handbook of Translation History*. London & New York: Routledge.

Schacker-Mill, Jennifer. 2000. "Otherness and Other-Worldliness. Edward W. Lane's Ethnographic Treatment of the Arabian Nights." *Journal of American Folklore* 113: 164–84.

Steiner, George. 1975. *After Babel. Aspects of Language and Translation*. London: Oxford University Press.

Trivedi, Harish. 2006. "In Our Own Time, On Our Own Terms. 'Translation' in India." In *Translating Others*, edited by Theo Hermans, 102–19. Manchester: St Jerome.

Venuti, Lawrence. 2009. "American Tradition." In *Routledge Encyclopedia of Translation Studies*, 2nd ed. Edited by Mona Baker and Gabriela Saldanha, 320–8. London & New York: Routledge.

Wakabayashi, Judy. 2005. "Translation in the East Asian Cultural Sphere. Shared Roots, Divergent Paths?" In *Asian Translation Traditions*, edited by Eva Hung and Judy Wakabayashi, 17–65. Manchester: St Jerome.

Wakabayashi, Judy. 2019a. "Time Matters: Conceptual and Methodological Considerations in Translation Timescapes." *Chronotopos* 1: 23–39.

Wolf, Michaela. 2012. *Die vielsprachige Seele Kakaniens. Übersetzen und Dolmetschen in der Habsburgmonarchie 1848 bis 1918*. Vienna: Böhlau.

Wolf, Michaela. 2015b. *The Habsburg Monarchy's Many-Languaged Soul. Translating and Interpreting, 1848–1918*. Translated by Kate Sturge. Amsterdam & Philadelphia: John Benjamins.

Zhou, Xiaoyan, and Sanjun Sun. 2017. "Bibliography-Based Quantitative Translation History." *Perspectives* 25: 98–119.

Websites

The French Book Trade in Enlightenment Europe (FBTEE): http://fbtee.uws.edu.au/main/

Perso-Indica: www.perso-indica.net/index.faces

Index Translationum: http://portal.unesco.org/culture/en/ev.php-URL_ID=7810&URL_DO=DO_TOPIC&URL_SECTION=201.html

Renaissance Cultural Crossroads Catalogue: www.dhi.ac.uk/rcc/index.php

Lexicon of Swedish Translators (*Svenskt Översättarlexikon*): https://litteraturbanken.se/översättarlexikon

Lexicon of Translators into German (Germersheimer Übersetzerlexikon): www.uelex.de

Lexicon of Translators into Dutch (Vertalerslexicon voor het Nederlandstalig gebied, VNLex): https://vertalerslexicon.nl

Digital Library and Bibliography for Literature in Translation (DLBT): https://dlbt.univie.ac.at/

3   Questions of Scale

As we saw in Chapter 1, Hayden White drew attention to the historical account as a narrative that was not just construed ('*invented* as much as *found*', as he put it) but also composed of words and figures of discourse. His work has been associated with what is known as the linguistic turn in the humanities in the final decades of the twentieth century. White himself (2013, 38, 40) preferred to speak of a discursive turn because he saw the linguistic constructs that historians devised as necessarily wrapped up in literary figures and tropes from the start.

Among historians, the interest in language and discourse led to questions of who speaks in narrative representations of the past, with what authority and to whom? The relevance of these questions becomes obvious when we think, for example, of conflicts that were decided by physical force. It was usually the vision of the victors that gained currency because they controlled the means of producing and spreading their version of events. Most histories of the sixteenth-century conquest of Mexico, for instance, are written from the point of view of the Spanish *conquistadores*. What about the vision of the vanquished? In the case of Mexico, the vanquished remained unheard for centuries until, in 1959, Miguel León-Portilla's *Visión de los vencidos* (translated by Lysander Kemp as *The Broken Spears*, 1962) pieced together surviving Aztec accounts to present an alternative narrative.

León-Portilla's book was an early example of what became known as history from below and more recently as minority history (Chakrabarty 2000, 97), the work of historians who sought to recover the voices of the downtrodden, the subaltern, the poor, those excluded from mainstream history. Another early instance, more concerned with recent history, was Oscar Lewis' *The Children of Sánchez* (1961), based on taped interviews in which a father and his four grown-up children spoke of their life of grinding poverty in a one-room tenement in a Mexico City slum. Later examples include *A People's History of the United States* (1980) by Howard Zinn, episodes of American history told, as far as the available documentation permitted, from the perspective of such groups as Native Americans, enslaved Africans, army deserters and factory workers. The Subaltern Studies Collective that emerged in India in the 1980s and subsequently spread to Latin America was similarly interested in local conditions and

DOI: 10.4324/9781315178134-3

in the agency of disenfranchised communities (Guha 2001; Rodríguez 2001; Chakrabarty 2000, 11–6).

Translation made its way into some of these books. Oscar Lewis conducted his interviews in Spanish, then translated and rearranged the transcripts for *The Children of Sánchez*, which was published in English, but neither Lewis himself nor the contemporary reviews of his book gave the issue much thought. For most historians at the time, translation was transparent. That attitude has begun to shift in recent decades but only slowly. The attention historians have paid to translation has increased as they have moved from local and national to transnational and cross-cultural issues. In the following pages I will address the question of scale in historical study, from micro to macro.

Microhistories

Microhistory shares with history from below the desire to give a voice to individuals of low social status. It emerged in the 1970s and received a favourable response from translation scholars when they noticed its existence thirty years on. As its name suggests, the distinguishing feature of microhistory is that it does history on a small scale: it typically consists of a single, narrowly focussed case study. At its best it can give an immediate, almost ethnographic sense of an individual's lived experience.

One way to understand the turn to microhistory is to see it as a reaction against an earlier generation of economic and social historians who presented grand panoramic views covering long stretches of time. Among the best-known examples of history in this vein is Fernand Braudel's *The Mediterranean*, first published in French in 1949. It surveyed the whole Mediterranean world in the sixteenth century and was envisaged as 'total history' (Braudel 1972, 1238): comprehensive, multilayered and complex. Part of this complexity was that it tracked three different velocities of temporal change. There was, first, the virtually unchanging physical environment (Braudel described the mountains, for instance, as 'conspicuous actors' resisting the language, religion and architecture of the plains; 1972, 29, 34–5), then the slow-changing time of social and economic conditions which he called the *longue durée*, and finally the series of rapid changes at the political level, merely the froth on the surface.

The Mediterranean was, and remains, a hugely impressive work of some 1,200 pages; its bibliography alone takes up 60 pages. The book took Braudel 20 years to research and write. The trouble is that most historians (and students of translation) lack the resources, the time or the stamina for an undertaking of this magnitude. Hence the attraction of the deliberately small scale of microhistory.

The starting point of microhistory, and one of its most famous exponents, is generally taken to be Carlo Ginzburg's *The Cheese and the Worms*, first published in Italian in 1976. Other classics include Emmanuel Le Roy Ladurie's *Montaillou* (published in French in 1975), Natalie Zemon Davis' *The Return of Martin Guerre* (1983) and Robert Darnton's *The Great Cat Massacre* (1984. Several of these books were based on court proceedings and transcripts of the detailed questioning of suspects, who were quite ordinary people. The archival source of *The Cheese and the Worms* was the trial of a sixteenth-century Italian miller known as Menocchio, who held decidedly unorthodox views about the origin of the universe (in the beginning, Menocchio told the court, 'earth, air, water and fire were mixed together; and out of that bulk a mass formed – just as cheese is made out of milk – and worms appeared in it, and these were the angels'; Ginzburg 1980, 6). A court case like this might have been a brief aside in a larger history of the Reformation in northern Italy, but Ginzburg was fascinated by the particulars of the case (1993, 22), tracing, for instance, the dozen or so books Menocchio mentioned during his trial, how he had obtained them, and how he appears to have interpreted what he read. Yet, for all this detail, the larger context – regional administrative structures, religious ideas circulating at the time, elements of popular culture – remained visible as well.

Le Roy Ladurie's *Montaillou* is even more resolutely focussed on the everyday. Its title refers to a tiny medieval village in the Pyrenees; the book was based on the interrrogations of its 250 or so inhabitants, most of them peasants and shepherds, by an inquisitor intent on rooting out heresy. Le Roy Ladurie, however, was less interested in what the villagers had to say about their religious beliefs than in the concrete detail of their daily lives. The farmers of Montaillou, for instance, lived under the same roof with their animals (pigs, mules, goats, sheep, oxen) and probably used the same door to go in and out (Le Roy Ladurie 1980, 40). The vivid portrayal of now forgotten individuals and households made *Montaillou* a commercial success. During the inquisitorial hearings on which the book reports, translation entered the scene as well: the accused spoke Occitan but their words were written down in Latin, which was orally back-translated into Occitan at a later stage to allow the accused to amend the record if they wished. The amended Latin text was the one eventually used by the court. However, this whole translation dimension was dealt with in a footnote in the book's introduction (Le Roy Ladurie 1980, xvii).

Broadly speaking, microhistories combine three elements: (1) their close range, with the lens trained on an individual or a restricted group, usually of low social rank, (2) the more distant larger structures around this focal point and (3) the emphasis on individuals as active agents in a complex environment (Magnússon and Szijártó 2013, 5–6). The single focus and the more dimly perceived wider canvas go together:

> Microhistorians try to show the historical actors' experiences and how they saw themselves and their lives and which meanings they attributed to things that had happened to them, while they also try to point to deep historical structures, long-lived ways of thinking and global processes using a retrospective analysis – factors that were absent from the actors' own horizons of interpretation. All this can only be brought together, without running the risk of over-simplifying the past, when historians investigate a narrowly defined subject.
>
> (Magnússon & Szijártó 2013, 7)

Microhistorians tend to combine narrative skill and an eye for the telling detail with an acute awareness of the fact that context is not everything. It constitutes the backdrop to what historical actors do and it conditions what they can think, but it does not determine their actions or ideas. For Robert Darnton, access to the past comes from instances of 'opacity' in historical documents, those moments when, despite all our knowledge of the past, something in the record seems inexplicable. In his most famous case study, such a moment came when he read about some apprentices in 1730s Paris who, in a macabre ritual, clubbed a large number of cats to death and thought this was hilariously funny. At moments like these, Darnton suggested, we meet 'the otherness in other cultures' (1984, 75–106, 261). This kind of singularity and wonder lies at the heart of microhistory.

Microhistory and translation

It is not hard to see why microhistory has been an attractive path to take for students of translation. Translators and interpreters tend to be the type of modest or marginal figures beloved of microhistorians. Researchers may find it rewarding to bring these frequently neglected mediators and their practices back from oblivion (Adamo 2006, 85–7). The reduced scale of microhistory also offers a convenient format for Masters dissertations, doctoral theses and other relatively inexpensive research projects of short to medium duration.

In addition, the reference in the quote above to 'the historical actors' experiences and how they saw themselves' is of particular relevance to situations involving translation across cultural divides and power imbalances. Stanley Ridge, for instance, has described the very different assumptions and self-perceptions at work during the trial, in the British Colony of Natal (South Africa) in 1874, of the indigenous chief Langalibalele. Following a conflict about guns, Langalibalele and his clan had tried to flee Natal but, in a firefight on the border, had killed several border guards. He was arrested and accused of rebellion. Langalibalele may have thought of his trial as an exercise in conflict resolution in accordance with Zulu custom but, as far as the British court was concerned, the charge was treason, and the written court record, wholly in English, reflected this. That record was later shown to contain highly prejudiced translations of the Zulu words and concepts used by the accused and several witnesses (Ridge 2009). Translation suppressed Langalibalele's experience and how he saw himself.

There are at least two other points of contact between microhistory and translation studies. One centres on the concept of thick description, a concept with a history. It was invented by the philosopher Gilbert Ryle, who, in an essay from the 1960s, described watching two boys who kept contracting the eyelids of their right eyes (Ryle 1971). What were the boys actually doing? Were they deliberately winking or involuntarily twitching, imitating or parodying a wink or a twitch, or perhaps rehearsing winks for later use? How much do we need to know to figure out what is really going on? A seemingly banal case like two boys winking or twitching, Ryle noted, called for a comprehensive or 'thick' description of its context. This idea was picked up by the anthropologist Clifford Geertz in *The Interpretation of Cultures* (1973), which opened with a chapter called 'Thick Description'. Geertz stressed that an anthropological account of even a small-scale event – his celebrated example concerned a cock-fight in Bali – required an engagement with the complex lifeworlds of unique communities. It was this emphasis on the detailed description of real lives and local networks that caught the attention of microhistorians (Magnússon and Szijártó 2013, 19, 127). In translation studies, Kwame Anthony Appiah grafted the term 'thick translation' onto Geertz' thick description to plead, in 1993, for the comprehensive contextualisation of translations from unfamiliar cultures (Appiah 2012).

New Historicism (Veeser 1989; Gallagher and Greenblatt 2000) operates in ways similar to anthropological thick description, and both are best thought of as orientations rather than schools or theories or methodologies. New Historicism is explicit about its debt to Clifford Geertz but belongs with literary studies rather than with history as such. It shares with microhistory the focus on apparently insignificant detail, on minor figures and non-canonical texts and on the need to fully contextualise small-scale phenomena. New Historicists claim that recovering cultural products hitherto regarded as marginal can recalibrate our appreciation of canonical works and authors as well. This leads to programmatic statements like: 'Works that have been hitherto denigrated or ignored can be treated as major achievements' (Gallagher and Greenblatt 2000, 10) – which should be music to a translation scholar's ears.

Archives and representativeness

Microhistory is not without its problems. One is eminently practical. Figures of minor rank and importance tend to be hard to locate in archives and other primary sources. These are usually about something else, and they are organised accordingly. Carlo Ginzburg and Le Roy Ladurie sifted through court records to extract the material for their stories. The source for Robert Darnton's great cat massacre was a passage of a few pages in an otherwise obscure eighteenth-century autobiography, while two other chapters in his book were based on manuscripts gathering dust in libraries. Rachel Lung (2015) has written on the ninth-century Sillan (Korean) interpreter Yu Sinŏn, who assisted the Japanese Buddhist monk Ennin during his travels in China in the 840s. What we know about Yu Sinŏn derives entirely from Ennin's diary, which today is valued not for what it says about Yu Sinŏn but for its information about popular Buddhism in Tang-dynasty China. Ennin's dealings with his interpreter had to be pieced together from remarks dispersed throughout the diary. Julia Wells (1998) wrote about the Khoena interpreter Krotoa (also known as Eva) who, in the 1650s and '60s, worked for the Dutch as they established the settlement known today as Cape Town. The story relies entirely on official Dutch reports and correspondence of the time, which, incidentally, Wells consulted not in the original but in English translation – including summaries rather than the full texts of some of the archival holdings – while also trying to read between the lines to tease out information not explicitly stated.

The issues associated with locating sources, combing through them and making sense of what they say are less than straightforward, so much so that they can become stories in themselves and be integrated into the researcher's account (Magnússon and Szijártó 2013, 24–5). In other words, describing the path that led to the historical narrative is a perfectly legitimate practice, and it lends the narrative a self-reflexive edge.

The other major problem of microhistory is that of scaling up, connecting the micro with the macro level. The issue is that of the wider relevance of any one particular case, which boils down to the question of representativeness and generalisation. Beyond this lies another matter: what does an accumulation of microhistories add up to?

Most microhistories are case studies, and historical case studies do not normally permit generalisation (Bell 2002, 273–4; Saldanha and O'Brien 2013, 233). This does not mean that larger issues cannot be raised or made visible, even if they are only glimpsed (Magnússon and Szijártó 2013, 17). Carlo Ginzburg described his Italian miller as 'symptomatic'; Menocchio's case, he argued, pointed to an oral popular culture that has left few written traces, and then only in documents penned by people from higher social classes (1980, 126). Rachel Lung, too, noted that her Sillan interpreter Yu Sinŏn was an official in the local administration in Chuzhou, making it likely that there were other cases like his (2015, 240). For Stanley Ridge, the case of Langalibalele shows how indigenous or minority voices are routinely subsumed in metropolitan interpretation (2009, 194).

Generalisation and contextualisation invariably involve grander narratives, degrees of abstraction and appeals to overarching structures, all of them essentially projections of our own time. They not only dull the colour and complexity that is visible on the ground but threaten to explain it away. Yet they cannot be avoided altogether if microhistory is to rise above the anecdotal. To resolve this dilemma, Robert Darnton stresses the need to go back and forth between texts and contexts. This, he admits, 'may not be much of a methodology' but has the advantage that 'it does not flatten out the idiosyncratic element in history' (1984, 262). Darnton is a key figure in book history, which sets great store by the specificity of each individual case. Sigurður Gylfi Magnússon (2003, 2017) goes further and champions what he calls the 'singularisation of history'. He deliberately limits contextualisation to the immediate environment so as not to be distracted from the particulars of the local. 'I apply microhistory', Magnússon writes, 'with the consciousness that the subject I am addressing is indirectly part of a much larger context – which does not, however, determine how life is lived at the local level' (2017, 330).

But microhistory can also be written in the margin of a larger history. In his account of the Dutch embassy to the Qing court in 1795, the historian Tonio Andrade wove microhistorical anecdotes into his broader narrative by teasing out a wealth of minor details from the archival record; they allowed him, as he put it, to 'write immersively' (2021: 7). Moreover, by writing his historical account in the present tense, Andrade invites his readers to get under the skin of the historical actors. An example with a direct bearing on translation is Sylvie Kleinman's study (2012) of the Irish revolutionary Wolfe Tone, who, also in the 1790s, went to Paris to seek French support for a rebellion against British rule in Ireland. Combing through the French National Archives, Kleinman was able to document the work of two Irish exiles in France, Nicholas Madgett and his nephew John Sullivan, who acted as interpreters, intelligencers and propagandists for the Irish cause. They remain shadowy figures, but their case also sheds light on the intricacies of political and bureaucratic contacts in both France and Ireland at the time.

Why microhistory?

Despite the concerns about representativeness and generalisation to which it gives rise, microhistory has much to offer historians of translation. Here is a quick list:

- It presents vivid accounts of lived experience, showing individuals as active agents and demonstrating the value of the particular. Its interest in detail and its localised perspective run counter to the broad-brush abstractions of theoretical models and grand narratives. Think, for instance, of the way in which polysystem theory speaks of translation as being potentially innovative when a culture is 'young' or 'weak' or 'in crisis' (Even-Zohar 1990, 47). From a microhistorical point of view, sweeping generalisations like these have only a tenuous grip on actual reality; as explanations of what happens on the ground, they are useless.
- It maintains that context is essential to understand individual phenomena but that it does not determine them. Its anthropological streak militates against using social conditions to explain beliefs and other aspects of culture (Darnton 1984, 258–9).
- Its focus on the particular and the idiosyncratic makes us recognise the alienness of the past and celebrate its difference and diversity, including its minor players (Adamo 2006, 91). In preferring thick description to hasty generalisation, microhistorical research slows down the process of meaning-making and remains alert to the role of such factors as emotions and material culture.
- It tends to write the negotiation with the sources into the historical account, making the researcher's voice part of the narrative and giving it a self-reflexive tinge (Magnússon and Szijártó 2013, 150–1). Sylvie Kleinman's study of her two Irish revolutionaries dealt as much with the gaps and silences in the archives as with what the documents actually said. Reporting on missionaries and technical experts collaborating in the translation of Western scientific works in the Jiangnan Arsenal of the late Qing

period in China, Rachel Lung wondered why various books on geology, botany and natural history were translated but Darwin's *Origin of Species* was not. The record had nothing to say on the matter, leaving Lung to speculate that the book's ungodly perspective was probably unacceptable to the missionaries who selected books for translation (Lung 2016, 46, 51). As it happens, her guess was borne out by other historical research: Yang Haiyan showed how one of the main missionary translators at the Arsenal, W.A.P. Martin, reckoned that the 'transformation of species' over time cannot have been the work of nature but must have been designed by an 'intelligent and wise Governor' (Yang 2013, 186) – an approach now known as 'intelligent design' that takes the sting out of Darwin's key idea.

Scaling Up

In the 1990s, a number of new historiographical trends emerged which became known under such labels as transnational history, transcultural history, global history, world history and *histoire croisée* or entangled (or connected) history. There are differences in emphasis between these trends, but they share a good deal of common ground. Some have points of contact with microhistory, including the perspective from below and the interest in marginal figures, but the stories now tend to involve circuits with a wide geographical reach. Clare Anderson's *Subaltern Lives* (2012), for example, tracks the lives and movements of people who left only fragmentary traces in the British colonial archives: convicts, wardens, indentured labourers and indigenous people around the nineteenth-century Indian Ocean (Anderson 2012, 6). World history, as the name indicates, stands at the opposite end of the scale from microhistory and tends to focus on very large-scale phenomena. Transnational history seeks to go beyond national borders. It is often hard to distinguish from global history, which also traces long-distance connections and trajectories, including globalisation processes. Both acknowledge their indebtedness to feminist and postcolonial history, which transgressed political, cultural and other boundaries from the beginning. Transcultural history, too, is interested in border crossings and in the foreign within the local. The term 'entangled history' has become the standard English translation for the French *histoire croisée*, which grew out of studies of cross-border cultural transfer.

I will begin with the family resemblances that tie these approaches together before homing in on some of the individual approaches.

Provincialising Europe

All these new trends are acutely aware that the modern discipline of history took shape in the nineteenth century, the heyday of European nationalism. That context led many historians to take the nation state as the self-evident unit for historical investigation, together with the idea that the world was comprised only of nations (Paisley and Scully 2019, 5–6). And since, in the nineteenth century, European colonialism covered a sizeable part of the globe, historians tended to look at the world from the vantage point of Europe as the centre of civilisation and of the world. That dominance also fostered the idea of a temporal lag between Europe and the rest of the world. Modernity – the industrial revolution, free trade, concepts of social justice and national sovereignty – was supposed to have happened in Europe first, leaving others trying to catch up with Europe (or, more recently, 'the West', meaning Europe and North America).

The fixation on the nation state as the default setting for historical study is known as *methodological nationalism*. Adopting Europe as the standard against which to measure others is called *eurocentrism*. For the new trends in historical study, methodological nationalism and eurocentrism stand for their 'negative heuristic': they are what these trends seek to avoid or sidestep (Bentley 2011, 4–9). And if both the nation state and Europe are to be decentred, centre and periphery models are no longer appropriate either (Paisley and Scully 2019, 4). In their stead we find an active interest in connections, circulation, circuits, interactions and networks.

Repudiating methodological nationalism does not mean denying the role of the nation state. Indeed, transnational, global and other such historians recognise that national structures have been, and continue to be, of vital importance at many levels, from politics and healthcare to education and research funding. The intention, however, is to look both within and beyond the confines of the nation state, to cross national borders, to explore alternative dimensions and trajectories (Paisley and Scully 2019, 7–8, 21). National borders have not become irrelevant, they are just not the only boundaries to be considered.

This also applies in the case of eurocentrism. Refusing eurocentrism is not a matter of denying or belittling the importance of Europe for the history of the world but of decentring it, treating Europe as only one part of the world among others and valorising local knowledges and traditions.

The decisive book in this respect, and one with a telling title, is Dipesh Chakrabarty's *Provincializing Europe* (2000). It argues that, while concepts like modernity, subjectivity, citizenship, sovereignty, democracy, capital, universal rights or scientific rationality may well be regarded today as universal, they originated in the particular time and place of Early Modern and Enlightenment Europe and were subsequently exported to the rest of the world together with European colonialism. The question is: can these concepts be both universal and rooted in a particular intellectual tradition? For Chakrabarty, the 'universal' is something unstable because, whenever or wherever it is put to work, it is adapted to local conditions. In that sense, he suggests, European thought is both indispensable and inadequate as a means to understand modernity worldwide (2000, 16).

Chakrabarty stands out among historians because translation is very much a part of his project. Universal ideas, he argues, are universal in that they travel, but because their application is always locally inflected, they must also contain elements that defy translation. Provincialising Europe is about inspecting the local modifications and imbrications of supposedly universal ideas.

One brief example will illustrate the point (Chakrabarty 2000, 119–29). In nineteenth-century Bengal, widows faced all manner of restrictions and sometimes even *sati*, the practice of widow burning. Prominent among those who were instrumental in bringing legislation to improve the lot of Bengali widows were Rammohun Roy and Iswarchandra Vidyasagar. In their writings they expressed sympathy with the suffering of widows, declaring that compassion was a natural and universal sentiment. The issue concerns the nature of this 'sympathy' or 'compassion'. The idea of sympathy, as discussed by European Enlightenment thinkers like Adam Smith and David Hume, assumes that we put ourselves in someone else's shoes by using our imagination, understood to be a universal mental faculty. At the end of the nineteenth century, however, the Bengali biographers of Roy and Vidyasagar explained this feeling of 'sympathy' in very different terms, not as a universal sentiment but as the strictly personal gift of *shahanubhuti*, a Sanskrit-derived Bengali word in which *shaha* means 'equal' and *anubhuti* means 'feelings'. The capacity for *shahanubhuti* comes from one's innate character as an individual possessing *hriday* or (roughly) 'heart'. Vidyasagar, said his biographer, was blessed because he was born with a heart full of *shahanubhuti* (Chakrabarty 2000, 128). *Shahanubhuti* translates into English as 'sympathy', but the dictionary equivalence hides an altogether different genealogy. In other words, and even though the dictionary would have us believe otherwise, the two terms do not match at all; they belong to different conceptual worlds, and some intellectuals in nineteenth-century Bengal were enmeshed in both of these worlds.

In a wide-ranging discussion of the history of translation in India, Harish Trivedi (2006) made a comparable move of provincialising Europe. He pointed out that, throughout the long history of pre-modern India, Indian works were translated into Chinese, Persian, Arabic and other languages, but never the other way round, from these languages into an Indian language – a remarkable 'history of non-translation' (Trivedi 2006, 106). Around the year 1000, however, the decline of Sanskrit and the rise of the modern Indian vernaculars saw classic texts like the *Ramayana* and the *Mahabharata* reworked in these languages. Should we treat these versions as being, in fact, translations? For Trivedi, this would be 'a very Western question to ask', if only, he says, because no one in India asks it (2006, 106–7). The question is 'very Western' because it imposes the original-and-copy mould of (European, Western) translation on retellings that simply do not fit that mould. They spring from and slot into an altogether different intellectual tradition. But we are straying here into conceptual history, the subject of the next chapter.

Connections, trajectories

Transnational, transcultural and global history is concerned primarily with 'the circulation of goods, technology and culture in the making of modernity'

(Paisley and Scully 2019, 1). The reference to modernity is relevant because, in practice, much of the research along these lines has restricted itself to roughly the last 500 years, when the density of long-distance connections greatly increased. Typically, historians of this ilk want to figure out how these connections were established and maintained, how they changed over time, whose interests they served and how they affected individual lives. As can be expected, transborder links often involve a multiplicity of languages, which means translation is never far away.

A good example of this type of history is Jon Sensbach's 2005 biography of Rebecca Protten (1718–80), a woman of mixed African and European descent, who was born into slavery on Antigua and grew up on the then Danish island of St Thomas (now part of the US Virgin Islands), where the main language at the time was a Dutch creole. She converted to Christianity, was freed and joined the Moravian church, preaching to the enslaved plantation workers. She travelled to Germany with her first husband, who died soon after their arrival there. Living in a Moravian community in Germany, she met her second husband, Christian Protten (1715–69), who was born in West Africa of an African mother and a Danish father. Rebecca and Christian Protten eventually ended up in the Danish fort Christiansborg (in today's Accra, Ghana), where they taught children of mixed parentage. They both died there. The Prottens lived their lives across continents, between the slave trade and Moravian piety, but also between and across languages. Both Rebecca and Christian Protten were multilingual (Dutch creole, Danish, German and two West African languages, Ga and Fante – indeed, Christian Protten wrote, in Danish, a grammar of Ga and Fante, as well as some liturgical translations). As Sensbach notes (2005, 213), individuals of mixed descent like the Prottens could become intermediaries and translators, but they also ran the risk of not being fully accepted anywhere.

Historical work of this kind is about human agency and mobility across borders and against a backdrop of larger emergent structures. The connections and transits themselves are of interest, together with the reasons why people crossed borders and languages and the effects of these crossings. Here is another example, in which translation plays a substantial part.

In February 1613, the Flemish Jesuit Nicolas Trigault (1577–1628) boarded a ship in Macau bound for Goa. He had been a missionary in China for barely two years when his superior sent him back to Europe on a propaganda tour aimed at gathering funds and support as well as new recruits for the China mission. At the time, the Jesuits were the only missionaries in China, and they numbered fewer than twenty in the whole country. Key to the publicity campaign would be an Italian manuscript Trigault carried with him. It contained a memoir written by Matteo Ricci, who had lived in China for nearly thirty years and had founded the Jesuit mission there. Trigault translated into Latin and reworked part of the memoir during the sea voyage from Macau to Goa and on to Hormuz in the Persian Gulf. From there he travelled overland via Basra and Aleppo. He arrived in Rome in October 1614 and completed his Latin version there. Printed in Augsburg in 1615 as *De christiana expeditione apud Sinas* ('On the Christian mission among the Chinese'), it proved an instant success, with reprints in several European cities within a few years. Trigault's own nephew made a French translation almost immediately. Versions in German, Spanish and Italian followed, as did a partial version in English. It was the first comprehensive and reliable account of China to reach Europe and, for this reason, a momentous book.

It served other, more mundane purposes as well. Trigault had also been tasked with securing the Pope's approval for ending the subordination of the China mission to the much larger Japan mission. This is probably why the cleverly designed frontispiece of *De christiana expeditione* shows two pillars of equal height with Francis Xavier, the Jesuits' revered first missionary to India and Japan, standing on one and, on the other, the then virtually unknown Matteo Ricci. The symbolism suggested parity between the two figures. The ploy worked and the Jesuits in China were granted their independence from Japan (Lewis 2021, 59). Trigault also obtained the Pope's permission for a Chinese translation of the Bible by Jesuits, but nothing came of this; instead the Jesuits, like other Catholic missionaries, translated liturgical works (Brockey 2007, 145).

Trigault toured the capitals of Europe and had his portrait painted by Peter Paul Rubens in Antwerp or Brussels. When he set sail from Lisbon in April 1618 to return to China, he had with him twenty-two fresh recruits (five died at sea, some were diverted to other missions, only seven ended up working in China). The ship also carried an estimated 700 to 800 European books, a small selection, yet it is sobering to reflect that they were virtually the only Western books available for translation in China for at least a decade. Yet, they fuelled a major translation project there as teams of Jesuits and Chinese converts set about translating scientific, mathematical, astronomical and other works for which the Chinese could see a practical use (Standaert 2003, 367, 379).

Global microhistory

The success of microhistory on one hand and of global and transnational history on the other led almost inevitably to the question of the relation between the micro and the global. This is what global microhistory is about (Bertrand and Calafat 2018; Ghobrial 2019). Some of it focuses on itinerant lives like those of Rebecca Protten and Nicolas Trigault, or more generally the lives of diplomats, merchants, soldiers, spies, missionaries, interpreters and various other brokers and mediators, all enmeshed in institutions that support them in one way or another. Other studies push back against global and transnational history's obsession with mobility and movement and, instead, explore the local dynamics of places caught between or situated in the far reaches of empires, the kind of 'contact zones' that Mary Louise Pratt spoke about as early as the 1980s (Pratt 1987, 60) and that Karen Thornber, mindful of the unstable and frequently ambiguous borders of these zones, refers to as 'contact nebulae' (Thornber 2009, 2).

An interesting twist on these differences and debates comes in the form of micro-spatial history (De Vito 2019), which is after 'connected singularities', local practices that are distinct yet connected to other locations and larger processes. For example, in the nineteenth century, enslaved individuals in a sugar plantation in Cuba and in a household in New Orleans faced different experiences and conditions but were connected not just through the institution of slavery but also through the flow of produce from one place to the other (De Vito 2019, 356–7). The approach invites comparisons and can readily be applied to the world of translation. The Jesuit missionaries mentioned above faced very different working conditions in places like Canada, Brazil, India, China and Ethiopia but maintained a remarkably efficient communication and propaganda network. Diplomatic and military interpreters are subject to comparable pressures regardless of where they are stationed, but their individual stories remain unique.

Entanglements

The term 'entangled history' is the widely accepted translation of the French *histoire croisée*, in which *croisée* means 'crossed, criss-crossed, entwined, interwoven, folded' or indeed 'entangled' (Werner and Zimmermann 2002, 618). Like microhistory, entangled history has received attention from translation studies scholars (Wolf 2015a; Batchelor 2017). Its affinity with transnational history is evident from its origin. It grew out of cross-border transfer studies but wanted to place more emphasis on processes, interactions and encounters at multiple levels rather than on static comparisons.

Among its key words are 'intersection' and 'reflexivity'. The former, 'intersection', means that everything – objects, people, ideas, structures, practices – exists by virtue of various other things coming together in a certain place and time, perhaps only for a while and as viewed from a certain angle. In the case of translation history, that could lead to a focus on how the actors, texts and institutions involved in producing translations found each other, how each was affected by the presence of the other elements and how, within this temporary constellation, translations took shape. 'Reflexivity' refers to the awareness that what one sees changes with the angle of vision. It makes a difference whether we look at a slice of history from the perspective of a historical actor or a student of history, or from the standpoint of macro- or microhistory. One direct implication for translation studies concerns the asymmetry in the researcher's position and competence. Most researchers are more at home in their native language than in a foreign one and they tend to identify more with (and be more defensive about) what they regard as their own historical and cultural environment than with a less familiar one. Reflexivity means being conscious of where you stand and how this affects what you observe.

Cristina Archetti (2019) has written a lightweight and very accessible application of entangled history to a specific case: the online provision of local news in English in several non-English-speaking European countries such as Norway and Spain. To understand how this particular form of journalism operates, Archetti considers what she calls the 'circulatory regime' of the various news outlets, the relatively stable set of connections that holds these outlets together. Her aim is to map the actors, technologies, collaborations, situations, locations, activities and events that make up the regime. To do this, she posits that the regime consists of three elements: actors, connections and connectors. The actors are primarily the news producers and consumers but include anyone who contributes to the regime, such as financiers and advertisers. Relationships and links, whether commercial or personal, are defined as connections. Connectors comprise all the structures and material means, such as social media and mutual expectations, that enable connections to be established and maintained. It is a simple set of concepts and they are applied flexibly: a customer's predilection for a certain type of news (i.e., an affect) is a connection; a customer's motivation is a connector, as is the entrepreneurial or journalistic culture within a company. The actual mapping of the 'circulatory regime' is based on a series of in-depth interviews with principal actors, with care being taken in the reporting that their perspective on things is not overshadowed by the investigator's comments. As a result, the negotiations and adjustments that keep the regime going gain prominence rather than the actual news outputs. Translation plays no part in Archetti's study, but it would not be hard to factor it in since the companies constantly need to translate local news sources into English.

The picture that emerges from an analysis like Archetti's is dynamic but also relatively harmonious. That does not have to be the case. Divergent experiences, stumbling blocks, power differentials, conflicted loyalties, acts of resistance and failures of communication can and should be built in as well (Bachmann-Medick 2008, 142–4; Lässig 2012, 195–6). They matter not only because they form part of the complexity of the world but also because they draw attention to translation as contingent, as something being constantly shaped and handled rather than a finished product or the proverbial bridge between cultures.

Speaking of contingent realities, adjustments, connections and intersections recalls another conceptual framework, that of actor–network theory. Although actor–network theory is a sociological approach, developed by people like Michel Callon, Bruno Latour and John Law, it has seen historical applications as well and seems compatible with entangled history. For both approaches, the key tenet is: follow the connections, spot the connectors, trace the network.

The distinctive features of actor–network theory are that

1. it treats the non-human world as being on a par with human actors;
2. it is interested in how things take shape when (human and non-human) actors come together to solve problems within shifting constellations;
3. it is interested in mediators, not in intermediaries, the difference being that intermediaries simply transport meaning or force, making the output predictable from the input, whereas mediators produce outputs that cannot be predicted in advance (Latour 2005, 39); and

4. it uses the concept of *translation* in a non-linguistic sense: translation, here, is the kind of shift that occurs when an actor substitutes one goal for another so as to secure cooperation.

A couple of very brief examples before we come to a historical application. A windmill is a machine resulting from the association of humans, stone, wood and canvas in an effort to co-opt the power of otherwise indifferent winds. It solves a problem in flour production that was beyond the reach of one person pounding wheat with a pestle (Latour 1987, 129). In the early twentieth century, large battleships had so much steel in them that their compasses went haywire. Elmer Sperry sold the idea of a gyrocompass to the US Navy. In fact, the gyro-compass was yet to be built, so the Navy invested in Sperry's research towards it – in actor–network theory terms, the shift from the Navy wanting a reliable compass to investing in Sperry's research is a translation (Latour 1987, 112).

John Law (2012) analysed the way the Portuguese, around 1500, managed to sail to India. The first adversary they had to overcome was Cape Bojador, a treacherous reef jutting into the Atlantic from the western Sahara, surrounded by adverse currents and winds. The Portuguese got round the Cape by building ocean-going ships that no longer had to hug the shore, by devising instruments such as compasses and sextants that enabled sailors to determine their latitude even in mid ocean, and by training navigators to work with these instruments. By assembling these disparate elements – ships, riggings, instruments, charts, handbooks, people, knowledge, the sun – they neutralised Cape Bojador. Having reached India's Malabar coast, the Portuguese then forced out Muslim merchants by using the superior firepower of their sturdy ships and gained a monopoly of the trade in Indian spices.

When, a good hundred years later, a missionary like Nicolas Trigault travelled between Europe and China, the global enterprise that was the Jesuit missionary endeavour relied on the system of long-distance connections established by Portugal and Spain. One study of this network (Harris 1996), which makes use of the actor–network theory, stresses that the ocean remained a formidable actor (it afforded Trigault the leisure to translate on the outward journey but, on the return leg, killed almost a quarter of his recruits, and this was no exception). At the same time, while in Rome, Trigault exploited his translation of Ricci's memoir to win papal support for an internal power struggle, wrenching the China mission from the Japan mission (by making the translation his ally, actor–network theory would say he also translated it). As he toured the capitals of Europe, enjoying the success of his recently published Latin book, he drew on the prestige of Jesuit schools and scholarship to raise money and win sponsors (again, translating these institutions). He was a mediator (not an intermediary) weaving multiple connections at several levels.

Hélène Buzelin (2006, 2007) has applied ideas of networks and entangle-ments to the world of literary translation in recent times, focusing as much on publishers, contracts, editors and payments as on translators. In one case, a trans-lator living in Paris approached a Canadian publisher with a recommendation to translate into French a short novel written in Portuguese by a Mozambican writer that had already been translated into English. The French rights were acquired and the translation proceeded by recruiting the English version alongside the Portuguese original because the translator was insufficiently familiar with Mozambican Portuguese. A French subsidy was obtained but it was conditional on changes being made to the translation, with the publisher leaning on the translator so as not to jeopardise future relations with the funder (Buzelin 2007, 156–8). Even a modestly sized study like this provides a view of a production process at the intersection of a variety of material and symbolic interests.

Alison Martin's *Nature Translated* (2018), on the translation of the work of the German explorer and naturalist Alexander von Humboldt in nineteenth-century Britain, paints a similarly networked picture, though without explicitly invoking frames such as entangled history or actor–network theory. Around 1850, for example, Elizabeth Sabine worked on her translations in the knowledge that another publisher was preparing rival and cheaper versions. One of the books was a multi-volume work appearing over several years, with translators and publishers sniping at each other in successive prefaces. Both publishers used their contacts to try and enlist the author's support for an authorised translation. Elizabeth Sabine had to translate at speed to beat the competition and was handsomely paid for doing so. On one occasion, her publisher decided on a title for commercial reasons, against the author's wishes (*Ansichten der Natur* became *Aspects of Nature*, the rival translation appeared within months as *Views of Nature*). The scientific terminology in the books proved as much an adversary as Cape Bojador had been to the fifteenth-century Portuguese. Since Elizabeth could not rely on the assistance of technical dictionaries (they did not yet exist), she mobilised other resources for her struggle with wayward words: the knowledge she had gained from earlier translations (books on magnetism, physics and meteorology), a recent French translation and, above all, her husband Edward Sabine, a prominent scientist who, in turn, had access to a large network of other expert informants (A. Martin 2018, 161–5, 188–99, 205, 236). For translators, dictionaries are equivalence-spewing machines; subject experts are walking dictionaries.

As these examples will have shown, entangled history and actor–network theory direct attention to

- processes and relations rather than static final entities – in other words, the production and marketing of translations rather than the finished products;
- interactions, intersections, networks, nodes and webs of relations, and not just at the level of the object of study: the researcher, too, has institutional and other entanglements to reckon with (Werner and Zimmermann 2006, 39–40); and
- material and symbolic interests at stake, along with the non-human and human actors to be confronted, co-opted or faced down.

The Whole World?

For some, world history is merely another term for transnational and global history. For others, the difference, although it remains relative, lies in world history's planetary scale – the historical equivalent of current geopolitical concerns. It also has a preference for very long time spans. Jared Diamond's *Guns, Germs and Steel* (1997), which became a bestseller, covers a period of over ten thousand years and seeks to explain why environmental factors such as geography, climate and the presence of animals that could be domesticated enabled Eurasian peoples to develop agriculture and, with it, immunity to certain diseases, leading, in turn, to technologies and social structures that supported imperial expansion.

Several periodisations have been suggested for world history. One proposal, by Jerry Bentley (1996), takes cross-cultural interaction as its main criterion and highlights processes such as mass migrations, empire building and long-distance trade. Its brushstrokes are very broad indeed. Here is a brief taste of its six epochs:

1. The first, from about 3500 to 2000 BCE, was predicated on transportation technologies resulting from the domestication of horses and the building of seaworthy vessels. This allowed societies in India, China, Mesopotamia and Egypt to trade with their neighbours, for example transporting copper and tin for bronze metallurgy.

2. Around 2000 BCE, spoke-wheeled chariots enabled military conquest and, from about 1100 BCE, iron tools and weapons were used throughout Eurasia and much of Africa. Agriculture led to population growth in settled societies in Europe, China, India and sub-Saharan Africa.

3. The period of classical civilisations (c. 500 BCE–500 CE) saw organised states that were much larger than their predecessors: the Han dynasty in China, the Maurya empire in India, Roman rule in the Mediterranean. Their transportation infrastructure – camels could carry goods and people once a suitable saddle had been invented between about 500 and 100 BCE – supported long-distance trade. These contacts facilitated not only the spread of cultural and religious traditions (Confucianism, Buddhism, Greek philosophy, Christianity) but also the dissemination of diseases, which fatally weakened both Han China and the Roman dominions in the first centuries CE.

4. Byzantium and Persia survived the collapse of the classical world, but at first the period from about 500 to 1000 CE witnessed reduced long-distance trade due to demographic loss and shrinking economies. Still, Tang China, the Byzantine empire in the eastern Mediterranean and the Abbasid Caliphate stretching from Mesopotamia to North Africa rebuilt trade routes and saw sustained interaction.

5. Nomadic empires controlled the Eurasian land mass from c. 1000 to c. 1500 CE: in the thirteenth century, the Mongols established the largest empire in human history, from Korea in the east to the Danube in the west. Trade

stimulated the diffusion of technological innovation and market economies but equally of the bubonic plague, which, in the fourteenth century, killed up to a third of the populations of Europe and China.

6. By about 1500 CE, Western Europe had accumulated a technological advantage that allowed it to dominate on a global scale, helped unexpectedly by diseases that decimated populations in the Americas and the Pacific. In view of current geopolitical developments, this sixth global epoch may be about to end.

As Bentley recognises (1996, 765), the model does not quite manage to be global. Its vision of pre-modern times encompasses Eurasia and parts of Africa but leaves out the Americas, the Pacific and Australia. On the other hand, it shows how material and biological factors play a part alongside trade and cultural contacts. Also, the use of cross-cultural interaction as the main criterion to define the different periods draws attention to the prevalence of intercultural communication throughout history. From a practical viewpoint, the period characteristics provide a large-scale backdrop but are of little value when we want to deal with particular cases. However, they also serve as a reminder of the different temporalities to which we saw Fernand Braudel drawing attention at the beginning of the present chapter: the surface history of rapid change and personal trajectories versus the *longue durée* of institutions, attitudes and economic regimes. The *longue durée* may be slow-moving but it does not stand still; individual lives and events can shed light on the larger processes surrounding them and vice versa.

Under the early Abbasid caliphs of the ninth century, the translation of scientific and philosophical texts from Syriac, Sanskrit, Pahlavi and Greek into Arabic constituted a major historical movement which affected almost every field of knowledge and made Baghdad an intellectual centre of the first order (Montgomery 2000, 93–118). It is against this background, which fits Bentley's fourth epoch above, that we can assess the work of individual translators such as Ḥunain ibn Isḥāq and others – as indeed both Myriam Salama-Carr (1990) and Scott Montgomery (2000, 118–32) have done.

Here is a modern example of a diplomatic interpreter as a participant in decisions that shaped world history. Paul Mantoux (1877–1956), a noted historian as well as an interpreter, had direct involvement in two of the most important series of international negotiations of the early twentieth century. Born in France, he wrote a book on the industrial revolution in England and taught at the University of London until the outbreak of the First World War. After the war, he was the sole interpreter, English to French and vice versa, for the so-called Council of Four – the group consisting of the American president and the French, British and Italian prime ministers – who met from March to June 1919 (they held around 300 meetings over 100 days) to decide the provisions of the Treaty of Versailles, which determined the post-war political order in Europe. He later published a two-volume account of these meetings, based on his own notes. Soon afterwards, he was involved in creating the League of Nations (the forerunner of the United Nations) and served as director of its political section for seven years before taking up teaching posts in Geneva and Paris (Roland 1999, 121–2; Baigorri-Jalón 2014, 32–3). Another way to appreciate the global significance of the events in which Mantoux took part is to reflect that the use of both French and English during the meetings of the Council of Four, in the Treaty of Versailles and in the League of Nations signalled the end, after two hundred years, of French as the dominant language of international diplomacy (Roland 1999, 122; Baigorri-Jalón 2014, 20–4).

We can also try to measure translation flows on a planetary scale. For all its shortcomings, the online Index Translationum can provide data that have at least indicative value. It allowed Johan Heilbron (1999) to assess the relative share of individual languages in the global production of translations in book form in the final decades of the twentieth century. He found that English had by far the largest share, about 40 percent, followed by French, German and Russian with about 10–12 percent each, all other languages having a share of 3 percent or less (Heilbron 1999, 434). He expressed these relative quantities in terms of a centre-and-periphery model: as regards their share in the global production of book translations, English was the most central language, French, German and Russian were semi-peripheral (or, of course, semi-central) and all other languages entirely peripheral. The dominance of English was due to translations from, rather than into, English – that is, most translating was taking place outside the Anglophone world. Heilbron also noted that, while there was a great variety in the kinds of books translated from more central languages, the proportion of translations in relation to the total book production in those central languages was low, and the central languages often acted as pivots for translations between languages with relatively small numbers of speakers.

There were other considerations, too, beyond proportions and percentages. The dominance of English correlated only loosely with economic, military and political clout but closely with cultural prestige and soft power. In the sciences, both Anglophone publications and publications in languages other than English all cited mostly Anglophone sources (Heilbron 1999, 439–40). Other researchers have pushed these ideas further. Karen Bennett has argued that the pre-eminence of English across the exact and human sciences leads to epistemic violence – that is, the suppression of forms of knowledge and scholarship that do not fit Anglophone academic traditions (K. Bennett 2007, 2015). Lawrence Venuti has lamented not just the relative paucity of translations into English but the fact that, in addition, many of these translations conform to Anglophone stylistic conventions to the point of virtually obscuring their foreign origin (Venuti 1995). In other words, the global prevalence of English, as both a recent and a current phenomenon, has consequences for the whole world.

Big Data

In their pamphlet *The History Manifesto*, Jo Guldi and David Armitage (2014) noted that increased computing power and archival digitisation have fuelled

renewed interest in big questions and in long-term and large-scale historical processes. As they pointed out, even a tool like Google's Ngram Viewer,
available since 2010 and based on Google's digitised corpus of books printed
between 1500 and 2019, offers a (very) rough guide to the rise and fall of ideas
(Guldi and Armitage 2014, 93). You can conduct a simple test yourself: check
the occurrence of the phrase 'the translator's invisibility' in the corpus since, say,
1950 and match it with the publication of Lawrence Venuti's best-known book.

Students of the history of translation are aware of the significance of the
digital revolution. Judy Wakabayashi (2019b) has written a comprehensive
survey of what digital humanities can offer translation history. In the style of
the *History Manifesto*, Zhou Xiaoyan and Sun Sanjun have pointed out that the
availability of digitised sources, online bibliographies and computing power
enables a quantitative translation history on the basis of just bibliographies,
because numeric data and statistical analysis can reveal long-term patterns and
larger structures (Zhou and Sun 2017, 99). The presentation of the results of this
type of study now makes use of visualisation tools like histograms, line charts,
bar charts, pie charts and more (Zhou and Sun 2017, 109).

Quantitative studies of translation are not new, but their scale has increased
dramatically in recent years. To give an impression of these changes, I will first
look at an early example and then introduce some more recent cases.

One chapter in Franco Moretti's *Atlas of the European Novel 1800–1900*
(1998) contains quantitative studies in which translations play the major part.
In one of these, Moretti analysed the catalogues of 14 circulating libraries in
England around 1850. The data were often incomplete or hard to compare but
still had indicative value. He found that, compared with the larger metropolitan
centres, provincial collections were not just smaller in size but also narrower
in scope. Whereas in London libraries two thirds of the holdings consisted of
non-fiction, in smaller towns three quarters or more of the books were fiction,
and most of these were canonical English novels, with only a few translations of
foreign works (Moretti 1998, 146–60). Later in the same chapter, Moretti used a
bibliographic sample of 104 British and 48 French novels belonging to different
genres to measure their diffusion, in translation, across several European countries. Here, too, he noted that size mattered: the smaller size of a national book
market did not just mean fewer items across the same spectrum of genres, it
meant less variety in what was imported. He also noted that the dominance
of French and British novels on the nineteenth-century European market and
their diffusion by means of translation was essentially conservative in that it led
to imitation, standardisation and greater uniformity (1998, 174–84).

The quantitative data Moretti worked with in 1998 – a total of 14 lending
libraries and about 150 novels – were impressive at the time, but he relied on
catalogues and bibliographies and did not engage with the actual texts of the
books in question. Less than fifteen years later, Ryan Heuser and Long Le-Khac
(2012) had at their disposal a digitised corpus of almost 3,000 British novels
published between 1785 and 1900, and they were able to skim the contents

of these books. The method they applied was called 'distant reading' (Moretti 2013), the opposite of the 'close reading' popular among literary scholars around the middle of the twentieth century. Close reading meant the minute textual analysis of poems or extracts with an eye for ambiguities and rhetorical effects. Distant reading means the computational processing of vast amounts of digitised text. Translation students familiar with corpus studies will recognise the approach: a tool such as keywords in context (KWIC) allows a similar exploration of the kind of words occurring in the vicinity of a keyword, and additional plug-ins such as Mosaic make it possible to view the results in a visually attractive and immediately insightful form.

The aim of Heuser and Long's study was to track discursive changes in fiction over the course of a century, from 1800 to 1900. To this end they sought out 'semantic cohorts', groups of semantically related words (also known as a semantic field) that share a common trajectory through history. In their corpus they observed, among other things, a steady decline in words relating to abstract values and social norms and a corresponding increase in concrete and physical words, suggesting that the traditional explicitly evaluative language of narration was making way for an indirect mode of presentation through concrete detail, a shift from telling to showing that would be continued in Modernist writing after 1900. The findings themselves confirmed what was already known. What made the study remarkable was the size and depth of the corpus and the application to it of a method that allowed changes in narrative presentation to be tracked over a period of a hundred years.

The corpora that students of translation have been working with have grown in a similar fashion. Some are now very substantial. A good example is the Genealogies of Knowledge project which ran from 2016 to 2020 at the University of Manchester.[1] Subtitled 'The Evolution and Contestation of Concepts across Time and Space', it sought to trace how the understanding of key political, cultural and scientific concepts (human rights, equality, evidence) had evolved and what part translation had played in this evolution. Its corpus is really a suite of corpora and comes in two parts. The historical part comprises almost 600 texts in four languages: Ancient Greek (105 texts), medieval Arabic (111 texts, including translations, commentaries and original texts), Latin (43 texts, from classical to medieval times) and modern English (332 texts from the nineteenth century onwards, including original texts and translations from French, German, Greek, Latin and other languages). The contemporary corpus consists of almost 3,000 born-digital documents in English published since 2010 and deriving for the most part from communities practising alternative politics. Access to the material is free but restricted, and the site comes with a user manual that explains the project's advanced corpus analysis and visualisation tools. Most of the studies generated by the project concern the history of concepts, which is the subject of the next chapter.

Translation researchers need not wait, of course, for corpora specially designed with translation in mind. All manner of historical archives have been digitised and made publicly available in various countries and languages, and some promise rich pickings for anyone with an interest in translation. To take just one example: the proceedings of London's central criminal court, known as the Old Bailey, are now on open access for the period from 1674 to 1913.[2] Described on its homepage as 'the largest body of texts detailing the lives of non-elite people ever published', the searchable database contains 120 million words relating to almost 200,000 criminal trials. A quick search for 'interpret*' yielded 1,830 hits, a narrower search for 'interpreter' yielded 1,166. The results can be sorted by type of offence, verdict and sentence. Just in case you're interested: the trials in which an interpreter was mentioned and a verdict of guilty was given ended with sentences of imprisonment in 610 cases (including 153 sentences of transportation to an overseas penal colony), death in 131 cases, corporal punishment in 16 cases and 'miscellaneous', which included branding and fines, in 68 cases.

Notes

1 http://genealogiesofknowledge.net/
2 www.oldbaileyonline.org/index.jsp

Further Reading

Luo, Wenyan. 2020. *Translation as Actor-Networking. Actors, Agencies and Networks in the Making of Arthur Waley's Translation of the Chinese 'Journey to the West'*. London & New York: Routledge.
This is currently the fullest exposition and application of actor–network theory to the history of translation. The opening chapter introduces the key concepts and principles informing the theoretical model. The rest of the book is a detailed study of the various stages in the production of Arthur Waley's English translation of *Journey to the West* in the 1940s, making use of the 200 or so letters exchanged between the various participants in the project.

Magnússon, Sigurður Gylfi, and István Szijártó. 2013. *What is Microhistory? Theory and Practice*. London & New York: Routledge.
A comprehensive introduction to microhistory. The first part, written by Szijártó, traces the history of microhistory from its Italian beginnings via French, German and English manifestations to its postmodern state, with close attention to differences and disagreements among microhistorians. The second part, by Magnússon, champions the author's idea of 'singularisation'.

Wakabayashi, Judy. 2019b. "Digital Approaches to Translation History." *Translation and Interpreting* 11: 132–45.
An eminently balanced and useful survey. It considers what digital humanities have to offer translation historians, discusses digital resources and analytical as well as visualisation tools, and covers concepts such as distant reading. It remains conscious of the limitations as well as the potential of digital approaches and stresses their complementarity to non-digital work.

Bibliography

Adamo, Sergia. 2006. "Microhistory of Translation." In *Charting the Future of Translation History*, edited by Georges Bastin and Paul Bandia, 81–100. Ottawa: University of Ottawa Press.

Anderson, Clare. 2012. *Subaltern Lives. Biographies of Colonialism in the Indian Ocean World 1790–1920*. Cambridge: Cambridge University Press.

Andrade, Tonio. 2021. *The Last Embassy. The Dutch Mission of 1795 and the Forgotten History of Western Encounters with China*. Princeton & Oxford: Princeton University Press.

Appiah, Kwame Anthony. 2012. "Thick Translation" [1993]. In *The Translation Studies Reader*, 3rd ed. Edited by Lawrence Venuti, 331–43. London & New York: Routledge.

Archetti, Cristina. 2019. "Mapping Transnational Journalism in the Age of Flows: Or How I Ditched 'Foreign Correspondence' and the 'Immigrant Press' and Started to Love *Histoire Croisée*." *Journalism Studies* 20: 2150–66.

Bachmann-Medick, Doris. 2008. "Übersetzung in der Weltgesellschaft. Impuls eines 'translational turn'." In *Kultur, Übersetzung, Lebenswelten. Beiträge zu aktuellen Paradigmen der Kulturwissenschaften*, edited by Andreas Gipper and Susanne Klengel, 141–60. Würzburg: Königshausen & Neumann.

Baigorri-Jalón, Jesús. 2014. *From Paris to Nuremberg. The Birth of Conference Interpreting*. Amsterdam & Philadelphia: John Benjamins.

Batchelor, Kathryn. 2017. "Introduction: *histoire croisée*, Microhistory and Translation History." In *Translating Frantz Fanon across Continents and Languages*, 1–16. London: Routledge.

Bell, David. 2002. "Total History and Microhistory: The French and Italian Paradigms." In *A Companion to Western Historical Thought*, edited by Lloyd Kramer and Sarah Maza, 262–76. London: Blackwell.

Bennett, Karen. 2007. "Epistemicide! The Tale of a Predatory Discourse." *The Translator* 13: 151–69.

Bennett, Karen. 2015. "Towards an Epistemological Monoculture: Mechanisms of Epistemicide in European Research Publication." In *English as a Scientific and Research Language*, edited by Ramón Plo Alastrué and Carmen Pérez-Llantada, 9–36. Berlin: De Gruyter.

Bentley, Jerry H. 1996. "Cross-Cultural Interaction and Periodization in World History." *The American Historical Review* 101: 749–70.

Bentley, Jerry H, ed. 2011. *The Oxford Handbook of World History*. Oxford: Oxford University Press.

Bertrand, Romain, and Guillaume Calafat. 2018. "La microhistoire globale: affaire(s) à suivre." *Annales* 73: 3–18.

Braudel, Fernand. 1972. *The Mediterranean and the Mediterranean World in the Age of Philip II*. Translated by Siân Reynolds. London: Collins. Original, French, 1949.

Brockey, Liam. 2007. *Journey to the East. The Jesuit Mission to China, 1579–1724*. Cambridge (Mass.) & London: Belknap Press of Harvard University Press.

Buzelin, Hélène. 2006. "Independent Publisher in the Networks of Translation." *TTR* 19: 135–73.

Buzelin, Hélène. 2007. "Translations 'in the making'." In *Constructing a Sociology of Translation*, edited by Michaela Wolf and Alexandra Fukari, 135–69. Amsterdam & Philadelphia: John Benjamins.

Chakrabarty, Dipesh. 2000. *Provincializing Europe. Postcolonial Thought and Historical Difference*. Princeton & Oxford: Princeton University Press.

Darnton, Robert. 1984. *The Great Cat Massacre and Other Episodes in French Cultural History*. New York: Basic Books.

Davis, Natalie Zemon. 1983. *The Return of Martin Guerre*. Cambridge (Mass.): Harvard University Press.

De Vito, Christian. 2019. "History without Scale: The Micro-Spatial Perspective." *Past and Present* 242: 348–72.

Diamond, Jared. 1997. *Guns, Germs and Steel. A Short History of Everybody for the Last 13,000 Years*. London: Jonathan Cape.

Even-Zohar, Itamar. 1990. "Polysystem Studies." Special issue of *Poetics Today* 11: 1.

Gallagher, Catherine, and Stephen Greenblatt. 2000. *Practicing New Historicism*. Chicago & London: University of Chicago Press.

Geertz, Clifford. 1973. *The Interpretation of Cultures. Selected Essays*. New York: BasicBooks.

Ghobrial, John-Paul. 2019. "Introduction: Seeing the World like a Microhistorian." *Past and Present* 242: 1–22.

Ginzburg, Carlo. 1980. *The Cheese and the Worms. The Cosmos of a Sixteenth-Century Miller*. Translated by John and Anne Tedeschi. London: Routledge & Kegan Paul. Original, Italian, 1976.

Ginzburg, Carlo. 1993. "Microhistory: Two or Three Things that I Know about It." Translated by John and Anne Tedeschi. *Critical Inquiry* 20: 10–35.

Guha, Ranajit. 2001. "Subaltern Studies: Projects for Our Time and Their Convergence." In *The Latin American Subaltern Studies Reader*, edited by Ileana Rodríguez and María Milagros López, 35–46. Durham (NC) & London: Duke University Press.

Guldi, Jo, and David Armitage. 2014. *The History Manifesto*. Cambridge: Cambridge University Press.

Harris, Steven. 1996. "Confession-Building, Long-Distance Networks, and the Organization of Jesuit Science." *Early Science and Medicine* 1: 287–318.

Heilbron, Johan. 1999. "Towards a Sociology of Translation. Book Translations as a Cultural World-System." *European Journal of Social Theory* 2: 429–44.

Heuser, Ryan, and Long Le-Khac. 2012. *A Quantitative Literary History of 2,958 Nineteenth-Century British Novels: The Semantic Cohort Method*. Stanford: Stanford Literary Lab.

Kleinman, Sylvie. 2012. "'Amidst Clamour and Confusion': Civilian and Military Linguists at War in the Franco-Irish Campaigns against Britain (1792–1804)." In *Languages and the Military. Alliances, Occupation and Peace Building*, edited by Hilary Footitt and Michael Kelly, 25–46. Basingstoke: Palgrave Macmillan.

Lässig, Simone. 2012. "Übersetzungen in der Geschichte – Geschichte als Übersetzung? Überlegungen zu einem analytischen Konzept und Forschungsgegenstand für die Geschichtswissenschaft." *Geschichte und Gesellschaft* 38: 189–216.

Latour, Bruno. 1987. *Science in Action. How to Follow Scientists and Engineers through Society*. Cambridge (Mass.): Harvard University Press.

Latour, Bruno. 2005. *Reassembling the Social. An Introduction to Actor-Network-Theory*. Oxford: Oxford University Press.

Law, John. 2012. "Technology and Heterogeneous Engineering. The Case of Portuguese Expansion." In *The Social Contruction of Technological Systems*, edited by Wiebe Bijker, Thomas Hughes and Trevor Pinch, 105–27. Cambridge (Mass.): MIT Press.

León-Portilla, Miguel. 1962. *The Broken Spears. The Aztec Account of the Conquest of Mexico*. Translated by Lysander Kemp. Boston: Beacon Press.

Le Roy Ladurie, Emmanuel. 1980. *Montaillou. Cathars and Catholics in a French Village 1294–1324*. Translated by Barbara Bray. Harmondsworth: Penguin.

Lewis, Nicholas. 2021. "Revisiting *De Christiana Expeditione* as an Artefact of Globalisation." *Itinerario* 45: 47–69.

Lewis, Oscar. 1961. *The Children of Sánchez. Autobiography of a Mexican Family.* New York: Random House.

Lung, Rachel. 2015. "Sillan Interpreters in 9th-century East Asian Exchanges." *Meta* 60: 238–55.

Lung, Rachel. 2016. "The Jiangnan Arsenal. A Microcosm of Translation and Ideological Transformation in 19th-century China." *Meta* 61: 37–52.

Luo, Wenyan. 2020. *Translation as Actor-Networking. Actors, Agencies and Networks in the Making of Arthur Waley's Translation of the Chinese "Journey to the West."* London & New York: Routledge.

Magnússon, Sigurður Gylfi. 2003. "The Singularization of History. Social History and Microhistory within the Postmodern State of Knowledge." *Journal of Social History* 36: 701–35.

Magnússon, Sigurður Gylfi. 2017. "Far-reaching Microhistory. The Use of Microhistorical Perspective in a Globalized World." *Rethinking History* 21: 312–41.

Magnússon, Sigurður Gylfi, and István Szijártó. 2013. *What is Microhistory? Theory and Practice.* London & New York: Routledge.

Martin, Alison. 2018. *Nature Translated. Alexander von Humboldt's Works in Nineteenth-Century Britain.* Edinburgh: Edinburgh University Press.

Montgomery, Scott. 2000. *Science in Translation. Movements of Knowledge through Cultures and Time.* Chicago & London: University of Chicago Press.

Moretti, Franco. 1998. *Atlas of the European Novel 1800–1900.* London & New York: Verso.

Moretti, Franco. 2013. *Distant Reading.* London: Verso.

Paisley, Fiona, and Pamela Scully. 2019. *Writing Transnational History.* London: Bloomsbury.

Pratt, Mary Louise. 1987. "Linguistic Utopias." In *The Linguistics of Writing. Arguments between Language and Literature*, edited by N. Farb, D. Attridge, A. Durant and C. McCabe, 48–66. New York: Methuen.

Ridge, Stanley. 2009. "Translating Against the Grain. Negotiation of Meaning in the Colonial Trial of Chief Langalibalele and its Aftermath." In *Decentering Translation Studies. India and Beyond*, edited by Judy Wakabayashi and Rita Kothari, 195–212. Amsterdam & Philadelphia: John Benjamins.

Rodríguez, Ileana. 2001. "Reading Subalterns Across Texts, Disciplines and Theories: From Representation to Recognition." In *The Latin American Subaltern Studies Reader*, edited by Ileana Rodríguez and María Milagros López, 1–32. Durham (NC) & London: Duke University Press.

Roland, Ruth. 1999. *Interpreters as Diplomats. A Diplomatic History of the Role of Interpreters in World Politics.* Ottawa: University of Ottawa Press.

Ryle, Gilbert. 1971. "The Thinking of Thoughts." In *Collected Papers. Vol. II: Collected Essays 1929–1968*, 480–96. London: Hutchinson.

Salama-Carr, Myriam. 1990. *La traduction à l'époque abbaside. L'école de Ḥunain ibn Isḥāq et son importance pour la traduction.* Paris: Didier.

Saldanha, Gabriela, and Sharon O'Brien. 2013. *Research Methodologies in Translation Studies.* Manchester: St Jerome.

Sensbach, Jon. 2005. *Rebecca's Revival. Creating Black Christianity in the Atlantic World.* Cambridge (Mass.) & London: Harvard University Press.

Standaert, Nicolas. 2003. "The Transmission of Renaissance Culture in Seventeenth-Century China." *Renaissance Studies* 17: 367–91.

Thornber, Karen. 2009. *Empire of Texts in Motion. Chinese, Korean, and Taiwanese Transculturation of Japanese Literature.* Cambridge (Mass.): Harvard University Asia Center.

Trivedi, Harish. 2006. "In Our Own Time, On Our Own Terms. 'Translation' in India." In *Translating Others*, edited by Theo Hermans, 102–19. Manchester: St Jerome.

Veeser, H. Aram, ed. 1989. *The New Historicism.* London & New York: Routledge.

Venuti, Lawrence. 1995. *The Translator's Invisibility. A History of Translation.* London & New York: Routledge.

Wakabayashi, Judy. 2019b. "Digital Approaches to Translation History." *Translation and Interpreting* 11: 132–45.

Wells, Julia. 1998. "Eva's Men. Gender and Power in the Establishment of the Cape of Good Hope, 1652–74." *Journal of African History* 39: 417–37.

Werner, Michael, and Bénédicte Zimmermann. 2002. "Vergleich, Transfer, Verflechtung. Der Ansatz der *histoire croisée* under die Herausforderung des Transnationalen." *Geschichte und Gesellschaft* 28: 607–36.

Werner, Michael, and Bénédicte Zimmermann. 2006. "*Histoire croisée* and the Challenge of Reflexivity." *History and Theory* 45: 30–50.

White, Hayden. 2013. "History as Fulfillment." In *Philosophy of History after Hayden White*, edited by Robert Doran, 35–46. London: Bloomsbury.

Wolf, Michaela. 2015a. "Histoire croisée." In *Researching Translation and Interpreting*, edited by Claudia Angelelli and Brian Baer, 229–35. London & New York: Routledge.

Yang, Haiyan. 2013. "Knowledge across Borders. The Early Communication of Evolution in China." In *The Circulation of Knowledge between Britain, India and China. The Early-Modern World to the Twentieth Century*, edited by Bernard Lightman, Gordon McOuat and Larry Stewart, 181–208. Leiden & Boston: Brill.

Zhou, Xiaoyan, and Sanjun Sun. 2017. "Bibliography-Based Quantitative Translation History." *Perspectives* 25: 98–119.

Zinn, Howard. 1980. *A People's History of the United States. 1492–Present.* London: Longman.

Websites

Genealogies of Knowledge: http://genealogiesofknowledge.net/
Old Bailey online: www.oldbaileyonline.org/index.jsp

4   Concepts

Writing about Athens as it was in the fifth century BCE, the ancient Greek historian Thucydides related a speech in which a local leader, a man named Pericles, glorified the city's political system by claiming that it constituted a democracy because (in a fairly literal translation) 'its government is in the hands not of the few but of the many'. What did he mean, exactly? Today the answer seems straightforward. Ancient Athens was run on the basis of the direct and equal participation of all its citizens in public decision-making. That is what, for Pericles and for Thucydides, 'democracy' meant. The citizens *were* the government, and this was cause for celebration – with the proviso that 'citizens' referred only to free male Athenians, excluding women, immigrants and the enslaved.

In Early Modern Europe things were different. Its political elites had a low opinion of democracy, which they associated with mob rule. In the preceding centuries, feudal lords had needed the support of the aristocracy only and ignored people of lower rank, but, by Early Modern times, the middle classes were in the ascendant. The ruling elites recognised this growing influence but had little faith in the political judgement of commoners. They also loathed the prospect of sharing power with the middle or, worse, the lower classes. Governments were therefore urged to take the welfare of the middle classes to heart while retaining power in their own hands. This understanding of democracy as a form of government broadly *for* the people but not *by* the people informed Early Modern translations of Pericles' speech. A 1753 English rendering had Pericles say that a democracy was 'committed not to the few, but to the whole body of the people': committed to the whole body of the people, yes, but not controlled by them. A version from as late as 1888 conveyed the same idea: a democracy 'tends towards the Many and not towards the Few', where 'tends towards' falls well short of 'is run by' (Lianeri 2002, 6, 16; H. Jones 2020a); in 1888 only about half the adult men in Britain could vote, depending on how much property they owned, and women still had no vote at all.

These translations were not wrong. The translators brought certain assumptions about the concept of democracy to their translations and read Thucydides through this lens. They could not do otherwise. At the same time, by using the concept as they did, both the 1753 and the 1888 translations

DOI: 10.4324/9781315178134-4

strengthened a particular idea of democracy in their respective contexts and thus contributed to the politics of the day.

Thucydides, Plato and Aristotle were each translated several times in nineteenth-century Britain. A number of these versions are available in digital form in the Genealogies of Knowledge project I mentioned in the previous chapter. A comparison of keywords across this sizeable corpus indicates that translators of Thucydides, Plato and Aristotle had a strong preference for the term 'statesman' when rendering Greek words that might also have been translated as 'politician' or 'politically engaged citizen' (H. Jones 2019, 236–7). The reason for preferring 'statesman' is almost certainly that many of the translators were close to the ruling elite of the day and shared this elite's concept of the statesman as a superior figure who knew better than the populace how to guide the nation. The prevalence of this idea of the statesman is attested in political writings of the time; the translators strengthened it by projecting it back in time onto the Greek authors they were translating (H. Jones 2019, 225, 238–9).

This is one way to illustrate the relevance of concepts. Other concepts matter in other ways. Thucydides' history of the Peloponnesian wars saw nine full or partial translations in nineteenth-century Britain. Comparing six of these (they each number around 200,000 words), Henry Jones (2020b) employed corpus tools to check their use of the word 'fact(s)'. His assumption was that, on the one hand, modern history fashioned itself as a science, rather than an art, in the latter half of the nineteenth century by insisting on values such as factual accuracy and objectivity, while, on the other, modern historians came to regard Thucydides as a methodological model, so there might be a link between the two. A connection duly appeared. Compared with Thomas Hobbes' version of 1629, the frequency with which nineteenth-century translators of Thucydides spoke of 'fact(s)' increased significantly. Not only that, the way the concept was used also changed. For Hobbes, a 'fact' had been 'something someone had done' (from the Latin *factum*, something done by someone); in a version from 1874, which showed the highest frequency of 'fact(s)' of all the translations studied, 'fact(s)' regularly became the grammatical subject of a sentence, gaining independent agency as 'facts speaking for themselves' (H. Jones 2020b, 75–6). In this way, a particular view of historiography as based on objective facts could find support in a translation that had an ancient Greek historian champion the same concept. The similarity was mostly illusory, but it provided the new historiography with a pedigree and thus aided its acceptance.

Concepts and Conceptual History

Concepts matter because, individually and collectively, we use them to draw distinctions and organise the world. We need them to build a mental picture of the world. To understand the organisation, beliefs and value systems of communities it is essential to understand their key concepts. The representation of cultural others likewise draws on conceptual grids and prevailing stores of concepts in our immediate environment, as we know from the use of stereo-types. Simply put, conceptual history is about the mental and linguistic vocabulary that shapes our world.

Concepts form part of what the postcolonial critic Edward Said calls the 'cultural archive' we carry around in our heads, the 'structure of attitude and reference' that results from our experience and knowledge and that, in turn, makes us see things in a certain way and take certain things for granted (Said 1993, xxiii–xxiv, 89).

We indicate concepts by means of words, but the exact difference between a concept and a word is hard to pin down – apart from the obvious fact that words have a material aspect while concepts, like meanings, remain abstract. Sometimes a concept can be signalled by two or more words, like 'nobility' and 'aristocracy', although it remains debatable to what extent such pairs can really be treated as synonyms. Words can carry more meanings than one, but concepts, too, can be ambiguous. Both words and concepts come and go; we no longer speak, for example, of 'non-aligned countries', a Cold War term. Occasionally a concept lacks a word. When John Milton wrote that he was doing 'things unattempted yet in prose or rhyme', he had a concept of originality but no word for it, because 'original(ity)' did not begin to be used with the meaning 'new, not derivative' until a hundred years later (Skinner 1989, 7–8; Ball 1998, 81). Sometimes words remain the same but their meanings change. Around 1700 the German word *Bürger* ('citizen') meant the inhabitant of a city, around 1800 it meant a citizen of a state and around 1900 a member of the bourgeoisie (Koselleck 2011, 17). 'Revolution' referred originally to planetary orbits, then to a return to an initial state (as when, following the English Civil War, Thomas Hobbes described the restoration of the monarchy in 1660 as a revolution, meaning that a series of upheavals had come full circle) and finally to a sudden social and political transformation in a process of linear – and no longer cyclical – change, as in the French or the Russian or the Chinese Revolution (Koselleck 1985, 39–54).

Concepts emerge in particular circumstances; as circumstances change, concepts change as well. They mutate as they pass from one generation to another or from one language to another. They also tend to occur in clusters; 'citizen' may cluster with 'nation', 'state', 'society', 'native', 'rights', and be contrasted with 'foreigner', 'visitor', 'migrant' and so on. But concepts do not simply register or reflect states of affairs. They legitimate them and authorise action. If particular groups want to impose their view of the world on others, they push the concepts that go with that view. Violent conflicts are invariably also wars of words, with a conceptual monopoly as the ultimate aim. Propaganda and indoctrination are ways of flooding people's minds with certain concepts to the exclusion of alternatives.

Different cultures develop different sets of concepts. Translation may involve the use of receptor language terms that evoke concepts different from those intended in the original context. James Robert Ballantyne, super-intendent of the Sanskrit College in Benares (Varanasi) in colonial India, provided an example of such a mismatch in the preface to his 1859 book *Christianity Contrasted with Hindū Philosophy*. The example concerned the opening line of the Bible: 'In the beginning God created the heaven and the earth' (according to the Authorised Version), meaning God created everything there is. A Sanskrit translation of the Bible made by Baptist missionaries had rendered this verse using the Sanskrit words *ākāśa* for 'heaven' and *pṛthivī* for 'earth'. Ballantyne pointed out that, in at least one school of Hindu philosophy, *ākāśa* ('ether') and *pṛthivī* were only two of the five elements that made up the world, the others being *ap* ('water'), *tejas* ('fire') and *vāyu* ('air'), so that the second verse of Genesis, 'And the spirit of God moved upon the face of the waters', made no sense because no water had yet been created (Ballantyne 1859, v–vi; Dodson 2005, 826). Cases of this kind are relatively common in cross-cultural translation.

The history of concepts is also known as the history of ideas, conceptual history and intellectual history. It is concerned with the evolution of concepts and the words used to refer to them. It traces the changes affecting both words and concepts as they figure in shifting lexical fields and social contexts. In practice, it is fair to say, conceptual historians have been interested primarily in political discourse.

Historical studies of this type face two methodological problems. One is that of the relation between concept and context. To understand a concept we have to understand the setting in which it is used, but to understand this setting we have to understand the concepts that are prevalent in it (Van Gelderen 1998, 234; Jay 2011, 559). The problem resembles the so-called hermeneutic circle: to understand something as part of a whole we have to understand the whole, but to understand the whole we have to understand the parts that make up the whole. There is no obvious solution to this problem, except to keep shuttling between part and whole, concept and context.

The other problem is more pertinent and immediate, and it involves translation. We only have our current concepts to interpret concepts employed in the past or in another language and culture. The concepts familiar to us in our own environment may not be adequate to grasp or describe alien concepts, yet our familiar concepts are all we have to interpret those distant concepts and to articulate our understanding of them (Lianeri 2006, 67–8; Pocock 2019, 3). The problem is one of translation. How can we translate alien concepts into our terms while respecting the specificity of an alien concept, including its embeddedness in sets of related concepts, discourses and practices? No easy answer is available, and much depends on the researcher's integrity and sense of responsibility.

Yet it was this latter problem that provided a starting point for modern conceptual history, which reacted against the assumption that concepts remained stable over time (so that, say, 'citizen' in a text from around 1400 was taken to mean what we mean by 'citizen' today) and that we could simply superimpose our modern concepts on past concepts (Koselleck 1985. 80). As Reinhart Koselleck put it: 'Any translation into one's own present implies a conceptual history' (1989, 309). By this he meant that modern historians needed to be able to translate into modern terms the concepts used in the past and that, vice versa, historians needed to design a terminology capable of doing justice to historical concepts.

This engagement with translation is one way of emphasising that historical concepts need to be handled with circumspection. It goes without saying that (as already suggested at the end of Chapter 2) the same circumspection is needed when we are dealing with historical concepts of translation and everything associated with them.

Reinhart Koselleck and Quentin Skinner

The groundwork for the modern history of concepts was laid in the closing decades of the previous century, when two distinct approaches, or 'schools', each with a relatively narrow focus, gained prominence: a German school with Reinhart Koselleck as its best-known exponent, and an Anglophone one around Quentin Skinner and J.G.A. Pocock. The two main centres were Heidelberg and Cambridge. Ironically, both schools developed independently of the other because their publications were not translated until the 1980s (Skinner 2016, 137). In their work, each school focused on European modernity and each touched on the issue of translation without really engaging with it. This has changed in recent years due to the rise of global intellectual history – about which more below.

Among the most impressive achievements of the German school of conceptual history is the large multi-authored lexicon *Geschichtliche Grundbegriffe* ('Basic historical concepts'), which runs to around 7,000 pages and was published in nine volumes between 1972 and 1990, including a two-volume multilingual index. The work is organised around 130 'basic concepts' (*Grundbegriffe*) such as aristocracy, civil society, progress, democracy, industry and liberalism (Koselleck 2011; Tribe 2016). Individual entries run from a few dozen pages to several hundred. The lexicon's focus is on Europe, and Germany in particular, in the period between roughly 1750 and 1850, the advent of modernity. It seeks to cover the concepts that were essential currency at particular historical junctures, such as 'reason' or 'progress' in Enlightenment Europe.

The central idea of the lexicon is that key concepts not only reflect historical processes but contribute to them. As Reinhart Koselleck put it: 'A concept is not simply indicative of the relations which it covers; it is also a factor within them' (1985, 86); and, in the same vein, Melvin Richter: 'Concepts both registered and affected the transformations of governmental, social, and economic structures' (1987, 252). In other words, concepts give us access to the way a community understands and articulates itself, but, in addition, the concepts people use to speak about their world also help to build that world, to hold it together or to challenge its values and institutions (Ifversen 2011, 66; Koselleck 2011, 8–9). Tracing conceptual change over time therefore yields insight into social and political change. For historians, this is the change that matters – they are not linguists or philologists. Indeed, the whole *Geschichtliche Grundbegriffe* project was envisaged as a contribution to social history.

The article on 'Crisis' that Koselleck (2006) wrote for the lexicon is a good example. It starts from the ancient Greek word *krisis* ('judgement', Latin *iudicium*), which comprised both assessment of a situation and decision-making in the form of a legal verdict, medical prognosis or political action. The article goes on to trace French, English and German usages from Early Modern times onwards, when 'crisis' acquired both a historical sense as a period of turbulence preceding a radical change and an economic sense, as when Marx and Engels spoke of the successive crises in the capitalist system that they thought would eventually lead to revolution. The article ends in the twentieth century, when 'crisis' becomes a common expression for just about any kind of disturbance. Among its contentions is that, in the run-up to the French Revolution, the new historical sense of the concept of crisis both reflected and enabled a novel understanding of political transformation.

As the 'Crisis' article shows, Koselleck references translation but only in passing (Pernau 2018, 13). This is true of the Cambridge school as well. Quentin Skinner, for instance, points out that words like *el estado, der Staat, l'état* or *lo stato* may figure as translations of 'the state', but to assume that they are equivalents 'presupposes what would have to be shown' (Skinner 2010, 26). It is an important point: the fact that we find x translated as y does not entitle us to consider y the equivalent of x. Translation does not guarantee equivalence. Skinner and Pocock, like Koselleck, draw on several languages (mostly Latin, French and Italian), but in practice they restrict themselves to one – English. This is not the case for historians working on transnational conceptual history, and I will return below to the question of 'semantic transparency' in cross-cultural contexts.

The main difference between the German and the Anglophone school of conceptual history is that, while the Germans looked at long stretches of time, the Anglophone school focused primarily on the way concepts were deployed in intellectual debates. This grounded concepts in the particulars of an actual situation in a way that book historians would approve of (Soll 2016).

Quentin Skinner's approach was symptomatic in this respect. In a couple of early and groundbreaking essays (Skinner 1969; 1970) he applied J.L. Austin's speech act theory – a theory that was quite new at the time – to historical material. To understand what someone in the past meant when they said something, Skinner argued, it is not enough to understand the meaning of that person's words or the context in which the words were uttered; it is essential also to understand what that person was trying to *do* by uttering those words in those circumstances. To give a trivial and non-historical example: someone says, 'It's cold in this room'. The remark may do no more than register the temperature in the room, but it may also be intended as a reproach ('you should have heated the room') or as a request ('can you turn the heating on, please'). In these latter two cases, the utterance does more than its words say: it calls for a response and constitutes a performative with a certain force – a gentle or stern

reproach, a casual or insistent request. The intent to use words in order to bring about a certain effect constitutes the illocutionary aspect of speech acts.

Language is used performatively when someone uses words in order to achieve something, including when this something lies beyond the semantics of the words in themselves. For Skinner, it is the performative quality of historical language use and the intention and agency of the speaker that have to be grasped if we are to understand how concepts were used in the past. In arguments and debates, concepts are deployed as tools, with the aim of persuading or getting the better of an interlocutor. Put differently: by looking on utterances as interventions in a context, we can get a sense of what someone was responding to or hoping to accomplish by saying what they said; in short, *why* they uttered *those* words in *that* context (Skinner 2002, 115).

The task is harder than it seems, mainly because speakers in the past were speaking to other people in the past and not to us. The historian merely 'overhears' past speakers talking to their contemporaries. Apart from having to know the conventions and the prevailing ideas and expectations alive in the environment in question – it makes a difference whether a given statement articulates a concept for the first time or merely rehearses a commonly held view – the historian also needs to be able to translate his or her understanding of the tenor and force of the past utterance into modern terms (Skinner 1970, 136). Here, too, Skinner evokes translation but without much consequence.

Skinner's work does not usually address the long time span that Koselleck covers. A typical essay ('Moral Principles and Social Change', Skinner 2002, 145–57) deals with the rhetoric used by merchants and early capitalists in sixteenth-century Britain to extend moral legitimacy to their economic practices. In the published writings of these groups, previously negative words like 'ambition' or 'shrewdness' acquired a positive charge, a religious term like 'providence' came to be associated with careful planning and foresight, and general terms like 'industriousness' and 'frugality' were applied to the world of finance and commerce. The essay documents various ways in which an appraisive vocabulary was made to serve the ideological interests of a rising social class. Skinner could easily have thrown translations of foreign works into the mix, but he didn't.

The attraction of Skinner's work, compared with Koselleck's, lies in its concrete detail and more manageable scale. Where Koselleck is often dauntingly abstract, referring to historical actors as little more than labels for the concepts they deploy, Skinner focuses on particular issues, situations and exchanges, allowing individuals and groups to gain a certain profile. The focus on people and their interactions aids the storytelling.

For students of translation history, the emphasis on the performative aspect of utterances is of importance even outside the context of conceptual history. It highlights the idea of translations being done for a reason, of translators who translate in order to intervene in a state of affairs or achieve a certain goal. To place a translation in its historical context, it is essential to understand what the

translator was trying to *do* by producing *this* translation in *these* circumstances and by framing the translated text in *this* way. Approaching translation from this angle turns the translator into an agent with an agenda that extends beyond translation. Put differently: translation is a speech act with a certain illocutionary force, an utterance made with intent.

Transnational Conceptual History

Like the other historical practices we saw in the previous chapter, conceptual history, too, soon went transnational. This happened in several ways at once. The ideas of the likes of Reinhart Koselleck and Quentin Skinner were taken up elsewhere, while others embarked on comparative studies; finally, the general turn to the global also affected conceptual history. Each of these developments brought translation to the fore along with an interest in mediators, interactions and cross-cultural networks.

Conceptual history on the move: Korea

In his account of conceptual history in Korea since the 1990s, Myoung-Kyu Park (2012) took his cue mainly from Koselleck. Part of the *Geschichtliche Grundbegriffe* appeared in Korean translation, and the early 2000s saw the launch of substantial research projects on 'basic concepts' in Korean and East Asian history (Park 2012, 42–4). The research showed that Western concepts entering Korea from the late nineteenth century onwards were never simply imported but invariably reshaped and put to local use (we saw Dipesh Chakrabarty making a very similar point in the previous chapter). The process of remodelling and appropriation was complicated partly by Korea's traditional orientation towards China and partly by Japan's rapid modernisation during the Meiji era (1868–1912). In concluding his survey of conceptual history in Korea, Park stressed this interrelatedness, pointing out that, while Korea shared a Confucian heritage with other East Asian countries, the way this heritage was transformed in the transition to modernity differed from country to country. As a result, translation into Korean tended to be multilayered, as Western concepts might pass through China or Japan on their way to Korea (Park 2012, 48). When one of Park's colleagues, Young-Sun Ha, traced the passage of the concept of 'civilisation' to Korea, he noted that Korean intellectuals around 1900 looked to both Japan and China for the new ideas that were transforming the Confucian mindset there (Ha 2011). In other words, the particular path that certain key concepts took as they entered Korea yields insight into the country's intellectual orientation at the time. These studies paid ample attention to translation, and they were the work of historians and political scientists. Koselleck may have worked primarily on Germany in the eighteenth and nineteenth centuries, but his approach proved fruitful in very different circumstances.

Comparative conceptual history

The concept of civilisation also featured as the main example in Pim den Boer's discussion of comparative conceptual history, even though he focused on its diffusion in eighteenth-century Europe (Den Boer 2001, 2007). Like his Korean colleagues, Den Boer highlighted the role of translation: the comparative history of concepts, he noted, investigates how, when and why certain key concepts are translated from one language into another, with particular attention to concepts that strike contemporaries as new, existing concepts that acquire new meanings, and concepts that prove hard to translate or that develop different connotations or functions in different languages (Den Boer 2001, 17; 2007, 210).

As Den Boer showed, the concept of civilisation emerged around the middle of the eighteenth century more or less simultaneously in Britain and France. Initially, it denoted a process of gradual refinement rather than a finished state, in line with Enlightenment thinking about progress. Its rapid spread across Western Europe turned it into a transnational key concept. It possessed the four features which Reinhart Koselleck identified as essential for key concepts: it had a temporal dimension (denoting growth towards a supposed future state), it could be deployed in political arguments (some ideas could be portrayed as furthering civilisation more than others), it entered general public discourse, and it was abstract enough to become part of ideological worldviews (Den Boer 2007, 213; Steinmetz 2012, 91–2). Replacing earlier words like 'civility' or 'politeness', it became the subject of analysis (distinguishing degrees of civilisation as developmental stages, for instance), it began to be used in the plural (in French since 1828) and, as a marker of a European sense of superiority, it was used to legitimise colonialism as bringing 'civilisational advancement' to the colonised (Den Boer 2001, 35, 55). Throughout its career, it reflected Europe's perception of itself, down to its more recent replacement with the less elitist concept of 'culture'. In fact, 'culture' had its own career as well, especially in German, where, in the nineteenth century, it no longer merely contrasted with 'nature' but came to be associated with *Bildung* (roughly 'education', including the moulding of one's character), thus drawing it closer to the idea of 'civilisation'. As a result, even into the twentieth century German books with *Kultur* in their title, such as Sigmund Freud's *Das Unbehagen in der Kultur*, often featured the word 'civilisation' in English or French translation (*Civilisation and its Discontents*; *Le malaise dans la civilisation*) (Sartori 2005, 678–9). As these interconnections between 'civilisation' and 'culture' also suggest, concepts constantly interact with other concepts; indeed, they derive their meaning from their relations with other concepts in complex sets.

Jörn Leonhard's comparative studies, which focus on the diffusion of the concept of liberalism in nineteenth-century Europe, explicitly foreground issues of translation. Tracing, for instance, the migration of the phrase *idées libérales* ('liberal ideas') from France to other parts of Europe (Leonhard 2008), he notes that, both in Germany (*liberale Ideen*) and Italy (*idee liberali*), the concept of 'liberal ideas' became part of political discussions about the place of religion in society, a dimension absent from the original French context. But whereas in Germany *liberale Ideen* were invoked to secure freedom of conscience, in Italy the Catholic Church associated *idee liberali* with atheism and implacably opposed them (2008, 55, 59–60). In other words, the German *liberale Ideen* and the Italian *idee liberali* may well look like simple calques of the French *idées liberales*, but they are in each case very different concepts because they play particular roles in always local configurations. As Leonhard stresses, it is not the original meaning of a concept that matters but the new functionality and semantic load the concept acquires as it migrates to new contexts (2008, 62). And just as Quentin Skinner reminded us in the previous section that seemingly close translations of 'the state' in different languages do not entitle us to presume they are equivalent in meaning, Leonhard insists that even calques are likely to cover very different content; to treat them as if they are equivalent would amount to 'semantic nominalism', ignoring the specific role the translated concepts are made to play in their new environment (2008, 49).

Not all comparative history of concepts involves translation at the primary level. For example, there are studies comparing the idea of history in ancient Greece and ancient China (Lianeri 2006) or the idea of a common humanity combined with cultural difference in the historians Herodotus, Sima Qian and Ibn Khaldun (Stuurman 2013). Both these studies concern historical actors who worked independently of the others. But both studies also happen to be written in English, so they still need to translate into English the key terms encountered in the primary texts in Greek, Chinese and Arabic. Both studies draw comparisons which are affected by the way the primary terms are pulled closer together or pushed further apart by their translation into English. As, in a different context, Lydia Liu noted in the opening sentence of her *Translingual Practice*: 'comparative scholarship that aims to *cross* cultures can do nothing but translate' (Liu 1995, 1).

How difficult the translation of concepts can be is illustrated in a case study by Vicente Rafael, a historian whose work has also been noticed by students of translation. The first chapter of Rafael's *Motherless Tongues* (2016, 22–42) considers ideas of sovereignty in the Philippines around 1900. The Philippines had been under Spanish colonial rule for several centuries when a revolution broke out in 1896, leading to a declaration of independence two years later. Although the country came under United States control soon afterwards, the years leading up to and during independence saw intense debates about the issue of sovereignty. The concept of sovereignty as the Spanish colonial regime used it stressed the sovereign's absolute power ('the ruler who makes the law cannot be subject to that law'). The 1898 declaration of independence, drawn up in Spanish by the Spanish-educated leaders of the revolution, spoke in terms of 'we', the representatives of the people, declaring 'them', the people, to be sovereign (Rafael 2016, 27–8). In doing so, the declaration remained within the understanding of sovereignty that had been current in colonial times.

Among revolutionary fighters, however, a very different concept took shape, and in Tagalog rather than in Spanish. It was embodied in words like *damayan*, denoting a kind of emotional closeness that comes from shared participation in work or grief (Rafael 2016, 39), and *kalayaan*, usually translated as 'freedom', although, as Rafael notes, 'there is no easy correspondence between these two words, *freedom* and *kalayaan*' (2016, 40). The Tagalog word connotes a caring relationship, like that between parent and child, together with a willingness to extend acts of generosity towards others. It embedded the idea of popular sovereignty in everyday experience (2016, 41–2).

Rafael's chapter is more contrastive than comparative, but it demonstrates that, in the cross-cultural study of concepts, language is irreducible and translation a very slippery tool. In that sense, his chapter echoes the *Dictionary of Untranslatables* that was initiated in French by Barbara Cassin in 2004 and subsequently adapted for an Anglophone audience (Cassin 2014). The dictionary covers the history of a number of philosophical terms and concepts across several European languages, from Greek and Roman Antiquity to the present day. The word 'untranslatable' in its title does not mean 'impossible to translate'; it refers merely to the bumps in the road, the lack of clear-cut equivalents, the always locally determined choices that translators make. Although the dictionary's scope is European rather than global and rarely addresses the historical context of individual translations, it is the largest work of its kind currently available and it highlights the provisionality and conditioning of all translating.

The global turn

With the turn to global perspectives, the mobility of concepts and their carriers – humans and texts, mostly – has come into view as well. As a result, attention is being paid to the various changes that accompany the transmission, migration and adaptation of concepts across borders and languages (Pernau 2018, 9–11). In investigating translation as part of these often complex processes of relocation, historians are not so much interested in whether translators in the past made the right or wrong choices in rendering certain concepts. Rather, the focus is on how translators perceived or created correspondences between foreign concepts and their own intellectual world as they chose, reshaped or coined words in their own tongue to accommodate the new ideas (Pernau 2018, 13–4). The guiding questions are: what made translators do what they did in the circumstances, and how did their creations fare subsequently?

In their survey of global intellectual history, Samuel Moyn and Andrew Sartori similarly stress the need to ditch the dull clichés that something is always lost in translation and that translation invariably fails. Following Lydia Liu (about whom more below), they note that the apparent difficulty of translation has not stopped attempts at it. They go on: 'Nor do historians need a perfect translation of local terms and concepts to examine the renderings that past actors have proposed and their consequences' (Moyn and Sartori 2013, 11). And they conclude:

> The translation model, at least in its recent versions, is less interested in the success of attempts at understanding than in the historical and often power-laden settings of enacted translations.
>
> (Moyn & Sartori 2013, 11–2)

'Enacted translations' is a useful term. For students of translation, it should also have a familiar ring. The call to study 'enacted translations' – that is, translations as they have actually been produced rather than as the researcher might have wished them to be – was at the heart of the descriptive paradigm in translation studies a generation earlier (Toury 1995; Hermans 1999). In one sense, Moyn and Sartori's reference to the historical and often power-laden settings of enacted translations merely catches up with the so-called cultural turn that descriptivism brought on in translation studies. The cultural turn, too, involved the investigation of what kind of understanding of a foreign work or concept was embodied in a given translation and how the translation could, in turn, be understood as an intervention in a given state of affairs – what the translator was trying to *do* by bringing out a translation. However, reducing the quotation above to the tenets of descriptivism and the cultural turn in translation studies would be selling the historians short. What they add is the emphasis on the setting. For them, it is not so much translation that matters as the entire dynamic constellation of which translation is just one part. That perspective is a reminder that translation is invariably a means to an end, an instrument deployed to solve a problem or attain a goal. Global historians recognise the relevance and power of translation, but they still have their eye firmly on the larger picture.

Translation and Travelling Concepts

The problem of semantic transparency

Douglas Howland has worked primarily on the process of modernisation in late nineteenth-century Japan and China and the migration of Western concepts to East Asia during that period. As a conceptual historian, he takes his cue explicitly from Reinhart Koselleck and Quentin Skinner (Howland 2002, 7–8, 25–9), but the cross-cultural nature of his research has made him acutely aware of issues of language and translation.

One key issue that he regards as problematic for conceptual historians is the assumption of what he calls 'semantic transparency' (Howland 2002, 5–7, 18–24; 2005, 18–25). He uses the term to refer to the common but naïve belief that words have fixed meanings, that these meanings can be identified and that they exist independently of language and usage. This belief leads to the assumption that, since meaning is transparent, words in different languages can unproblematically refer to the same meaning: all we have to do is replace a word in one language with an equivalent word in another language so that the meaning remains the same. This kind of word replacement is commonly known as translation. The belief in semantic transparency entails the view that a given culture can absorb or adopt foreign ideas as they are, provided they are translated correctly. Researchers such as historians or students of translation can subsequently verify whether the imports have been correctly understood or not.

The belief in semantic transparency is misguided. Students of translation theory will have noticed that semantic transparency as Howland outlines it is similar to what the French deconstructionist philosopher Jacques Derrida calls the 'transcendental signified'. For Derrida, too, the 'transcendental signified' refers to meaning (the 'signified') considered as something that exists independently of its material carrier (the physical word or 'signifier') and that should therefore be capable of being transported intact from one language to another. In his own work, Derrida demonstrated the untenability of the idea of a transcendental signified by adopting a style of writing that constantly reminds the reader of the form and materiality of the signifier, so that meaning remains firmly tied to a very particular handling of language.

Earlier in this chapter, we also saw both Quentin Skinner and Jörn Leonhard point out that the fact that x is translated as y does not permit us to assume that x and y are equivalent; to do so 'presupposes what would have to be shown' (Skinner 2010, 26) and would constitute 'semantic nominalism' (Leonhard 2008, 49). Howland agrees. Meaning, he argues, is not a fixed attribute of words. On the contrary, it is generated in usage, in discourse and debate, which is also why words and concepts do not appear in isolation but as part of semantic fields that mutate over time. Semantic transparency is an illusion. We cannot simply assume to 'know' the meaning of a word or a concept, not even in our own language with its many variants and variations, let alone in another language, and least of all in our own or another language as it was used in the past. Neither is there an invariant in translation that could somehow be pinned down. In particular, the translation of concepts between cultures that do not have a long history of close contact cannot be based on and does not bring about equivalence.

Instead, Howland suggests, the historian should investigate 'the historical conditions of transcultural understanding' (2005, 27) and pay close attention to the historical translator's discourse. One application of this approach is his study of Nakamura Keiu's Japanese translation of John Stuart Mill's *On Liberty* (1859) as *Jiyū no ri* ('The principle of liberty'; 1871). The study opens a window on the complexities of Japan's modernisation in the latter half of the nineteenth century.

Mill understood liberty as the right of individuals to pursue whatever they want, as long as their actions do not harm others. The exercise of this liberty insisted on freedom of speech and association and on minimal interference from government and society. Conformity and public morality, Mill argued, were obnoxious ways of imposing the tyranny of the majority.

Mill's Japanese translator Nakamura Keiu (1832–91) descended from a samurai family, was sent to study in England from 1866 to 1868, and returned to Japan immediately after the Meiji restoration of 1868. He supported the Meiji programme of modernisation by introducing Western ideas to Japan. Apart from Mill's *On Liberty*, he also translated Samuel Smiles' popular *Self-Help*, which advocated individualism and self-reliance. His work helped create a new political discourse during a revolutionary period (Howland 2005, 27).

In translating *On Liberty*, as Howland describes it (2002, 2005, 2012), Nakamura made a number of conceptual adjustments, two of which may be picked out here. First, because traditionally the people of Japan had been divided into four classes, the language lacked a general abstraction to designate 'society' as a whole. To translate Mill's 'society', Nakamura used half a dozen different words with meanings such as 'public', 'people' or 'social group', and he recast Mill's concept of civil liberty by imagining – in an addition of his own devising – the state as a village in which the inhabitants governed themselves. Whereas Mill saw society as threatening to encroach on individual freedom, Nakamura obviated the need for a concept of society by projecting the idea of a self-governing village in which only the government – and not 'society' – could threaten the individual's freedom (Howland 2005, 64–6; 2012, 180–5). His version recalibrated the entire balance between the individual and those forces that can limit individual liberty.

The other conceptual adjustment stemmed from the fact that, in nineteenth-century Japan, 'liberty' connoted selfishness. Westernising intellectuals therefore preferred to relate liberty to private and religious belief rather than to the public sphere (Howland 2002, 23; 2005, 7). To this, Nakamura added a very particular inflection. Whereas Mill had been wary of the oppressive conformism of Christianity in England, Nakamura, in a series of additions woven into his translation, recommended Christianity as a tool for self-improvement and thus a corrective to selfishness (Howland 2002, 106–7; 2012, 187). His move had a political edge as well. Christianity had been banned in the early seventeenth century by the Tokugawa shogunate; the ban was reiterated in 1868. Around this time, attempts were also made to install Shintō as the national doctrine of Japan (Howland 2002, 176). Nakamura himself would be publicly baptised in 1874. In Mill's libertarian ideas, he saw a way of advocating freedom of thought, which would have to include freedom of religious belief.

On individualism

In the remainder of this chapter, I want to report on a couple of other case studies involving concepts in a translingual context. Both case studies concern China. The first, by Zhu Yifan and Kyung Hye Kim, strikes me as very much a translation studies study, and it shows both the strengths and the limitations of that approach. The second, by Lydia Liu, is arguably closer to a historian's understanding of history.

The article by Zhu Yifan and Kyung Hye Kim (Zhu and Kim 2020) investigates the changing meanings of the concept of 'individualism' in China after 1900. It surveys the various Chinese words used to render the concept when it first reached China and then takes a closer look at the predominant term, *geren zhuyi*, by inspecting the words that tend to cluster around it, the company it keeps, also known as its semantic prosody.

When the term 'individualism' first appeared as a new coinage in France (as *individualisme*) and then England in the early nineteenth century, it referred to the idea of anti-social self-centredness; only later in the century did it gain more positive connotations. The concept entered China in the early 1900s. English–Chinese dictionaries rendered it variously as *liji* ('selfishness'), *duli* ('self-reliance'), *geren pingquan zhuyi* ('equal rights doctrine') and, with a neologism, *geren zhuyi* ('doctrine of the individual'), which became the standard translation. For the anti-traditionalist writers of the New Culture movement of the 1910s – as the Qing dynasty was being replaced by the Republic of China – *geren zhuyi* stood for healthy self-interest, as opposed to the alleged oppressiveness of patriarchal and feudal structures.

Zhu and Kim explore the history of *geren zhuyi* after 1910 with the help of two large diachronic corpora. One is a parallel corpus consisting of English donor texts (over 10 million words) and their Chinese translations (over 19 million characters) covering different genres in the period from 1910 to 2010. The other is the huge monolingual Diachronic Chinese Corpus (over 66 million characters for the years 1911 to 1949 and more than 400 million characters for the period 1949 through to 2009). The results show that, in the decades before 1949, *geren zhuyi* was charged with a variety of meanings in discussions on a wide range of topics; predictably, during the Mao era after 1949, the term carried a mostly negative load, showing more positive meanings again from the 1980s onwards.

The article's strength lies in the time span covered – a hundred years or so – and the use made of very sizeable corpora. This allows the identification of the period 1911–1949 as a problem era because, in that period, conflicting meanings and associations can be shown to co-exist. But semantic prosodies only take us so far. The words co-occurring with a given term say little about the kind of argument or exchange that the historical actors were conducting. To be fair, Zhu and Kim were after the semantic prosody of *geren zhuyi*, not the wider historical context. A *historical* study would probably take the data spewed out by the corpus tool as a starting point and home in, first, on the webs of synonyms and antonyms that form around key terms, then on the debates and reflections in which these webs are deployed, and finally on the various interests at stake in the debates and reflections. An approach informed by Quentin Skinner's work would probably focus on the debates and on who was trying to achieve what by wielding the concept of *geren zhuyi*. An approach following Reinhart Koselleck might investigate how *geren zhuyi* related to other concepts that helped define modernity in twentieth-century China.

Lydia Liu's chapter 'The Discourse of Individualism' in her *Translingual Practice* (Liu 1995, 77–99) is, in this sense, more a historical than a translation studies exercise. It focuses on a much shorter period – the 1910s only – and on just one term, the use of *geren zhuyi* in journalistic disputes about self and nation. It highlights the modernisers' championing of individualism in their indictment of traditional Chinese culture but stresses that this valorisation did not happen at the expense of collectivism or nationalism (1995, 95). It also points to the emergence of first-person and autobiographical fiction while, at the same time, the Communist Party rejected individualism as part of bourgeois ideology. Liu echoes Quentin Skinner when she points out that 'it is not enough to grasp what a discourse says. One must be attentive to what the discourse does as well' (1995, 97). The Communist Party's attack on bourgeois individualism, for instance, positioned the party in relation to the Nationalists, to warlords and to imperialist powers alike, and it opened up an avenue to the rhetoric of social collectivism. In other words, the concept of individualism, trailing its foreign pedigree, quickly became enmeshed in complex local interactions, experiments and conflicts. To understand translation historically means to recognise its role as one part of a much broader dynamic and to bring that dynamic into view.

On barbarians?

Lydia Liu is one of the few translation studies scholars whose work has been noted and appreciated by historians, as shown by the inclusion of one of her essays in a reader such as *Global Conceptual History* (Pernau and Sachsenmaier 2016). Among her best-known studies is that on the Chinese character *yi* and its problematic translation as 'barbarian' (Liu 2004, 31–69).

The starting point is Article 51 of the 1858 Anglo–Chinese Treaty of Tianjin. The article stipulated that the character *yi*, translated as 'barbarian' in the same article, 'shall not be applied to the Government or subjects of Her Britannic Majesty in any Chinese official document issued by the Chinese Authorities' (Liu 2004, 32). What did this prohibition mean and what lay behind it?

Before the 1830s, *yi* simply meant 'foreign' or 'foreigner', as attested in Robert Morrison's Chinese–English dictionary of 1815. When, shortly before the outbreak of the first Opium War in 1840, the Imperial Commissioner Lin Zexu wrote to Queen Victoria calling on her to halt the opium trade, the English translation of his letter also consistently rendered *yi* as 'foreign' or 'foreigner(s)' (Liu 2004, 229–41). In the course of the 1830s, however, British officials had begun to argue that the term was offensive and even injurious, and they translated it increasingly as 'barbarian'. Ever since the failed Macartney embassy to the Qing court in 1793, when the ambassador famously refused to kowtow before the emperor and was sent packing, the presumed arrogance of the Qing had been a thorn in the side of the British. They claimed, for instance, that having to address the Chinese authorities in a written genre known as *bing*, 'petitions', put them in a position of inferiority. After Britain won the first Opium War, the 1842 Treaty of Nanjing put official correspondence on 'a footing of perfect equality' (Article 11) by imposing terms like *shao hui* ('communication'), *shen chen* ('statement') and *zha xing* ('declaration') to replace *bing* (Liu 2004, 51–3). During the negotiations preceding the treaty, the British plenipotentiary had also signalled his unhappiness with the Chinese use of *yi*, but the term was not yet banned. The second Opium War, which resulted in the Treaty of Tianjin, sealed its fate. Although the ban applied only to designating British subjects as *yi* (the treaties with the United States, France and Russia, for example, have no corresponding provision), it was so effective that the word *yi* subsequently disappeared from the language (Liu 2004, 38–40).

By insisting that *yi* meant 'barbarian', the British officials in effect annulled the alternative and inoffensive translation of *yi* as 'foreign(er)'. More importantly perhaps, the 'footing of perfect equality' on which the British set such a price was the regime of international law which had been taking shape in Europe since the middle of the seventeenth century. Deemed universally applicable despite being a European invention, international law regarded all sovereign states as equal (Liu 1999; 2004, 108–39). This idea proved incompatible with the Qing court's perception of foreign powers as mere tributaries.

But the Qing lost the Opium Wars, and the simultaneous imposition of 'barbarian' as the sole translation of *yi* and the ban on using *yi* to refer to British subjects formed part of a much larger shift that dragged China into a world of modern diplomacy based on the concept of international law. The Chinese translation (1864) of Henry Wheaton's *Elements of International Law* (1836) was a key moment in this process. It created new compounds by combining existing Confucian terms and investing them with meanings that matched the new legal and diplomatic context (Liu 1999; 2004, 108–39). As Liu points out (1999, 148–9; 2004, 132–3), the use of these neologisms – words like *quanli* for 'rights', *xingfa* for 'natural law', *gongfa* for 'public law, law of nations' – made it clear that translation was not a matter of applying existing equivalents. These equivalents did not exist prior to the translation (Liu 2004, 109). On the contrary, the translation constituted an obvious case of language engineering inasmuch as the neologisms proposed, or conjured up, a tentative matching of sorts, with the potential subsequently to crystallise into dictionary equivalents if they caught on.

The situation was also rife with irony. International law proclaimed the idea of the equality of nations, but China was forced to accept that equality from a position not of equality but of weakness, following a series of military defeats and unequal treaties. In one of these treaties, Britain imposed its own exclusive translation on a Chinese word and prohibited the Chinese from using a word in their own language on the grounds of its wilfully chosen translation into English.

These ironies only serve to highlight the fact that the migration and creation of concepts happens under certain conditions. As noted earlier, concepts by themselves do not travel, they are carried around inside human heads and by material media such as books, magazines and treaties. They never appear in isolation either, but always as part of larger clusters and constellations. In the contacts and exchanges that enable concepts to spread and transmute across cultures, translation plays a vital role. While it remains instrumental, serving whatever goals the historical actors see fit, its effects remain incalculable.

Further Reading

Burke, Martin, and Melvin Richter, eds. 2012. *Why Concepts Matter. Translating Social and Political Thought*. Leiden & Boston: Brill.
This collection contains essays by a couple of translation studies scholars (Jeremy Munday, Anthony Pym) but mostly by historians and social scientists. Its focus is on the migration of concepts and the cross-cultural representation of ideas. Individual contributions explore historical cases of self-translation by political philosophers such as Jean Bodin and Thomas Hobbes, the translation of sociological concepts in the work of Emile Durkheim and Max Weber, and the activities of nineteenth-century East Asian translators, notably Liang Qichao in China and Nakamura Keiu in Japan.

Pernau, Margrit, and Dominic Sachsenmaier, eds. 2016. *Global Conceptual History. A Reader*. London: Bloomsbury.
A collection geared primarily towards the German tradition of conceptual history, including two essays by Reinhart Koselleck himself, as well as an accessible short piece by Quentin Skinner and an assessment of 40 years of German conceptual history by Willibald Steinmetz. It also contains essays by Lydia Liu (the introduction to her 1999 collection *Tokens of Exchange*), Jörg Leonhard (on the concept of 'liberal' in early nineteenth-century Europe) and Andrew Sartori (on 'culture' in a global context). Other case studies concern concepts in the Arab world around 1900, in East African newspapers of the 1920s and in popular Hindi cinema of the 1970s and '80s.

Liu, Lydia. 2004. *The Clash of Empires. The Invention of China in Modern World Making*. Cambridge & London: Harvard University Press.
The six substantial essays in this collection are mostly about China in the nineteenth century. One, 'The Birth of a Super-Sign', covers the troubled history of the translation of the Chinese character *yi* as 'barbarian', while another, 'Translating International Law', describes the circumstances around the Chinese translation of Henry Wheaton's *Elements of International Law* (this latter essay overlaps with Liu's earlier piece, 'Legislating the Universal', in the edited collection *Tokens of Exchange*).

Bibliography

Ball, Terence. 1998. "Conceptual History and the History of Political Thought." In *History of Concepts: Comparative Perspectives*, edited by Ian Hampsher-Monk, Karin Tilmans and Frank van Vree, 75–86. Amsterdam: Amsterdam University Press.
Ballantyne, James R. 1859. *Christianity Contrasted with Hindū Philosophy*. London: James Madden.
Cassin, Barbara, ed. 2014. *Dictionary of Untranslatables. A Philosophical Lexicon*. Translated by Steven Rendall et al. Princeton & Oxford: Princeton University Press.

Den Boer, Pim. 2001. "Vergelijkende begripsgeschiedenis." In *Beschaving. Een geschiedenis van de begrippen hoofsheid, heusheid, beschaving en cultuur*, edited by Pim den Boer, 15–78. Amsterdam: Amsterdam University Press.

Den Boer, Pim. 2007. "Towards a Comparative History of Concepts: Civilisation and *beschaving*." *Contributions to the History of Concepts* 3: 207–33.

Dodson, Michael. 2005. "Translating Science, Translating Empire. The Power of Language in Colonial India." *Comparative Studies in Society and History* 47: 809–35.

Ha, Young-Sun. 2011. "The Global Diffusion of the Western Concept of Civilisation to Nineteenth-Century Korea." In *Cultural Transfers in Dispute. Representations in Asia, Europe and the Arab World since the Middle Ages*, edited by Jörg Feuchter, Friedhelm Hoffmann and Bee Yun, 283–98. Frankfurt & New York: Campus.

Hermans, Theo. 1999. *Translation in Systems. Descriptive and Systemic Approaches Explained*. Manchester: St Jerome.

Howland, Douglas. 2002. *Translating the West. Language and Political Reason in Nineteenth-Century Japan*. Honolulu: University of Hawai'i Press.

Howland, Douglas. 2005. *Personal Liberty and Public Good. The Introduction of John Stuart Mill to Japan and China*. Toronto: Toronto University Press.

Howland, Douglas. 2012. "The Public Limits of Liberty: Nakamura Keiu's Translation of J.S. Mill." In *Why Concepts Matter. Translating Social and Political Thought*, edited by Martin Burke and Melvin Richter, 177–92. Leiden & Boston: Brill.

Ifversen, Jan. 2011. "About Key Concepts and How to Study Them." *Contributions to the History of Concepts* 6: 65–88.

Jay, Martin. 2011. "Historical Explanation and the Event. Reflections on the Limits of Contextualization." *New Literary History* 42: 557–71.

Jones, Henry. 2019. "Searching for Statesmanship. A Corpus-Based Analysis of Translated Political Discourse." *Polis* 36: 216–41.

Jones, Henry. 2020a. "Jowett's Thucydides. A Corpus-Based Analysis of Translation as Political Intervention." *Translation Studies* 13: 333–51.

Jones, Henry. 2020b. "Retranslating Thucydides as a Scientific Historian." *Target* 32: 59–82.

Koselleck, Reinhart. 1985. *Futures Past. On the Semantics of Historical Time*. Translated by Keith Tribe. Cambridge (Mass.): MIT Press.

Koselleck, Reinhart. 1989. "Social History and Conceptual History." *International Journal of Politics, Culture and Society* 2: 308–25.

Koselleck, Reinhart. 2006. "Crisis." Translated by Michaela Richter. *Journal of the History of Ideas* 67: 357–400.

Koselleck, Reinhart. 2011. "Introduction and Prefaces to the *Geschichtliche Grundbegriffe*." Translated by Michaela Richter. *Contributions to the History of Concepts* 6: 1–37.

Leonhard, Jörn. 2008. "Von der Wortimitation zur semantischen Integration. Übersetzung als Kulturtransfer." In *Über-setzen*, edited by Ulrike Gleixneer, 45–63. Essen: Klartext.

Lianeri, Alexandra. 2002. "Translation and the Establishment of Liberal Democracy in Nineteenth-Century England: Constructing the Political as an Interpretive Act." In *Translation and Power*, edited by Maria Tymoczko and Edwin Gentzler, 1–24. Amherst & Boston: University of Massachusetts Press.

Lianeri, Alexandra. 2006. "Translation and the Language(s) of Historiography. Understanding Ancient Greek and Chinese Ideas of History." In *Translating Others*, edited by Theo Hermans, 67–86. Manchester: St Jerome.

Liu, Lydia. 1995. *Translingual Practice. Literature, National Culture and Translated Modernity. China 1900–1937*. Stanford: Stanford University Press.

Liu, Lydia. 1999. "Legislating the Universal. The Circulation of International Law in the Nineteenth Century." In *Tokens of Exchange. The Problem of Translation in Global Circulations*, edited by Lydia Liu, 127–64. Durham & London: Duke University Press.

Liu, Lydia. 2004. *The Clash of Empires. The Invention of China in Modern World Making*. Cambridge (Mass.) & London: Harvard University Press.

Moyn, Samuel, and Andrew Sartori. 2013. "Approaches to Global Intellectual History." In *Global Intellectual History*, edited by Samuel Moyn and Andrew Sartori, 3–20. New York: Columbia University Press.

Park, Myoung-Kyu. 2012. "Conceptual History in Korea. Its Development and Prospects." *Contributions to the History of Concepts* 7: 36–50.

Pernau, Margrit. 2018. "Einführung: Neue Wege der Begriffsgeschichte." *Geschichte und Gesellschaft* 44: 5–28.

Pernau, Margrit, and Dominic Sachsenmaier, eds. 2016. *Global Conceptual History. A Reader*, 1–27. London: Bloomsbury.

Pocock, J.G.A. 2019. "On the Unglobality of Contexts. Cambridge Methods and the History of Political Thought." *Global Intellectual History* 4: 1–14.

Rafael, Vicente. 2016. *Motherless Tongues. The Insurgency of Language amid Wars of Translation*. Durham: Duke University Press.

Richter, Melvin. 1987. "*Begriffsgeschichte* and the History of Ideas." *Journal of the History of Ideas* 48: 247–63.

Said, Edward. 1993. *Culture and Imperialism*. London: Vintage.

Sartori, Edward. 2005. "The Resonance of 'Culture'. Framing a Problem in Global Concept-History." *Comparative Studies in Society and History* 47: 676–99.

Skinner, Quentin. 1969. "Meaning and Understanding in the History of Ideas." *History and Theory* 8: 3–53.

Skinner, Quentin. 1970. "Conventions and the Understanding of Speech Acts." *The Philosophical Quarterly* 20: 118–38.

Skinner, Quentin. 1989. "Language and Political Change." In *Political Innovation and Conceptual Change*, edited by Terence Ball, James Farr and Russell Hanson, 6–23. Cambridge: Cambridge University Press.

Skinner, Quentin. 2002. *Visions of Politics. Volume 1: Regarding Method*. Cambridge: Cambridge University Press.

Skinner, Quentin. 2010. "The Sovereign State: A Genealogy." In *Sovereignty in Fragments. The Past, Present and Future of a Contested Concept*, edited by Hent Kalmo and Quentin Skinner, 26–46. Cambridge: Cambridge University Press.

Skinner, Quentin. 2016. "Rhetoric and Conceptual Change" [1999]. In *Global Conceptual History. A Reader*, edited by Margrit Pernau and Dominic Sachsenmaier, 135–48. London: Bloomsbury.

Soll, Jacob. 2016. "Intellectual History and History of the Book." In *A Companion to Intellectual History*, edited by Richard Whatmore and Brian Young, 72–82. Chichester: John Wiley & Sons.

Steinmetz, Willibald. 2012. "Some Thoughts on a History of Twentieth-Century German Basic Concepts." *Contributions to the History of Concepts* 7: 87–100.

Stuurman, Siep. 2013. "Common Humanity and Cultural Difference on the Sedentary-Nomadic Border. Herodotus, Sima Qian and Ibn Khaldun." In *Global Intellectual History*, edited by Samuel Moyn and Andrew Sartori, 33–58. New York: Columbia University Press.

Toury, Gideon. 1995. *Descriptive Translation Studies and Beyond*. Amsterdam & Philadelphia: John Benjamins.

Tribe, Keith. 2016. "Intellectual History as *Begriffsgeschichte*." In *A Companion to Intellectual History*, edited by Richard Whatmore and Brian Young, 61–71. Chichester: John Wiley & Sons.

Van Gelderen, Martin. 1998. "Between Cambridge and Heidelberg. Concepts, Languages and Images in Intellectual History." In *History of Concepts: Comparative Perspectives*, edited by Ian Hampsher-Monk, Karin Tilmans and Frank van Vree, 227–38. Amsterdam: Amsterdam University Press.

Zhu, Yifan, and Kyung Hye Kim. 2020. "The Individual on the Move. Redefining 'individualism' in China." *Translation and Interpreting Studies* 15: 161–82.

5   Memory

Memory is both the ability to call to mind something from the past (as in: 'I can remember that day') and the mental image of the thing that is recalled (as in: 'I have good memories of that day'). Memory viewed in this way is personal memory, the memory I have of something.

Strictly speaking, only individuals can remember. Collective entities such as groups, communities, societies or cultures do not remember as such. Personal memories, however, can be shared with others. For individual memories to become social, they have to be communicated. It may then become apparent that a number of individual memories converge or overlap; conversely, we could say that a particular memory is distributed among several individuals. In this way, collective memories are formed. Whereas the workings of personal memory have been studied by psychologists, memory studies emerged as a separate field of study in the early twentieth century, when the sociologist Maurice Halbwachs and the art historian Aby Warburg began to explore the idea of collective memory. Today, collective memory is more commonly called cultural memory.

Memory brings back the past. History, too, is the past as remembered and articulated in the present. As we saw in previous chapters, most historians are preoccupied with making sense of the documentary record that the past has left behind, and they write up their interpretations in the form of historical narratives. But the act of remembering itself deserves attention as well. It pulls the past into the present and makes us aware of what the past means for the present. In this sense, memory can be described as history actively remembered. Memory studies are about the kind of remembering in which the past is kept alive in the present.

Some memories may be so traumatic that individuals repress them. They may also be so personal or so intense that they defy being put into words. Ruling elites, for their part, may seek to suppress memories that do not fit their agenda. Memory studies bring us up against these extremes as well. At the same time, both individuals and collectives may feel that their past as they remember it has made them into who they are. In this sense, memory is often seen as constitutive of identity. Considerations like these can help explain why memory studies, once they took off, quickly grew into a flourishing field of study.

DOI: 10.4324/9781315178134-5

Memory studies emerged as a branch of historical study towards the end of the previous century. They are concerned both with acts of remembrance and with representations of the past. Understood in this broad sense, memory studies obviously overlap with the practice of history as such. But there is a difference. Memory studies are interested in the significance of the past for the present. In the representation of the past, it is not the represented past that matters but what the representation tells us about the present.

There is an obvious point of contact between memory and translation inasmuch as translation hauls pre-existing discourses into the present. In Siobhan Brownlie's words, interlingual translation 'has the memory of texts at its heart' (2016, 14). The distance in time between a base text and its translation may be counted in seconds, as in simultaneous interpreting, or in centuries. The wider the gap, the more evident it is that translation constitutes an act of recalling the past to repurpose it in and for the present. Translators in Early Modern Europe, for instance, regularly spoke of their work as bringing ancient authors back from the dead or from oblivion, and the more libertine among them took pride in writing as their author would have written 'had he lived in our age and in our country', as John Dryden put it in 1680 (Hermans 1985, 125–6).

Despite parallels like these, memory studies, like other branches of historical study, only recently began to pay attention to translation. In what follows, I will first outline the basics of memory studies before turning to transcultural perspectives and issues of translation.

Memory Studies

In order to be able to remember a few things, we need to forget a great many other things. We also tend to remember those things or events that mean something to us. In other words, memory is highly selective and coloured by affect. It is also notoriously unreliable. In most cases, memory is not really concerned with the detail of what happened or the accuracy of the recalling (there is a major exception, as we shall see). Instead, it tells us how the past was experienced. Its affective quality is an essential ingredient.

The difference between personal and collective memory is that between memory in the head and memory in the world. Somewhere between these two lies what Jan Assmann (2008) calls communicative memory, which is not as public as collective or cultural memory but depends on communicative interaction within a relatively closed circle like a family. My mother lived as a young woman through the Nazi occupation of Belgium during the Second World War. She would tell us about life on the farm in those years. I never recorded her stories and, now that she has passed away, I remember them only imperfectly. Her grandchildren remember them even less. Communicative memory has a limited range and typically lasts for only a couple of generations, the time span we refer to as 'living memory'. Cultural memory, by contrast, is more institutionalised, more durable and objectified in symbolic forms such as books, monuments and commemorative rituals. It is also at some remove from the actual experience and kept alive by those who are no longer eyewitnesses. This makes cultural memory a matter of vicarious recollection (Rigney 2005, 12).

Memory needs a medium in which to take shape. Personal memories form in the brain. Socially shared memories need means of communication such as words, still or moving images, statues, places, ceremonial acts of remembrance, and so on. The choice of medium is important because each medium configures the past in a certain way. A written narrative presents past events differently from, say, a historical painting or a TV documentary. Since different media configure a past event in different ways, changing the medium also reconfigures the event (Brodzki 2007, 4).

Narrative is an essential part of communicative and cultural memory. Family photographs and national monuments need to be explained, contextualised and narrated to retain their social function as shared testimonies. Public memory sites normally feature various converging representations in different media. These representations condense a range of memories into a 'site' of memory. I have visited two former concentration camps in my life, Dachau and Auschwitz. In both cases, the guidebooks, the words spoken by the guide, the onscreen images, the buildings, the barbed wire and the objects that have been preserved combined to tell the story of these sites and what happened there.

Memories require frequent repetition if they are to be kept alive. This led Aleida Assmann (2008) to distinguish between active and passive cultural memory. Passive cultural memory is what is preserved in archives or in museum storerooms, where items are kept but not put on display. Active cultural memory is what the museum exhibits for the public to see. Depending on circumstances, artefacts may move from the display to the storeroom and vice versa. The archive contains the things that are deemed sufficiently important to be preserved but not important enough to enter the public domain. It has the potential to be activated but remains inert for now. Canonical objects, by contrast, constitute a culture's active working memory. Canonical memory sites attract repeated representations in different media and over a relatively long period of time. In the 1980s and after, the historian Pierre Nora made his name by writing at length about 'sites of memory' (*lieux de mémoire*) in France, historic objects and locations where the national past was actively remembered as a shared experience and where the persistence of the past in the present was brought home. Because the remembering that these memory sites elicit has emotional as well as cognitive appeal, it fosters a sense of national identity and belonging.

As memory drags the past into the present, the perspective from the present shapes the perception of the past. In the case of collective memory, the present is always the present of a particular group, whether this is a community of online activists, a commercial company or a national government. In institutional and ideological contexts, this also means that the present can be framed in a certain way by associating it with a carefully selected slice of the past. For example, when the COVID-19 pandemic first reached Britain in the spring of 2020, the government invoked the spirit of the Second World War, framing COVID as an aggressive enemy in order to encourage people to be resilient and disciplined in difficult times. In many countries in the world, the history curriculum for schools comprises a highly selective effort to promulgate a collective memory as part of a national identity project (Wertsch 2008, 59). The idea of tradition or of a 'memory culture' may be understood as the set of memorial practices maintained by a particular group.

As these examples suggest, in the case of cultural memory it is important to ask who is controlling or promoting the remembering, whose voice is heard and whose past is being leveraged (Carrier and Kabalek 2014, 51). Complex and conflicted histories mean that events can often be seen from more angles than one and the received version may be open to challenge. In addition, as Astrid Erll and Ann Rigney point out (2009, 2), views of the past reflect changing values, so that even canonical memory sites have a history.

A good example is what happened to the statue of Edward Colston in Bristol. Colston (1636–1721) had been a wealthy merchant who had generously financed hospitals, schools and almshouses in Bristol and elsewhere. In 1895 he was honoured with a statue in the centre of Bristol for his philanthropic contribution to the life of the city. The problem was that part of Colston's wealth had come from his involvement in the slave trade. Objections to the statue came to a head during the Black Lives Matter demonstrations in 2020, when a crowd pulled the statue from its pedestal and dumped it in Bristol Harbour. The town council had it retrieved from the mud a week later. It was eventually put into a museum in its defaced state so as to allow public debate about its symbolism. Clearly, the way Colston was remembered in 2020 was no longer the same as it had been in 1895.

A very different case is discussed by Aleida Assmann (2018), who emphasises active forgetting as the deliberate erasure of the past. The violent events that accompanied the establishment of the state of Israel in 1948 are known to Israelis as the War of Independence but to Palestinians as the Catastrophe, a memory of flight, expulsion and loss. As subsequent decades saw new Israeli settlements being built on land where Palestinian villages had been devastated, Israelis chose to forget the Palestinian past of these places. For Palestinians in the diaspora without a hope or right of return, the memory of their now buried villages becomes ever more remote.

Cases like these show that collective memories can be contested, that there is room for non-hegemonic countermemories and that, consequently, it would be advisable to think about memory in less static terms than those suggested by the ideas of a national memory or a memory culture. As memory studies deepened and diversified, they recognised these complexities. One way forward was to shift attention from memory as a product to memory as a process. This meant focusing on the production and transmission of memory, on remembering as a shared cultural practice and on acts of remembrance seen as performatives – that is, as communicative acts aiming to bring about affective and cognitive effects (Rigney 2015, 68).

There were other developments, too. As the digital age progressed, memories were being recycled from one medium to another with increasing ease and speed. It was soon recognised that these media were not mere conduits. For most people today, the memory of the Second World War is shaped by feature films, TV documentaries and online images and texts. These media, and the narrative forms they permit, help shape what is remembered and how (Rigney 2015, 65).

This phenomenon was captured in the term 'remediation', defined as 'the continuous transcription of memory content into different media' (Erll 2017, 313–4). Canonical sites of memory had always used several media at once. The digital age enabled memories of all sorts to be articulated and transmitted in an array of media. Interlingual translation may be seen in this context as one type of remediation. Some memory researchers even regard translation as synonymous with remediation, speaking of the translation of content from older to newer media or from one medium to another, such as print to moving image (Rigney 2015, 69).

In her book *Can These Bones Live?* (2007), Bella Brodzki works with a similarly broad understanding of translation, which she describes as 'a process of transporting and transposing meanings, both vertically and horizontally, within the same language, as well as across different languages, cultures, genres, and modes of artistic expression' (2007, 12) – which is very much the kind of process that memory studies describe as remediation. One of Brodzki's case studies concerns a French Holocaust survivor memoir published in 1987, Claude Morhange-Bégué's *Chamberet: Recollections from an Ordinary Childhood*, translated from the French by Austryn Wainhouse from an unpublished manuscript. Chamberet is the French village where, in 1944, the eight-year-old Claude was living with her mother when the mother was arrested and deported to Auschwitz, from where she returned after the war with an obsessive urge to talk about her ordeal. The daughter's memoir records her own sense of loss at the time of the arrest but also her identification with her mother's suffering and her helplessness at the sight of a mother broken by life in the camp. For Brodzki, the memoir constitutes an act of intralingual translation of the mother's oral narrative (2007, 123).

Transcultural Memory

In the first decade or so of the present century, memory studies went through the same transcultural turn that, as we saw in previous chapters, affected the study of history along with other humanities disciplines. The new orientation meant a change in scale and focus, but it also brought new ideas, and it put translation on the memory studies map.

A decisive essay in this respect was Astrid Erll's 'Travelling Memory' (2011). The author voiced criticism of the restricted idea of cultural memory as national remembrance in the style of Pierre Nora, an approach that Erll (2011, 6–7) associated with the methodological nationalism we encountered in Chapter 3.

Instead, Erll pointed to the porosity of national borders, to individuals wearing several identities and professing several allegiances at once, to the pervasiveness of global media and to demographic mobility giving rise to diasporic memories. In that context, she argued, memory is best conceived as something unstable and fluid, in need of constant remediation. Even ostensibly stable memories change over time, or they only appear stable because they have been made serviceable to certain ends (2011, 14–5).

Erll distinguished five dimensions of movement: (1) carriers, meaning humans moving around, including travel and migration; (2) media, with modern technology enabling both the globalisation and localisation of memory; (3) contents, usually to be derived from images and narratives; (4) practices, such as the international rituals that emerged after the First World War around the tomb of the Unknown Soldier; and (5) forms, such as the eminently transportable images of the fall of the Berlin Wall in November 1989 standing as condensed narratives of the end of the Cold War in Europe (2011, 12–3). While these dimensions do not explicitly address translation, the emphasis on mobility and transportability leave plenty of room for it.

Astrid Erll herself has written about the different ways in which the 'Indian Mutiny', or the 'Indian Rebellion', of 1857 has been remembered in Britain and in India – beginning with the name given to the events: mutiny or rebellion (Erll 2009). Her study focuses on a bloody episode that took place in Cawnpore (now Kanpur, in Uttar Pradesh, northern India), where the British station had been besieged by rebels who offered the British safe passage. Whether through deceit or confusion, however, the evacuation turned into a massacre. When, subsequently, a British relief force approached Cawnpore, a number of British women who had been taken prisoner by the rebels were murdered. This, in turn, led to brutal reprisals by the British.

For her study, Erll draws on the notion of remediation and, in addition, the related idea of 'premediation', understood as the filter or lens through which we perceive the world and process new impressions. Premediation consists of existing modes of representation, or, slightly more technically, 'the fact that existent media which circulate in a given society provide schemata for new experience and its representation' (Erll 2009, 111). The concept is similar to that of a conceptual grid or the cultural archive mentioned in the previous chapter, except that it puts more emphasis on existing representations and the material form or medium in which these representations appear.

The Cawnpore episode obviously constitutes a contested and therefore an unstable memory, inasmuch as the events have not only been remembered differently in India and in Britain but remembered differently at different times. Pre- and post-independence India and imperial and postcolonial Britain produced their own memorial practices (2009, 109–10). First, reports in British newspapers in 1857 contained wildly exaggerated claims of Indian treachery and cruelty; the language in these reports filtered the events through Gothic horror fiction (premediation). The earliest account by a British soldier, though not himself an eyewitness to the killings, was printed in India within months.

Parts of this account appeared in *The Times* newspaper and it was copied a year later, sometimes verbatim, in Charles Ball's *History of the Indian Mutiny* – the first of many subsequent remediations. An Indian perspective appeared in the novel *Shunkur* (1877–8) by Shoshee Chunder Dutt, which tells of the fictional peasant Shunkur whose wife is raped by two fugitive British soldiers and who joins the Indian rebellion to take revenge. In some scenes, Dutt follows the earliest printed account, but the novel's storyline also seems to echo (that is, may be premediated by) scenes from the Indian epic *Mahabharata*, lending it an altogether different symbolic dimension. In the 1880s, popular fiction in Britain frequently rehearsed the Cawnpore episode (more remediation), enriching the narrative with visual illustrations and invariably contrasting British valour with Indian villainy. Finally, a 2005 Bollywood film, *The Rising*, reverses the picture presented in the imperialist English fictions of the 1880s and celebrates the Cawnpore episode as heralding Indian independence.

Concepts like remediation and premediation help us understand and structure memory chains like this. Although Erll does not invoke translation, it is not hard to see how translation interacts with remediation and premediation. A change of language and context affects both, as translated texts enter new sets of existing representations that filter perceptions. Translators read their base texts with certain preconceptions in mind and, in turn, write words that appeal to existing genres and evoke intertextual echoes in the translating language. Readers for their part may recognise the patterns created by the translator or discern patterns and echoes of their own. Retranslations involve both remediation and premediation.

Astrid Erll's study of the Indian Rebellion/Mutiny of 1857 shows not only evolving memories but also memories interacting with each other, sometimes in complex ways. The 2005 Bollywood film *The Rising*, for instance, recalls both the Cawnpore episode and Indian independence and remains aware of British representations. To characterise complexities of this kind, Michael Rothberg (2009) speaks of 'multidirectional memories'. The term designates multilayered collective memories that exist simultaneously in different locations and are constantly renegotiated through social interaction. Memories of one event may be cross-referenced with memories of another, as in the case of *The Rising* associating the 1857 Rebellion with Indian Independence; or, to take one of Rothberg's own examples, memories of the Holocaust may be intertwined with memories of decolonisation.

Multidirectional memory means linking memories of events or things from different places or times. Two chapters of Rothberg's book show how, during the Algerian War of Independence (1954–62), associations with the Holocaust were triggered by reports in the French press about the use of torture and so-called 'regroupment centres' (effectively concentration camps) by the French state. The nodal point in Rothberg's chapters on the topic is the year 1961. In that year, the trial of Adolf Eichmann was taking place in Jerusalem, marking the beginning of the discourse on the uniqueness of the Holocaust as an event without equal in history. Also in 1961, Jean Rouch and Edgar Morin released their experimental documentary film *Chronique d'un été* ('Chronicle of a Summer') which featured, among scenes of daily life in Paris, conversations associating the violence in Algeria with the Nazi death camps. And in this same year, Charlotte Delbo, a former member of the French Communist resistance during the Second World War, published a book ironically titled *Les belles lettres* in which she reprinted letters published in the French press about the Algerian war, interspersed with her own observations as a survivor of Auschwitz. Rothberg's point in tracing and making these connections is that the emergence of Holocaust memory and the unfolding of decolonisation are interlinked processes and that recognising the connection between them aids our understanding of both (Rothberg 2009, 200).

Rothberg sees the idea of multidirectional memory as appropriate for today's multicultural and transnational world (2009, 21). Alison Landsberg (2004) bases her approach on modern mass media such as moving images or interactive museum displays. In this context, she speaks of 'prosthetic memories', memories that are 'not the product of lived experience' but instead are 'derived from engagement with a mediated representation' (Landsberg 2004, 20). She argues that filmic images and techniques, in particular, have become so sophisticated that they enable viewers 'to *experience* an event or a past without having actually lived through it' (2004, 48; original emphasis). Watching a film like Steve McQueen's *12 Years a Slave* may elicit such intense empathy with its main character that the spectator 'does not simply apprehend a historical narrative but takes on a more personal, deeply felt memory of a past event through which he or she did not live' (2004, 2). The memory is 'prosthetic' because it has been obtained at second hand: it is based on the film, which, in turn, is based on a written narrative derived from an oral autobiographical account. The film's persuasiveness results in part from details that are not, in fact, in the written narrative. As Landsberg notes, 'mass mediated memories are not premised on any claim of authenticity' (2004, 9).

Does Landsberg have too much faith in the power of a medium like cinema to give viewers the experience of an event without them actually having experienced that event? Surely watching *12 Years a Slave* is a far cry from the physical and mental experience of slavery? Yet this is precisely how cultural memory works: vicariously, at a distance. Once personal and communicative memories have transitioned to collective or cultural memories, they become vicarious memories, kept alive and transmitted by those who are no longer eyewitnesses. What Landsberg calls a prosthetic memory is a particularly vivid vicarious memory that touches us emotionally. As Ann Rigney points out in another context, testimonies can offer the receiver who was not a witness a vicarious experience through empathy with the historical actor (Rigney 2015, 73).

Translations of testimonies, too, typically offer their readers a vicarious experience. They not only remediate the original testimony and enable it to enter new cultural environments, they also enable the receiver to feel empathy with the original speaker – provided the translator positions him- or herself in alignment with this speaker (Hermans 2014). When a translated testimony invites reading as if it were the unmediated original, readers may feel the witness is speaking directly to them; as one reviewer said of the translation of Elie Wiesel's Holocaust survivor testimony: 'to listen to the witness is to become a witness' (in Davies 2018, 59). At the same time, translations insert texts that originated in one cultural context into another cultural context. As a result, the memories evoked in these texts almost inevitably become multidirectional, as the different contexts are likely to interact and both translators and recipients with different backgrounds will make new connections that are meaningful to them (Brownlie 2016, 77). In all these ways, translation is not just enmeshed in the complexities of transcultural memory, it contributes to them.

Memory and Translation

Memory studies at first neglected translation (Deane-Cox 2013, 309). This is not surprising, since in its early days the field focused on national traditions conveniently construed as homogenous and monolingual. The work of Pierra Nora on 'sites of memory' in France is an example. The arrival of transcultural memory studies has changed all that, as they were interested in memory formation across different communities, traditions and languages (Carrier and Kabalek 2014, 50–7). Translation has a significant role in the migration, mutation and maintenance of memories that transcend linguistic boundaries.

The emergence of transcultural memory studies followed on the heels of another development: the Holocaust becoming a transnational cultural memory. The Holocaust – the systematic persecution and murder of millions of Jews and others by the Nazi regime during the Second World War – occupies a special place in memory studies. The extreme nature of the events themselves made their memory traumatic for the survivors, who, if they were able to speak about them at all, often struggled to put them into words. A traumatic experience that defies expression in conventional language marks the limit of the idea of premediation, as no pre-given mould is available or felt to be appropriate for its articulation. The Holocaust is the most paradigmatic case of an unspeakable experience (Rigney 2015, 72).

Yet many testimonies have been produced, and they play an extraordinarily large role in current understandings of the Holocaust. Also, with the passing of time, the eyewitnesses gradually disappeared and the Holocaust as constituted by individual first-hand accounts transitioned to a cultural and transcultural memory. That transition coincided with the emergence of the Holocaust as a universal symbol of evil.

Translation accompanied the Holocaust from the beginning. The world of the camps was already multilingual, as people from different parts of Europe found themselves thrown together while the language of the guards was German. Postwar Holocaust testimonies were written up in at least twenty languages, making many of them dependent on translation to reach a wider readership (Davies 2018, 2). As a transcultural memory, the Holocaust is unthinkable without translation (Davies 2018, 209; Seidman 2006, 207).

The translation of Holocaust documents shows several special features that are directly connected with the gravity and uniqueness of the genre. Among these are the following:

- The authenticity of the testimony and the integrity of the voice of the witness are issues of such prominence that translators tend to go out of their way not to compromise them. Prefaces to translated Holocaust testimonies often stress such things as the strict accuracy of the rendering, the authorisation given by the witness, or the translator's personal or emotional closeness to the witness in order to claim that translation has not affected the authenticity of the testimony. Paratextual comments like these 'are designed to draw attention to translation in order to neutralize it' (Davies 2018, 44). The dilemma is stark: when the eyewitness's first-hand account passes through the hands of a translator, the testimony cannot remain untouched, yet the ethical imperative is for it to be preserved intact (Davies 2014, 176–7; 2018, 45–51). The anxiety about translation potentially undermining the authenticity of the survivor's memory is similar to – but much more acute than – the unease felt by some historians when faced with the element of fictionalisation affecting the historical narrative, as discussed in Chapter 1.
- In the context of this preoccupation with authenticity and integrity, the idea emerged of the translator as 'secondary witness' (Deane-Cox 2013). A secondary witness is someone who listens to a witness with empathy and helps to record and transmit the testimony. This could be a family member or close friend of the witness, a journalist or indeed a translator. Yet for all the empathy that a translator may feel, he or she still cannot identify with the witness whose experience is far too extreme for that, but neither should the translator try to assimilate what the witness says into their own world of experience (Deane-Cox 2013, 312–3).
- As the idea of the translator as secondary witness suggests, ethical demands powerfully affect the translation of Holocaust documents. These demands are not always met, opening up gaps between theory and practice that can be approached from ideological, religious, genre and other perspectives (Davies 2018, 15).
- Holocaust survivors who act as self-translators tend not to show the kind of creativity generally associated with self-translation but to concentrate on the accuracy of the rendering, sometimes out of a desire to keep personal control of the testimony, at other times in order to counter Holocaust deniers (Davies 2018, 42).

A critical look at the textual history of Elie Wiesel's Holocaust testimony reveals the anxiety about the authenticity of memory that accompanies the genre (Seidman 2006, 216–36; Davies 2018, 58–97). Wiesel's testimony as an Auschwitz survivor gained iconic status through the publication in France of *La Nuit* in 1958 and its English translation by Stella Rodway as *Night* in 1960.

For decades, most Anglophone critics read the English version as if it was the original. Its status as a translation became salient, however, in 2006 with the publication of a new English translation by the author's wife, Marion Wiesel. The translation corrected some minor factual errors in the French text of 1958, but it also contained a preface by Elie Wiesel himself in which he spoke of a – by then largely forgotten – Yiddish original published in Buenos Aires in 1956. This original derived from a much longer manuscript that had been further abbreviated and put into French as *La Nuit* by Wiesel himself together with the French publisher. The factual corrections in the English retranslation of 2006 led in turn, a year later, to a revision of the French text, which had now become an original that was no longer the original.

These complications raise a series of issues concerning what constitutes the original testimony, the closeness of each version of it to the actual experience, the changes in Wiesel's own memory over time, the position of the translator in relation to the author, and the element of stylisation and fictionalisation leaving its mark on each reworking of the narrative. Translation plays an unsettling part in the transmission of Holocaust testimony.

While the Holocaust occupies a distinct place in memory studies and confronts translators with very specific issues, the interface between memory and translation is much broader. Siobhan Brownlie (2016) has offered a comprehensive survey of different aspects of this interface. She starts with personal memory as typically laid down in autobiographies and then considers different media as well as different forms of collective memory. She sees, for instance, electronic memory tools, including translation memories, as extensions of individual and collective memory. Textual memory is 'the way in which memory of earlier texts is embedded and elaborated on in subsequent texts' (2016, 77). This includes retranslations but also the way in which, for example, legal or scientific texts continually refer back to and build on earlier texts. Intertextuality is the hallmark of textual memory. Among collective forms of memory is group memory, which could be applied to translators united by a shared interest or ideology, and institutional memory, which applies to organisations, from private companies to international bodies like the United Nations or the European Union, and their translation and interpreting divisions. Brownlie also highlights the idea of tradition; because traditions tend to be tied to certain communities and are often signified by implicit means such as gestures or allusions, they are potentially problematic for translation if there is no shared cultural memory (2016, 16). In discussing national and transnational memory, Brownlie gives the example of the extraordinary popularity of Walter Scott's historical novels in nineteenth-century Europe. In places like Catalonia, Poland and Hungary, the novels stoked nationalist sentiment because readers were quick to draw parallels between Scotland and their own region – an obvious case of translation facilitating multidirectional memory (2016, 114–5).

The uses of collective memory in a national context led James Wertsch to come up with new concepts that have also proved useful for students of translation. Wertsch observed that national narratives of the past may form particular traditions that shape collective memories (2002, 60–2; 2008, 66–7). On this basis, he developed the idea of 'schematic narrative templates', which are narrative patterns that can be applied to different episodes of the national past and which constitute what Wertsch calls a collective 'deep memory' (2008, 70). For instance, the schema 'peaceful existence disrupted by external aggression which causes great hardship but is finally overcome' is available to many societies but has been applied in Russian schools and media to several historical episodes of Russian history, from the Mongol invasion in the thirteenth century and the Swedish invasion in the eighteenth to Napoleon and Hitler; state sponsorship of the schema has made it especially effective (Wertsch 2002, 93–4).

In an innovative piece of research, Anneleen Spiessens has applied Wertsch's idea of deep memory and its attendant schematic narrative template to a body of ideologically motivated translations. Her study (Spiessens 2019) concerns the way memory can be seen to serve a political agenda. Its object is a semi-official Russian website that featured regular translations of French and English-language newspaper reports about the Russian annexation of the Crimea between February and March 2014. The Crimean Peninsula had been part of Ukraine since 1954, and the Russian annexation remains unrecognised by the United Nations. The study combines a corpus-based approach to news translation with Wertsch's concepts. Its corpus consisted of 770 articles in either English or French, published at the time of the annexation, together with 39 Russian translations. As these figures suggest, only a small proportion of the original articles was translated. The Russian website had usually selected articles that evoked Russia's role in the Second World War, part of the 'deep memory' promoted by the Russian state. The effect of this selection was strengthened by a further selection in favour of articles making reference to Ukrainian collaboration with Nazi Germany during the War. Translation as such played its part, too. An article that compared the annexation of Crimea with the *Anschluss* (Nazi Germany's annexation of Austria in 1938) was translated with this inconvenient reference removed. In one case a photograph was substituted, a picture of a gunman at an airport being replaced by one of pro-Russian demonstrators holding a banner requesting Russia's assistance in the fight against fascism. The narrow selection of articles for translation and the translational adjustments combined to paint a picture of Russia liberating the Crimea as a way of countering the threat posed by a fascist Ukraine.

In itself, this kind of selective translation practised for political purposes is not new. Mona Baker, for example, has commented on the Middle East Media and Research Institute (MEMRI), an American organisation which has links with the Israeli far right and monitors the Middle East press, selecting for translation the most extreme views so as to portray the Arab world in general in a negative light (Baker 2010). In Spiessens' case study it is the appeal to memory that stands out. As she shows, the gatekeeping and remediation at work in the Russian translations enhanced, for the Russian audience, the deep memory of their country's role in the Second World War. This in turn enabled the application of the schematic narrative template of aggression and resistance in which Ukraine was implicitly cast as a Nazi or fascist threat that Russia was facing down by liberating Crimea. Whereas the original English and French articles aired a variety of opinions but generally opposed the annexation of Crimea, the Russian selection largely emasculated this opposition by foregrounding a set of historical references that presented Russia once more in the role of heroic saviour (Spiessens 2019, 416), thus serving the aims of self-legitimation and propaganda. It is a striking illustration of the role of translation in ideological memory-work. (It may be worth adding that, when the Russian army attacked Ukraine at the end of February 2022, the Russian government justified its invasion by appealing to the same tried and tested schema, casting Russia as facing an aggressive Ukrainian regime that had to be neutralised.)

Further Reading

Brownlie, Siobhan. 2016. *Mapping Memory in Translation*. Basingstoke & New York: Palgrave Macmillan.
A wide-ranging exploration of different kinds of overlap between memory and translation, each chapter illustrated with a case study.

Davies, Peter. 2017. "Ethics and the Translation of Holocaust Lives." In *Translating Holocaust Lives*, edited by Jean Boase-Beier, Peter Davies, Andrea Hammel and Marion Winters, 23–43. London: Bloomsbury.
A thoughtful discussion of the ethics of translating Holocaust testimonies. It pays attention to the real-life situation of translators faced with sometimes impossible demands, but it also explores the broader points of contact between translation studies and Holocaust studies.

Davies, Peter. 2018. *Witness between Languages. The Translation of Holocaust Testimonies in Context*. Rochester: Camden House.
The most comprehensive and theoretically nuanced account currently available of the interaction between Holocaust testimonies and translation, with a range of individual case studies. These concern Elie Wiesel's *Night*, Krystyna Żywulska's self-translation of her Polish testimony into German, the various translations of court statements by and interviews with Filip Müller, who served in a crematorium squad in Auschwitz and then Birkenau, and translations of two Russian testimonies, one by Vassily Grossman about the Treblinka concentration camp, the other by Anatoly Kuznetsov about the September 1941 massacre at Babi Yar.

Erll, Astrid. 2011. "Travelling Memory." *Parallax* 17 (4): 4–18.
A short but incisive essay that marked the transition from twentieth-century traditional memory studies, which operated with static concepts in national contexts, to the transcultural memory studies of the twenty-first century.

Bibliography

Assmann, Aleida. 2008. "Canon and Archive." In *Cultural Memory Studies. An International and Interdisciplinary Handbook*, edited by Astrid Erll, Ansgar Nünning and Sarah Young, 97–108. Berlin & New York: Walter de Gruyter.
Assmann, Aleida. 2018. "One Land and Three Narratives: Palestinian Sites of Memory in Israel." *Memory Studies* 11: 287–300.

Assmann, Jan. 2008. "Communicative and Cultural Memory." In *Cultural Memory Studies. An International and Interdisciplinary Handbook*, edited by Astrid Erll, Ansgar Nünning and Sarah Young, 109–18. Berlin & New York: Walter de Gruyter.

Baker, Mona. 2010. "Narratives of Terrorism and Security. Accurate Translations, Suspicious Frames." *Critical Studies on Terrorism* 3: 347–64.

Brodzki, Bella. 2007. *Can These Bones Live? Translation, Survival and Cultural Memory*. Stanford: Stanford University Press.

Brownlie, Siobhan. 2016. *Mapping Memory in Translation*. Basingstoke & New York: Palgrave Macmillan.

Carrier, Peter, and Kobi Kabalek. 2014. "Cultural Memory and Transcultural Memory – A Conceptual Analysis." In *The Transcultural Turn. Interrogating Memory Between and Beyond Borders*, edited by Lucy Bond and Jessica Rapson, 39–60. Berlin & Boston: De Gruyter.

Davies, Peter. 2014. "Testimony and Translation." *Translation and Literature* 23: 170–84.

Davies, Peter. 2017. "Ethics and the Translation of Holocaust Lives." In *Translating Holocaust Lives*, edited by Jean Boase-Beier, Peter Davies, Andrea Hammel and Marion Winters, 23–43. London: Bloomsbury.

Davies, Peter. 2018. *Witness between Languages. The Translation of Holocaust Testimonies in Context*. Rochester: Camden House.

Deane-Cox, Sharon. 2013. "The Translator as Secondary Witness. Mediating Memory in Antelme's *L'espèce humaine*." *Translation Studies* 6: 309–23.

Erll, Astrid. 2009. "Remembering across Time, Space and Cultures: Premediation, Remediation and the 'Indian Mutiny'." In *Mediation, Remediation and the Dynamics of Cultural Memory*, edited by Astrid Erll & Anne Rigney, 109–38. Berlin & New York: Walter de Gruyter.

Erll, Astrid. 2011. "Travelling Memory." *Parallax* 17 (4): 4–18.

Erll, Astrid. 2017. "Media and the Dynamics of Memory." In *Handbook of Culture and Memory*, edited by Brady Wagoner, 305–24. New York: Oxford University Press.

Erll, Astrid, and Ann Rigney. 2009. "Introduction. Cultural Memory and its Dynamics." In *Mediation, Remediation and the Dynamics of Cultural Memory*, edited by Astrid Erll and Anne Rigney, 1–11. Berlin & New York: Walter de Gruyter.

Hermans, Theo. 1985. "Images of Translation. Metaphor and Imagery in the Renaissance Discourse on Translation." In *The Manipulation of Literature. Studies in Literary Translation*, edited by Theo Hermans, 103–35. London & Sydney: Croom Helm.

Hermans, Theo. 2014. "Positioning Translators. Voices, Views and Values in Translation." *Language and Literature* 23: 285–301.

Landsberg, Alison. 2004. *Prosthetic Memory. The Transformation of American Remembrance in the Age of Mass Culture*. New York: Columbia University Press.

Rigney, Ann. 2005. "Plenitude, Scarcity and the Circulation of Cultural Memory." *Journal of European Studies* 35: 11–28.

Rigney, Ann. 2015. "Cultural Memory Studies." In *Routledge International Handbook of Memory Studies*, edited by Anna Lisa Tota and Trever Hagen, 65–76. London & New York: Routledge.

Rothberg, Michael. 2009. *Multidirectional Memory. Remembering the Holocaust in the Age of Decolonization*. Stanford: Stanford University Press.

Said, Edward. 1993. *Culture and Imperialism*. London: Vintage.

Seidman, Naomi. 2006. *Faithful Renderings: Jewish–Christian Difference and the Politics of Translation*. Chicago & London: University of Chicago Press.

Spiessens, Anneleen. 2019. "Deep Memory during the Crimean Crisis. References to the Great Patriotic War in Russian News Translation." *Target* 31: 398–419.

Wertsch, James. 2002. *Voices of Collective Remembering*. Cambridge: Cambridge University Press.

Wertsch, James. 2008. "Blank Spots in Collective Memory. A Case Study of Russia." *Annals of the American Academy of Political and Social Science* 617: 58–71.

6   Translation as History

Around 1658, the Dutch artist Johannes Vermeer produced a painting known as *Officer and Laughing Girl* (or as *Cavalier and Laughing Woman*). It shows a man, viewed from the back, sitting at a table with a smiling young woman. A half-open window to the left illuminates the girl but not the man. We can enjoy the scene for what it is and admire the artist's technique, his handling of composition and light, for instance. We can also examine the painting for historical clues. The man in the foreground is wearing a black broad-rimmed hat of the kind that was fashionable in Europe at the time. The felt used in hats like these came from beaver fur imported from eastern Canada, where beaver hunters equipped with modern firearms were doing a roaring trade. The officer in the painting appears to be courting the girl. Such a scene of flirtation in a domestic setting, without a matron present to watch over the young woman, would have been most unusual half a century earlier and points to shifting social customs among the Dutch middle classes. On the wall behind the two figures is a large map, which we can identify as one printed in Amsterdam by Willem Blaeu in 1621. It shows part of Holland, including over thirty ships, a sign of the country's formidable seaborne power at this time (Brook 2008, 26–53). All these clues allow us to connect the painting with the time and place of its manufacture. It is just a matter of looking.

In one sense, this is quite basic. Watching a feature film made in the last hundred years or so, we can usually date it to within a decade by such clues as the wear and tear on the reel itself, the quality of the soundtrack, the camera technique, the way the characters move and speak, the clothes they wear, their hairstyles and the type of kettles, cars or telephones they use.

In another sense, however, reading a painting or a film in this way is anything but basic. Vermeer may or may not have been aware of, or have cared, where the felt in the hat of the man he was painting came from, or how the social customs among middle class people in his native Delft were changing. As for the map on the wall, Vermeer used it in several of his paintings and we have no idea what he meant by it. Reading the painting for historical clues is very much anchored in the here and now of today's spectator, who interprets the artwork independently of any intentions Vermeer may have had, especially as these intentions are now inaccessible to us in any case. In other words, reading

DOI: 10.4324/9781315178134-6

a work from the past – a painting, a film, a piece of writing – for the traces it carries of its historical moment is, to an extent, a reading against the grain. It does not seek to reconstruct what its author subjectively intended – although, as we shall see, intention remains part of the picture. Instead, it seeks to understand the object as a product of its time and place, and to do so from today's vantage point. We can also read translations in this way and historicise them. That is what this chapter is about.

Layers of Time

Semantic autonomy

A good starting point for this kind of exercise is the philosopher Paul Ricoeur's idea of semantic autonomy, together with the related ideas of distantiation and appropriation. Ricoeur developed these ideas as early as the 1970s.

Ricoeur suggests we begin by thinking of a spoken conversation in which both speaker and hearer are physically present in the same space. The speaker can point to a table and say 'this table', the ostensive deictic reference being evident to both speaker and hearer. The meaning of what the speaker says is both what he or she says and what he or she intends to say. If any uncertainty arises as to the speaker's meaning, the hearer can ask: 'What do you mean?', and chances are that things will be clarified so that, to all intents and purposes, what the speaker says ends up coinciding with, or close to, what he or she intends to say.

Written discourse typically involves the separation of author and reader in time and space. Deictic references no longer function unproblematically (when you read 'this table' here on this page, which table and which page am I talking about?). Authors cannot anticipate their potential readers and readers can no longer ask authors what they meant. The result of this distantiation is that the meaning of a text cannot be traced back to the author's intention as it was at the time of writing. As Ricoeur put it in an essay from 1975:

> [...] writing renders the text autonomous with respect to the intention of the author. What the text signifies no longer coincides with what the author meant; henceforth, textual meaning and psychological meaning have different destinies.
>
> (2016, 101)

Or again, more fully, in an essay from 1988:

> The meaning of what has been written down is henceforth separate from the possible intentions of its author and hence removed from any kind of psychologizing critique. What we can call the *semantic autonomy* of the text means that the text unfolds a history distinct from that of its author. The ambiguity of the notion of signification reflects this situation. To signify

can mean what the text signifies or what the author meant to signify (in English: what does the text mean? What do you mean?).

(Ricoeur 2013, 12–3; italics in original)

Semantic autonomy is Ricoeur's term for the fact that, in written discourse, the meaning of a text proceeds from the text itself rather than from some subjective intention behind or outside it. In other words, what the author means is there in the text, in its verbal composition and thrust. As we also saw in Chapter 3 with respect to Quentin Skinner, intention is still part of the picture, but it cannot be construed outside the text as a criterion for what the text means. Thinking of meaning in this way enables a textual and non-psychological understanding of intention.

The distantiation that marks written discourse, detaching it from its writer, brings about the semantic autonomy of the text. Its counterpart is the appropriation that comes with reading and interpretation. Reading takes place in the reader's here and now, which confronts the there and then of the text. Because readers can only engage with distant texts from the particular historical position they themselves occupy, reading and interpretation constitute acts of appropriation. This does not entail readers simply projecting their own selves onto the text. On the contrary, appropriation is 'understanding at and through distance' (Ricoeur 2016, 105). Reading negotiates but does not negate the strangeness of the distant text. For Ricoeur, reading is a form of appropriation that both suppresses and preserves distance (1976, 43). This duality, as Sarah Maitland reminds us in her discussion of Ricoeur, makes up the text's double historical reference, to the world of the writer and to the world of the reader (Maitland 2017, 62). If we read texts on the lookout for traces of history or for the way they are embedded in their context, that search is dictated by contemporary concerns.

Layering

Reflections like Ricoeur's can provide a conceptual basis for historicising translations. There may, however, be a need to add a level of complexity that is specific to translations, adaptations and similar ostensibly intertextual discourses. We can, of course, read translations as texts by themselves, but when we read them as translations, they necessarily refer to the anterior texts for which they act as proxies. Translations, that is, gesture towards at least two different moments in time, that of their own production and that of the originals they are evoking. The researcher studying a translation from his or her own historical position adds a third moment in time. Studying translations historically is therefore a matter of triangulation. Chronologically, there is first the moment of the original, then the moment of the translation looking back at the original, and thirdly the moment of the researcher looking back at the way the translation looks back at the original. (In some cases, the researcher may also look back directly at the original, but this is very much secondary: the important thing is not what the researcher thinks the original was about but what the translator made of the original and how the researcher construes that construction.)

If this is the basic scheme, further complications abound. Here are two brief examples.

In the early seventeenth-century Dutch Republic, Hugo Grotius (or Hugo de Groot) made a Latin translation of a collection of ancient and Byzantine Greek poetry known as the Greek Anthology. One short poem in this collection (De Bosch 1795, 480–1; Van Dam 2021) begins with two lines which may be rendered in English prose as: 'I can't stand people who dislike all young poets, even those who write "Sing, Muse, the wrath"'. The last few words are, in Greek, a direct quotation of the opening words of the most famous of all Greek poems, the *Iliad*, by the archetypal epic poet Homer. In his Latin version, Grotius did not translate the quotation but instead conjured up a substitute. He wrote something like: 'I can't stand people who dislike all young poets, even those who write "Arms and the man"'. These last few words, in Latin, are also a quotation, not from Homer but from Virgil's *Aeneid*, the quintessentially Latin epic which, in its turn, had been conceived by Virgil as a creative imitation of Homer. Grotius' choice is ingenious because, for the canonical Greek verse that was quoted in the Greek original, his Latin substitutes a canonical Latin verse which itself harks back, indirectly, to the same Greek poem quoted in the Greek original.

The Latin version does in Latin what the Greek original does in Greek, but with the added twist that the Virgil quote gestures towards Homer as well. To appreciate this added twist, however, we have to read the Latin as a translation of a specific Greek verse. The Greek poem has two historical layers: its time of writing plus Homer. If we read Grotius' Latin as a poem in its own right, it also has two layers: its time of writing plus Virgil, without much need to throw into relief the latent Homeric echo. It is only when we read the Latin poem as a translation of the Greek that the connection between Virgil and Homer leaps to the fore and Grotius' verse acquires an extra layer as well as a degree of translatorial intentionality.

Viewing the Latin poem as a translation from today's perspective reveals yet another historical moment. Grotius did not simply translate the Greek Anthology but a particular version of it, the so-called Planudean anthology, compiled by the Byzantine grammarian Maximus Planudes in the early fourteenth century and the only version available to Grotius and most of his contemporaries. Today, the older and larger 'Palatine' version is much better known. This means that Grotius' translation contains four very specific historical layers: 1 Grotius; 2 the Planudean anthology; 3 Virgil; 4 Homer. And if today's researcher wants to apply a modern term like 'intertextuality' to this case, a fifth layer is made visible.

My second example comes from roughly the same part of the world but half a century earlier. In 1567, one Jacop vande Velde (now wholly forgotten) produced a polemical book, translating into Dutch a fourth-century Greek treatise written by the church father Athanasius against the Arians, whom Athanasius condemned as heretics. Vande Velde was a Catholic apologist who vehemently opposed the rise of Protestantism in the Low Countries at this time. He regarded all Protestants as heretics. A year earlier, in 1566, Protestants had appropriated a number of Catholic churches for their own services and destroyed statues of Catholic saints in the process, which is why the event quickly became known as the Iconoclasm. Vande Velde raged against these heretical iconoclasts.

The translation (Athanasius 1567) brings a series of historical moments into view. The thrust of Vande Velde's argument lies in the parallel he draws between Athanasius' polemic against the Arians and his own polemic against the Protestants. Where Athanasius accuses the Arians of desecrating churches and sacraments, Vande Velde peppers his translation with marginal notes denouncing the very similar destruction wrought by the heretics of his own day. As part of his attack on the Arians, Athanasius refers to several Biblical stories, all of which naturally predate his own time; these references remain embedded in the translation. Vande Velde, however, did not translate Athanasius from the original Greek but from a Latin translation by Desiderius Erasmus published in 1522, adding a further historical moment. In his preface, moreover, Vande Velde says he is writing to counter a confession by a Protestant who had been tried and executed a year earlier; the condemned man had mentioned Vande Velde by name and cast doubt on his orthodoxy, so Vande Velde is now eager to clear his name. This last point gives his translation a double agenda – lambasting heretics but proving his own orthodoxy as well – and ties it to its year of publication much more firmly than was the case with Grotius' Greek Anthology. More importantly, perhaps, the different ways in which historical moments are imbricated in the translation suggest that, while we may begin by simply peeling away historical layers one by one, we should go on from there to gauge their weight and significance.

Interlinking translations

There are, of course, numerous other ways of reminding ourselves of the historicity of translations and the particular intricacies that spring from it. Apart from considering the way in which a translation or its paratexts relate to the original and to the translation's immediate context, we can also look into the relation between new translations and existing translations. This viewpoint highlights translation as a historically unfolding series, new translations responding to or taking account of previous translations. Vande Velde's reliance on Erasmus' Latin rendering of Athanasius is a case in point. It is an indirect translation, with Erasmus as the relay or pivot or intermediate version, itself located within its historical moment. Chains of indirect translation can involve more than just two steps. In 1550, Thomas Nicholls published an English translation of Thucydides that was based on the French version of 1527 by Claude de Seyssel which was itself based on the Latin version by Lorenzo Valla of the original Greek. An anonymous Dutch Qur'an of 1641, purportedly printed in Hamburg but almost certainly in Amsterdam, derived from a German version that derived from an Italian version that derived from a medieval Latin version of the Arabic text.

The point here is not to lament progressive straying from the source but to appreciate the circumstances that led to the apparent acceptability of indirectness in translation. Late nineteenth-century China was aware of the need to translate from Western languages but possessed few intellectuals sufficiently well versed in both a Western language and classical Chinese to translate directly by themselves, so the solution consisted of either tandem translation (one person translating orally, the other taking care of the writing) or translating via Japanese, which was relatively convenient because Japanese already used a number of Chinese characters. As one Chinese intellectual put it, by translating Western works via Japanese, the West served as the ox, Japan was the peasant and China could enjoy the harvest (Hill 2013, 35).

Retranslations are equally obvious illustrations of the way successive translations interlink over time. They may be produced for a variety of reasons. Ignorance might be one of them, a translator being unaware of an already existing version, in which case the direct intertextual link is not with this pre-existing version but with other translations more generally. Another reason might be competition among publishers vying to dump their translations on the market as quickly as possible, as we saw in Chapter 2 with reference to the German 'translation factories' and in Chapter 3 with reference to Alexander von Humboldt in English. The most common reason to produce a retranslation is a sense of dissatisfaction with one or more previous versions. In this latter case, Anthony Pym (1998, 82–3) speaks of active retranslations, whereas the first two cases would be passive retranslations. Naturally, retranslations that challenge specific predecessors have received most attention. When Lawrence Venuti (2004) argues that retranslations are value-creating exercises because they have to justify their existence by affirming a critical difference with a predecessor, he is referring exclusively to retranslations that identify the pre-existing versions they are responding to (as indeed he makes perfectly clear; 2004, 25). From the researcher's point of view, what matters is not so much the later translator's subjective intentions but the way in which the later text can be construed as bearing on its predecessor (whether the later translator was aware of this or not) and the historical embedding of both texts. This is perhaps the main lesson to be taken away from Ricoeur's notion of semantic autonomy.

If active retranslations advertise their historical filiation, they only make explicit something that inheres in all translating. All translations build on earlier translations and thus carry within them a history of translating. We can translate only because there are pre-existing translations, as shown with particular clarity in electronic tools such as translation memories or statistical and neural translation systems (Rozmyslowicz 2019, 34).

Reading for Traces

We can read translations for the different historical layers they contain. We can also read them as products of their time. In this latter case we are looking for the way their environment impinged on them. Of course, the environment

· includes just about everything, from genre conventions and ideological debates to material conditions and personal experience. In practice, researchers will need to select a domain to focus on. The point is to look for those traces that tie a translation to the world around it. The traces will typically be textual in nature. The exercise then becomes a matter of assessing how the language of the translation connects with some of the discourses swirling around it. The aim may be, in the first instance, to document the translation's dependence on surrounding discourses. But it is possible to be rather more ambitious and to see an individual translation as intervening in a state of affairs by addressing current issues or contributing to a debate. The rest of this chapter is devoted to these two approaches.

Seven Agamemnons

The archetypal essay illustrating the first approach is Reuben Brower's 'Seven Agamemnons', which dates all the way back to 1959. Brower's essay appeared in the collection *On Translation*, which he edited and which also contained Roman Jakobson's famous 'On Linguistic Aspects of Translation' and Willard Van Orman Quine's philosophical reflections on the indeterminacy of translation.

Brower's 'Seven Agamemnons' is concerned with verse translation. It posits that, by and large, literary translators have little choice but to speak in the language and poetic idiom available to them at the time they are writing. This permits a symptomatic reading: poetic translations correlate with the literary conventions prevalent in a certain time and place. To prove his claim, Brower compares several English translations of a brief passage from an ancient Greek play, the *Agamemnon* of Aeschylus. Brower's analysis does not aim to compare the English translations with the Greek original. In fact, he does not even quote the original Greek passage but instead uses a modern English rendering as his control sample. By the same token, it does not matter to him that one of his translations is not actually based on the Greek but on an intermediate Latin version. His attention is focused on the language used in the English translations and how that usage echoes the kind of poetry being written at the time the translation was made. He reads the translations in light of the poetic language in vogue around them. He proceeds by marking the contrasting poetic idioms of the various translations and then contextualising each version's distinctive features. Let me pick up some elements of Brower's analysis.

The passage he focuses on is taken from a speech by a herald who reports to the court on a violent storm that destroyed a Greek fleet. The oldest English version he considers dates from 1581. It is not based directly on Aeschylus but on a Latin version by Seneca, who, Brower suggests, had much in common with English writers of the Elizabethan age. In this rendering, the storm has become much more intense than it is in the Greek (or in the control sample) due to the English being both heavily rhetorical (through the use of assonances, alliterations, paradoxes and hyperboles) and expansive (with added circumstantial detail, repetitions and doublets of the 'grunt and groan' type). By contrast, a version from 1777, the height of the neoclassical period, is remarkably uniform and flat in tone. Here, the herald speaks the measured language of the court, and instead of striking metaphors we find plain statements. For example, whereas, in other versions, the morning after the storm sees a sea 'bedecked' or 'carpeted' or even 'flowering' with corpses and wreckage, the 1777 version simply registers bodies and wreckage floating in the water.

Among the twentieth-century versions that Brower discusses is one from 1928 by Gilbert Murray, which overlays the scene with Biblical language and Christian terminology (it speaks of a 'blessed sun' and of 'Saviour Fortune'; Brower 1959, 189–90) and one from 1936 by Louis MacNeice, which is conversational in tone, avoids any recognisable poetic vocabulary and evokes emotion not by using emotive words but by soberly stating the events that happened. As Brower notes, MacNeice's version, like the others, 'reflects the definition of proper poetic practice which was prevalent at the time it was written' (1959, 194).

The one version that stands out is by Robert Browning, from 1877. Its insistent literalisms make the English look like Greek. When the herald describes the onset of the storm as an ominously heaving sea and the prose rendering in the Loeb Classical Library says that 'there arose a terrible wave of troubles' (Aeschylus 2009, 77), Browning speaks of 'bad-wave-outbreak evils' – a bold choice, and one that risks leaving readers puzzled (Brower 1959, 187). Browning's language consistently eschews the poeticisms of its day in favour of mirroring the Greek, a feature Brower links not with a particular literary school or trend but with what he calls the 'nineteenth-century dream' of reproducing the past 'as it actually was' (Brower 1959, 188–9). This last phrase inevitably recalls the well-known statement by Leopold von Ranke that (as we saw in Chapter 1) came to be associated with a positivist historiography intent on factual accuracy. Brower, that is, reads Browning not as reflecting but as rejecting the literary idiom of his day and places him instead in a historiographical orbit.

Brower's study can be criticised on several grounds. He seems to have a fairly monolithic view of what constitutes the dominant poetic idiom in English at a given moment, with little appreciation of possible diversity. He sees translation as merely passively reflecting the literary norms of the day, with the ensuing risk that we project our knowledge of those norms onto the translation in question, merely confirming our pre-existing knowledge. He shows little appreciation of the potential of translation to actively shape a novel discourse. His approach also seems to falter when it comes to Browning, who does not toe the line and for whose language Brower needed to identify an alternative mould.

But for all that, and certainly in 1959, Brower's essay was remarkable. He did not carry out a standard comparison of original and translation but considered the language of the translations in the context of the poetic usage of the time the translations were made. In other words, he read the translations for what they could tell him about their embedding in a particular moment of – in this case literary – history. Most interesting of all, for our present purposes, is that he was looking for textual traces, the close or more remote echoes that tie individual translations to the texts around them – previous and current translations and ways of translating, stylistic and rhetorical conventions in relevant genres, discourses about representing the past or about leveraging the past for the present.

Kinds of traces

Historicising translations by means of textual connections is a task comprising many facets. In an essay of 1992, Armin Paul Frank listed a number of references and relations that may be consciously or unconsciously inscribed on translations. They are 'elements of history immanent in translation' and constitute 'the historicity of individual translations' (Frank 1992, 383, 384). Frank identified a whole gamut of such references and relations, including the following:

1. The most obvious is the relation to the original which the translation purports to represent. This is, in Frank's words (1992, 383), the 'constitutive relation' underpinning all translation, at least in principle. All the other references and relations may apply in some measure, or not at all, depending on the individual case. They include:
2. Traces of earlier translations (followed, avoided, challenged, modified, inflected), ranging from the specific to the generic, as discussed in Chapter 3, and as perhaps most evident in computerised translation memories and statistical translation systems.
3. Traces of receptor-language usage, as in the use of stylistic habits, clichés, period slang and similar devices, as Reuben Brower showed in his 'Seven Agamemnons' above.
4. Traces of other writings, whether in the receptor or in another language. See the example of Hugo Grotius, above. In translating Marlene van Niekerk's novel *Agaat* from Afrikaans to English, the translator Michiel Heyns sought to match the original's rich intertextuality by creating alternative references and allusions drawn from English canonical writers (Meintjes 2009, 78). But the category obviously stretches much further and can include any type of writing in any language.
5. Traces of the translator's personal experience or knowledge, as evidenced, for instance, in the apt or inept use of technical terms. As we saw in Chapter 3, Elizabeth Sabine marshalled her earlier translation experience along with her husband's personal contacts to help her find terminological solutions to problems posed by Alexander von Humboldt's *Ansichten der Natur*.
6. Traces of the translator's (or publisher's, or commissioner's) attitude towards the task. Martin Luther reckoned that once a Biblical passage had been properly understood, it could be rendered in plain everyday language, but other translators, while in theological agreement with Luther, took a diametrically opposite line as regards translation and insisted on strict literalism out of respect for the divine word. English translators of Boccaccio and the *Jin Ping Mei* rendered sexually charged passages they deemed offensive

into Latin or French so their average readers would not understand them (Hermans 2007, 60–4; 2014, 291). A translator may also just lose interest in the job. When, around 1600, the Flemish translator Karel van Mander had come to the end of Book 12 of his translation of the *Iliad*, he decided to put down his pen because 'having reached the half-way stage, I got tired of the journey' (Smit 1975, 295, 301–2).

7. Traces of the translator's working conditions, such as signs of haste, or the translator having made use of particular dictionaries, reference works, manuals and the like. In 1924, as psychoanalysis was becoming institutionalised, Ernest Jones compiled a *Glossary for the Use of Translators of Psycho-Analytical Works* to serve as a guide for translators of Sigmund Freud's writings into English (E. Jones 1924); the *Glossary* left its mark on the standard English-language edition of Freud's collected works translated by James Strachey and others between 1953 and 1974 (R. Steiner 1987, 50).

8. Traces of pressure from commissioners, patrons, authorities or other controlling bodies, such as a commissioning editor, a publisher, a state censor or a church. As we saw in Chapter 1, the absence of explanatory notes or interpretive comments in Thomas Bridges' Yámana gospels was due directly to the role of the British and Foreign Bible Society in seeing the translations into print.

Naturally, a checklist like this can do little more than scratch the surface. It suggests there are more aspects and dimensions to this than we might have thought. Most aspects can be taken a great deal further. For instance, Ernest Jones' 1924 *Glossary* proposed, with varying degrees of emphasis, translational equivalents for individual Freudian terms. The most famous one, emphatically recommended, was 'cathexis', rather than the more normal-looking 'investment' or 'charge', to render Freud's *Besetzung* (E. Jones 1924, 6). Some of these terms, like 'cathexis', entered psychoanalytic parlance, others were contested and subsequently rejected (notably 'instinct' or 'impulse' for *Trieb*, now usually rendered as 'drive'). But the *Glossary* itself belongs to its own historical moment. It was part of Ernest Jones' attempts not only to control future English translations of psychoanalytic work but also to have psychoanalysis recognised as a serious scientific endeavour and to secure his own position in the increasingly international psychoanalytic movement (R. Steiner 1987, 1991, 1994). The glossary, in other words, served multiple ends and, in turn, slotted into a series of other activities on Jones' part. Its impact on specific translations is just one aspect of this more complex picture. Conversely, a single trace, such as 'cathexis' or 'drive' when used in a psychoanalytic context, can trail a long and bushy tail behind it.

Translation as Intervention: A Model

The traces I have been discussing are intertextual connections, tentacles reaching into the past as well as into the world around specific translations.

They serve as reminders that translators make choices and decisions in a context that comprises a historical as well as a contemporary dimension. But it is also clear that we need not think of translations only as reflecting prevailing discourses. They feed into them as well, indeed they are designed to act on the world around them and would have little purpose without that design. Studying translations in their historical context, then, means recognising them as active interventions in existing states of affairs and identifying the relevant traces.

A theoretical model of translation as intervention will help us understand this aspect of the historicity of translations. The next few paragraphs sketch such a model in seven steps (there is a fuller version in Hermans 2014). It casts the translator as reporting to an audience what someone else has said, and it asks recipients of a translation to focus both on the translator's reporting and on the reported words.

1. Translation constitutes a form of reported speech. A translator tells us what someone else said previously. In principle, the whole range of types of reported speech is available, from indirect speech (think of the amateur interpreter in a health setting who tells the doctor, 'She says her stomach hurts' when the client had said, in another language, something like 'My stomach hurts') to fully mimetic direct quotation (think of a consecutive interpreter who mimics the first speaker's intonation, pitch, posture and gestures as well as the propositional content of the speaker's words). Prototypically, translation comes to us in the form of direct speech, in that a translator does not merely inform us of what a heterolingual author said but imitates that author speaking in his or her own name, albeit now by means of words we can understand in our own language. Because quotations do not have to be verbatim, the shift in language leaves the status of translation as direct reported speech unaffected (Clark and Gerrig 1990, 777–99). When, additionally, a translation is done in a manner that Jiří Levý called illusionist and Lawrence Venuti calls domesticating, it allows us to imagine – that is, it creates the illusion of – the original speaker addressing us directly through the translation.

2. For the recipient, the use of direct speech involves a shift in his or her focus of attention. This shift is known as a deictic shift. When I am speaking to you here and now, you recognise my words as coming from me. When, in the course of talking to you, I quote, say, Hayden White, you adjust your focus of attention to Hayden White now speaking through me. That adjustment is the deictic shift. For the recipient, the deictic centre of an utterance is the 'I-here-now' of the speaker. When the speaker quotes someone else's words, the deictic centre temporarily shifts to this secondary speaker nestled within the first speaker's discourse. In other words, the deictic shift is caused by the fact that reported speech requires a reporting speech and constitutes an inset in it. Reported speech is necessarily embedded in a framing discourse or, at the very least, a framing communicative situation – this last caution is necessary because I may quote someone without announcing

that I'm going to quote; usually, however, there will be a clue to signal that a quotation is coming or under way.

3. As reported speech, and prototypically as direct quotation, translation shows the same structure as other reported speech. There must be a framing discourse, with the actual translation, as direct speech, set into this frame. The framing discourse of individual translations may be extensive and comprise, say, a translator's preface and annotations in addition to a title page announcing the translation; it may also be minimal, such as the bare indication that there is a translation to follow; or it may be merely implied, as in the case of international news broadcasts reporting a foreign politician's words in our own language without it being explicitly stated that the words we hear have been translated. The framing discourse of a translation forms part of what is called the translation's paratext (Batchelor 2018). In this paratextual frame, the translator speaks in his or her own name. As soon as the translation gets under way, the translator adopts the original author's speaking position. The transition from the paratextual frame to what we might call the performance of translation brings with it a discursive and deictic shift known as first-person displacement (the term is Anthony Pym's, 2004, 8), meaning that, if the translated author speaks in the first person in the translation, this is not the first person of the translator's preface. Even though we know the translator wrote the 'I' that we may read on the page in both the paratext and the translation, our familiarity with reading translations (or hearing interpreters perform) accommodates the fact that, in the paratext, the translator speaks in his or her own name, whereas in the translation, the translator adopts the speaking position of the original author.

4. Two important things follow from this. First, the paratextual framing discourse belongs not to the original author but to the translator (or whoever acts for the translator in presenting the translation to its intended audience). This framing discourse is, in effect, the main discourse reaching the audience; the translation is an inset in it. This means we can recast one of the traditional perceptions of translation. Instead of picturing a heterolingual author speaking through a disembodied translator, we can now envisage a communicative situation in which a translator, as reporter, directly addresses an audience and, as part of this discourse, lets the heterolingual author speak in the audience's language. The translator is the main communicator, and the actual translation is embedded in this communication.

5. Second, in a typical translation, two communications, not one, reach the recipient simultaneously. One is the framing discourse, that of the translator presenting the translated text. Wrapped inside this discourse is the translated text, in which the translator lets the author speak by adopting that author's speaking position. Inevitably, the meaning or import of the inset is affected by the surrounding discourse. This is most obvious in cases where someone quotes or translates an utterance they have reservations about, but approval or studied neutrality or indeed any other attitude equally inflects the words quoted or translated. As a result, translated discourse is ambivalent. During

the performance of translation, the audience shifts the deictic centre to the author speaking through the translator, but the translator's framing discourse, like a background hum, continues to accompany the translated words. All translations come with the translator's value judgement attached, even if that judgement remains implicit or is no more than perfunctory. As a simple but stark illustration, think of Hitler's *Mein Kampf* translated by a pro-Nazi translator happy to merge his or her voice with the author's or to disappear behind it, and by an anti-Nazi translator keen to remind the reader in paratextual comments that he or she rejects the author's views.

6. An approach like this enables a view of translation as intervention. Reading translations as interventions means paying attention not just to the translated discourse but to its frame as well, moving from one to the other to see how each bears on the other. It makes the translator the main communicator and the primary focus of the reader's attention. The translator enables the author to speak but is likely to be guided by motives very different from the author's. The translator's attitude towards what he or she is translating matters if we want to understand what this translator intended to achieve by producing this translation, in this form, in these circumstances and for this intended audience.

7. Approaching translations with this duality in mind means adopting the mode of reading that J.R. Martin and Peter White in *The Language of Evaluation* (2005) call 'tactical', as opposed to a 'compliant' reading. A compliant reading of a translation is one that accommodates the reading position invited by the text. Most routine translations, in many languages, are so-called illusionist or domesticating translations, which endeavour, through their presentation and style of writing, to make their readers forget that they are translations. The reading position they invite, or naturalise, allows the reader to imagine he or she is reading the original. Accepting this invitation results in a compliant reading. A tactical reading, by contrast, does not adopt the reading position naturalised by the text but seeks to remain forensic. It keeps the framing discourse in mind, toggles between the frame and the translation itself and remains aware that, in the translation, the translator is constantly putting words into the author's mouth even while adopting that author's speaking position. In other words, a tactical reading looks for evidence to determine the translator's positioning and agenda. In the case of historical translations, this means looking for evidence that can reveal the translator's agency at a particular historical juncture.

The approach described here is compatible with the notions of framing and renarration associated with the socio-narrative model mentioned in Chapter 1, and it chimes with Quentin Skinner's position as outlined in Chapter 3. Calling on speech act theory, Skinner pointed to the illocutionary aspect of historical speech acts: what someone was trying to achieve by uttering certain words in certain circumstances. This question of intent also applies to translators and their translations. Note that 'intent' here takes account of what Paul Ricoeur said about the semantic autonomy of written texts, including historical texts. It refers not to an irretrievable subjective inclination but to the presumed intent that the available evidence permits us to construe. The intent that resides in translations is what Julia Richter, in Chapter 2, called the translator's motive. As also suggested in Chapter 2, the basic descriptor of a historical translation event is the triad of motive, means and opportunity.

Translation as Intervention: Illustrations

Finally, some illustrations. The first two are very brief; the third one covers somewhat more ground. All could be extended. The difference in scale and the potential for further extension suggests that, as the view broadens out from a given translation to the world from which it stems and with which it interacts, the focus of attention moves with it and, rather than just contextualising a given translation, we begin to apprehend a larger historical constellation and the role of translation within it. This comes close to the approach Christopher Rundle envisaged in Chapter 2 when he spoke of trying to understand a slice of history by considering the place of translation in it – as opposed to trying to understand translation by studying its historical manifestations.

Germany in 1938

The first illustration is low key. In one chapter of her book *The Alien Within*, Kate Sturge (2004, 126–47) reads a German translation, published in 1938, of a historical novel by Hugh Walpole, *The Fortress* (1932), a family saga set in the countryside in northern England during the nineteenth century. The translator was Vivian Rodewald-Grebin, about whom next to nothing is known but who, with about a dozen published titles to her name, was probably an occasional rather than a professional translator.

The translation comes without translatorial paratexts and appears to be an unremarkable routine job of popular fiction translation. Indeed, the most remarkable thing about it is its appearance in Germany in 1938. At this time, the Nazi regime was firmly in charge and the entire cultural sector was subject to state censorship. The fact that the translation passed the censor means it contained nothing overtly offensive to the regime. The genre probably helped, as Nazi ideology approved of fiction about rural communities held together by kinship bonds and ties to land and nation.

Even without recourse to a textual comparison between the translation and its base text, we can appreciate this translation as an intervention with intent. It is a very modest intervention with a somewhat uncertain ascription of intent, but that happens to be the nature of the case – a humdrum novel, no paratexts to speak of, virtually unknown translator. No doubt, however, the novel's appearance in translation strengthened the regime, if ever so marginally, and the translator's agency contributed to this, whether or not she was actively in sympathy with or indifferent to the regime's ideology.

When Kate Sturge checked the translation against the original, the comparison added a measure of nuance to this picture. Some findings accorded with expectations regarding the translation of popular fiction (such as simplification of the narrative presentation) or suggested conformity with Nazi ideology (some scenes of male bonding, with their hint of homosexuality, were toned down). Less true to form, however, was that the city was not being painted in negative colours in this mostly rural novel and that the protagonists were bourgeois landowners rather than peasants. This suggests, either for the popular fiction genre as a whole or for this novel in particular, a degree of permissiveness, or perhaps more laxity on the censor's part than might have been expected. This last conclusion would accord with other parts of Kate Sturge's study, which found the whole Nazi apparatus of cultural control to be a highly complex, not always consistent and at times chaotic system.

Even in the absence of an explicit framing discourse, then, the historical embedding of a routine case like this is clear enough. We read the clues against relevant expectations regarding genre and ideology, and we assign agency and intent as the evidence permits. The translator, as an agent with a voice, seems content to remain inconspicuous and to let the translated narrative speak for itself, at most nudging it towards conformity. The translation passing the censor turns out to be the key event. The textual traces point to a web of institutional practices, ideological pronouncements and cultural criticism. The relation between the translation and its base text echoes, in a small way, the complexity of the discourses surrounding the published book.

Beyond this, other possible avenues open up. One option might be to explore other work by Vivian Rodewald-Grebin. In a translation published in 1933 of a short story by William Faulkner, she rendered the word 'Jew' as *Yankee* (Nicolaisen and Göske 2008, 64), the decision to replace a politically charged word with a relatively innocuous one suggesting no great sympathy with Nazi ideas. This makes it at least possible that Rodewald-Grebin's translations in subsequent years had motives other than ideological. Most of these translations concerned popular fiction and, as regards this genre, it seems unlikely that the picture painted by Kate Sturge will change much. In picking as a representative sample the average translation of an average book in a low-key genre, Sturge made a judicious choice.

As an intervention, Rodewald-Grebin's translation is a very minor affair. Its minimal paratextual frame did little more than recommend the book as comfortable entertainment, and its narrative presentation invited a compliant reading. If we read it against the background of prevailing political conditions, we can appreciate it as confirming Nazi ideology in its own modest way – whether out of conviction or not is hard to tell.

Why the earth stood still in China

The second example is paradoxical because it suggests that non-translation, too, can be a form of intervention.

In 1637, the Italian Jesuit missionary Giulio Aleni had a little book printed in China called *Xifang dawen* ('Questions and answers about the West'), a brief and accessible description of Europe for the Chinese, who, at the time, knew next to nothing about Europe. Two of Aleni's statements in this book are of interest. One explains that Europe is divided into many nations but, when a war occurs, the Pope intervenes to stop the fighting. The other is about cosmology and has the earth sitting 'in the middle of the sky like the yolk of an egg in its shell' (Mish 1964, 43, 65).

Both statements are remarkable. As for the Pope keeping the peace in Europe, by the time Aleni's book appeared in print in 1637, the Thirty Years' War had been raging across the continent for almost twenty years. It was the most murderous conflict Europe had seen until then. Although Aleni had been in China since 1613, the Jesuits' excellent global communication network makes it extremely unlikely he was not aware of these events. It obviously fitted his missionary agenda to portray Europe as peaceful and the Pope as its central political figure.

His cosmological statement is even more curious, and it bears on translation as well as on Aleni's status as a missionary. Aleni was a trained scientist; he had studied astronomy at the Jesuit college in Rome before moving to China. He must have known that the earth-centred view of the planetary system had been contested and discredited. Copernicus had suggested a heliocentric model almost a hundred years earlier and this model had been gaining ground among scientists in Europe for decades, most famously through the work of Galileo. Why did Aleni not even mention heliocentrism? The reason is that the Catholic Church condemned it outright, forbade its teaching and had Galileo placed under house arrest. While the scientific revolution later in the century took the heliocentric view for granted (Newton's work would be unthinkable without it), the Jesuits in China, many of them trained scientists like Aleni but bound by a vow of obedience to the Pope, continued to translate European astronomical books expounding an increasingly outdated earth-centred view of the universe. By not translating modern scientists such as Galileo, Kepler, Huygens or Newton, Jesuits made the earth stand still in China and let the sun orbit the earth. When the Catholic Church finally, in 1757, removed Galileo's works from the index of forbidden books and a Jesuit was able to describe the heliocentric system to Chinese scientists, they refused to believe it because it contradicted what the Jesuits had been telling them for over a hundred years (Mungello 1989, 26–8; Montgomery 2000, 206–7).

China ca. 1900

Let me explore the final illustration a bit more fully. It revolves around some early works of the prolific Chinese translator Lin Shu (1852–1924). In an essay from 1998, Martha Cheung looked closely at the religious elements in the Chinese translation of *Uncle Tom's Cabin* by Lin Shu and his collaborator Wei Yi published in 1901 (Cheung 1998). The translation appeared in print at a time when China had suffered a series of military defeats (only a year earlier, Western and Japanese troops had looted Beijing in the wake of the Boxer Rebellion), the ruling Qing dynasty was crumbling (it was overthrown in 1911) and Chinese intellectuals were talking about the need for reform on the basis of so-called Western learning – ideas about law, politics, economics and culture that hailed from Western Europe and North America and that, according to these intellectuals, could and should be used to reinvigorate the country and shape it into a modern nation able to resist Western encroachment.

In her analysis, Cheung stressed the explicit political aims of the translation as the translators stated them in their prefaces and notes. Her study shows that, while the Chinese version of *Uncle Tom's Cabin* kept some of the frequent Christian references that were there in the original, others were consistently omitted or secularised. This practice contrasted with Lin Shu's version of *Robinson Crusoe* which he made just a few years later (now with Zeng Zonggong as his collaborator), in which all the Christian elements were preserved, so much so that Lin Shu apologised for them in his preface (Wong 1999, 33). In the translation of *Uncle Tom's Cabin*, then, Christianity was downplayed, and the effect of this, Cheung argued, was ideological. In the original novel, the Christian perspective served to elicit sympathy with the suffering of enslaved people, as indeed Harriet Beecher Stowe stated in her own preface in 1851. Because the translation downgraded the element of Christian compassion, the political message of oppression and anti-imperialism gained greater visibility.

Most contemporary Chinese readers will not have been in a position to assess the extent to which the translators had muted the original novel's Christian dimension. They will, however, have been able to see the relevance of the translators' framing of the story. While the original novel is concerned solely with the fate of African enslaved people in the US, Lin Shu and Wei Yi's prefaces and notes highlighted the misery of Chinese labourers in both North and South America, a plight they saw as symptomatic of China's political weakness in general. As the translated narrative unfolds, the frame that contains it still makes itself felt. It is the parallel between the suffering of the African slaves and the Chinese coolies that gives the translation its political thrust in the context in which it was deployed.

Cheung's study is of methodological interest. While the role of the translation as a political intervention at a particular historical juncture is clear enough, Cheung will not be drawn on whether, in reducing the size of the Christian dimension in the novel, the translators acted intentionally or not. Instead, she respects the translation's semantic autonomy and describes the effect, as she sees it, of the translators' handling of the Christian references. Needless to say, this effect is a textual effect; how the translation came across to actual readers is an altogether different question.

In order to be able to speak of the Chinese translation of *Uncle Tom's Cabin* as downplaying the Christian dimension, Cheung had to resort to a comparison with the original text. Having noted the reduced role of religion in the translation, she was then able to correlate the relatively greater prominence of the political aspect with the translators' own emphasis, in their preface, on their patriotic mission. This meant, however, that the textual links between the translation and its political and intellectual context remained somewhat vague.

In this respect, the study of Lin Shu by Michael Gibbs Hill (2013) provides a firmer footing. One chapter in Hill's book considers two early translations, *Uncle Tom's Cabin* (1901) and Aesop's *Fables* (1903), by Lin Shu and his collaborators. It offers a masterclass in placing a translation in a historical context by tracing keywords that connect the translation with the discourses surrounding it (Hill 2013, 50–96).

Lin Shu's version of Aesop's *Fables* appeared as an illustrated book in which each fable was followed by a moral that formed part of the original, plus an additional commentary by Lin Shu himself (writing as Weilu). Most of the translator's commentaries applied the relevant fable to China's condition.

The translation's material presentation already tells us a great deal about what the publisher and the translators hoped to achieve with it. Advertisements for the book as well as the book's design and layout presented it as an elementary textbook for use in schools. The publisher, the Commercial Press in Shanghai, brought out a number of similar readers around this time with great success, and the translation of Aesop's *Fables* visually resembled these other readers (Hill 2013, 81). The translator's preface also highlighted the book's usefulness for educating children, although it remains uncertain if it was ever used in schools. Both the advertisements and the translator's preface stressed that, in the West, the fables had always served as pedagogical tools (Hill 2013, 82).

The connection with contemporary discourses about China's relation with the West is visible in the texts themselves. The book is 'nothing less than a primer of master terms and concepts central to the writings of many late-Qing intellectuals and reformers' (Hill 2013, 83).

For instance, in one story (Hill 2013, 83–4), a lamb becomes separated from its flock and is devoured by a wolf. The moral explains that tyrants will kill even the innocent when they can. The translator's commentary adds to this that powerful states are like a pack of wolves and they will destroy weak countries under any pretext. In the Chinese, the word for both the 'flock' of lambs and the 'pack' of wolves is *qun* ('group, crowd'). It appears both in the translated story and in the translator's commentary on the story, which makes it unlikely the repetition is a coincidence. As Hill explains, around 1900 the word *qun* had acquired political meanings, and leading intellectuals interpreted *qun* as 'community' or 'society', the collective that brings safety and is the necessary ingredient for building a cohesive nation. Well-known cultural figures such as Liang Qichao and Yan Fu used it in this sense. For example, in a commentary in his famous translation (1898) of Thomas Huxley's *Evolution and Ethics*, Yan Fu noted: 'People form groups for safety and benefit […]. Those who form groups well will survive' (Hill 2013, 68, 111).

The word had also figured in Lin Shu's translation of *Uncle Tom's Cabin*, together with a number of other terms such as *gongfa* ('international law') and *gongli* ('universal justice' or 'universal principle'), terms representative of the new ideas on social and political organisation entering China at the time (Hill 2013, 68–70).

By tracing these keywords in the translations, their paratexts and the discourses of other intellectuals of the period, we can build a web of interconnecting concepts, making the translations part of an ongoing public discussion of national importance. At the same time, we can piece together a network of individuals, as writers – including translators – position themselves in relation to fellow travellers and ideological opponents. In this case, Lin Shu seems to align himself with political reformers who saw themselves as modernisers. The keywords are the nodes we need to connect to see the networks emerge and mutate.

I have picked up only a couple of elements from Hill's much richer analysis, which also covers such things as Lin Shu's writing style and its affiliations – another way of tying the translation to other texts around and before it. Also, the picture above is at best a snapshot representing a moment in time; in fact, in later years, Lin Shu became an icon of conservatism, as indeed Hill (2013, 156–91) also shows at length.

All the same, the potential opened up by a study like Hill's is vast. It enables us to make connections with the transmission of Western science and the self-strengthening movement that were both part of the modernisation of China in the closing decades of the nineteenth century. We caught a glimpse of the beginning of this process at the end of Chapter 4, when I reviewed Lydia Liu's work on the introduction of international law to China.

In a methodologically important move, Liu described the 1864 Chinese translation of Henry Wheaton's *Elements of International Law* as a three-fold event: textual, diplomatic and epistemological (2004, 110, 194). It was a textual event in that it created a new, neologistic vocabulary in Chinese under conditions of minimal equivalence with the concepts in the base text (Liu 2004, 109). It was a diplomatic event in that it was prepared and published in Beijing under the auspices of Prince Gong's newly established foreign affairs office (the *Zongli yamen*) and pushed China into an international order of nation states (Liu 2004, 114). It was an epistemological event in that it made China look upon itself and the world differently, even though initially the Qing court, in contrast with the Meiji regime in Japan, remained unwilling to embrace the new concepts (Dudden 2004, 173). The combination of these various dimensions – textual, political, cultural, intellectual – supplies us with the necessary hooks to fix a translation into a broader historical context. It enables us to see a translation as an intervention on more levels than one.

One of the direct links between Lin Shu's early translations and the intellectual discourse surrounding and preceding them is in the person of Xu Jianyin (1845–1901), who, like his father Xu Shou (1818–84), was a mathematician and engineer and a prolific translator of Western science books. Like Liang Qichao, Xu Jianyin came to favour political reform and was involved in the abortive Hundred Days' Reform in 1898. A year earlier, Xu and Yan Fu had written in Liang's newspaper in Shanghai about the need for translations of Western knowledge to aid China's modernisation (Wright 1995, 83).

In 1896, Xu had been sent to the Fuzhou Navy Yard, from which Yan Fu had graduated with a science degree 25 years earlier. The Fuzhou shipyard was one of a range of shipbuilding and weapons manufacturing plants set up at the time to strengthen the country's military and industrial capacity. The largest and most famous of these plants was the Jiangnan Arsenal in Shanghai. It had been established in 1865 by Zeng Guofan, the Qing general who had been instrumental in putting down the Taiping Rebellion that devastated China between 1850 and 1864, a period that also saw the Second Opium War (1856–60). Xu Jianyin and his father Xu Shou were among those who persuaded the general in 1868 to create a translation department at the Jiangnan Arsenal (A. Bennett 1967, 19–20; Lung 2016, 39–40). In a memorial to the throne, Zeng Guofan summed up the connection between science, manufacture and translation:

> Now translation is the foundation of modern manufacture. Mathematics is used by foreigners as the mother of manufacturing science. Its wonder is explained by works and drawing. Being handicapped by the difficulty of language, although we know how to manufacture things, we are unable to understand the principles of manufacturing.
>
> (A. Bennett 1967, 21)

Manufacture, and especially the manufacture of armaments, was what mattered to the general. He knew from experience that manufacturing skill alone was insufficient. In 1863, he had ordered the first steamship built in China, but, although Xu Shou had taken part in its construction, the result had been disappointing due to a lack of proper understanding of the technology involved. It made Zeng and those around him realise that, if China was to possess industrial machinery and modern weapons, a much more thorough grasp of Western science and engineering was needed than could be garnered from self-study (Wang 2010, 49–53). That is why, for Zeng, manufacture, mathematics and translation went together, and why he agreed that the Jiangnan Arsenal should have a translation department.

From 1871, the Arsenal published a long series of translations of Western scientific works. Many of these resulted from collaborative translation efforts. Thus, Xu Shou and the head of the Arsenal's translation department, John Fryer, worked together in much the same way as Lin Shu and his collaborators, with Fryer translating orally and Xu putting his words into literary written form (Wright 1995, 67–9; Lung 2016, 43–4). Xu Shou's son Xu Jianyin was attached to the Jiangnan Arsenal from 1874 to 1877. Around 1890, Liang Qichao purchased many of the translations published at the Arsenal. Later that decade, he declared in the preface to his *Catalogue of Western Books*: 'If the nation wishes to strengthen itself, then translation of Western books must form the basis for this' (in Hill 2013, 29). Many of the intellectuals around him shared the belief that translation was crucial to the nation's destiny. Translation doesn't get much bigger than that.

Lin Shu, of course, translated fiction, not science or engineering. The link between the kind of translations done at the Jiangnan Arsenal and Lin Shu's work is provided by figures such as Yan Fu and Liang Qichao. After China's defeat in the Sino-Japanese War of 1894–5, Yan Fu wrote of the need to translate works in the realm of ideas and values as well as technology (Hill 2013, 28–9). In 1898, following the failure of the Hundred Days' Reform, Liang Qichao had fled to Japan. There he immediately founded a magazine, in which he began to serialise his own translation of a Japanese political novel. In the preface, he appealed to Chinese patriots and emphasised the power of fiction to influence public opinion (Hashimoto 2017, 228). The paratexts by Lin Shu and Wei Yi to their translation of *Uncle Tom's Cabin* echo these sentiments.

We must leave the examples. The above paragraphs have sought to illustrate, however briefly, one way of historicising translations, starting with certain keywords linking a given translation to other texts in its vicinity and prehistory. These intertextual traces anchored the translation in its context and gave access to a broader constellation of institutions, ideas, individuals and interests. Exactly where to start and how to proceed in each case will depend on the available evidence, including previous research (such as the studies by Kate Sturge, Martha Cheung and Michael Gibbs Hill that I relied on for two of the three illustrations above). But no matter how it is conducted, the approach results in a recognition of the historical depth visible behind individual translations and an appreciation of the way they actively engage with existing states of affairs.

Further Reading

Brower, Reuben. 1959. "Seven Agamemnons." In *On Translation*, edited by Reuben Brower, 173–95. Cambridge (Mass.): Harvard University Press. Reprinted in Brower, Reuben. 1974. *Mirror on Mirror: Translation, Imitation, Parody*, 159–80. Cambridge (Mass.): Harvard University Press.

Although Brower's essay restricts itself to poetry, is now mainly of historical interest and should be read with a critical eye, its methodology remains remarkable for the way in which the author explains the shape of individual translations with reference to the dominant poetics of the time. The procedure might work both ways. Brower seeks to infer the shape of mainstream translations from prevailing discourses. Should we also, vice versa, be able to read translations as weathervanes pointing to broader stylistic and other conventions?

Hill, Michael Gibbs. 2013. *Lin Shu, Inc. Translation and the Making of Modern Chinese Culture*. Oxford: Oxford University Press.

This eminently thoughtful study of Lin Shu surveys his entire career but focuses on the translator's interventions in a series of public debates during the late Qing and early Republican period. The book is instructive for its handling of theoretical concepts and for the way it combines detailed textual analysis with a broader historical brush.

Lung, Rachel. 2016. "The Jiangnan Arsenal. A Microcosm of Translation and Ideological Transformation in 19th-century China." *Meta* 61: 37–52.

By describing the Jiangnan Arsenal as the site of both intense translation activity and ideological transformation, Rachel Lung is able to integrate the microhistorical detail of the Arsenal's translation department with the much larger changes taking place in China at the time. The study demonstrates how we can understand key aspects of a historical period by assessing the significance of translation within it.

Bibliography

Aeschylus. 2009. *Oresteia: Agamemnon. Libation-Bearers. Eumenides.* Edited and translated by Alan Sommerstein. Cambridge (Mass.): Harvard University Press.

Athanasius. 1567. *Den brief van die heilige bisschop van Alexandrien Athanasius.* Translated by Jacop vande Velde. Bruges: Pieter de Clerck.

Batchelor, Kathryn. 2018. *Translation and Paratexts.* London & New York: Routledge.

Bennett, Adrian Arthur. 1967. *John Fryer. The Introduction of Western Science and Technology into Nineteenth-Century China.* Cambridge (Mass.): Harvard University Asia Center.

Brook, Timothy. 2008. *Vermeer's Hat. The Seventeenth Century and the Dawn of the Global World.* London: Profile Books.

Brower, Reuben. 1959. "Seven Agamemnons." In *On Translation*, edited by Reuben Brower, 173–95. Cambridge (Mass.): Harvard University Press. Reprinted in Brower, Reuben. 1974. *Mirror on Mirror: Translation, Imitation, Parody*, 159–80. Cambridge (Mass.): Harvard University Press.

Cheung, Martha. 1998. "The Discourse of Occidentalism? Wei Yi and Lin Shu's Treatment of Religious Material in their Translation of *Uncle Tom's Cabin.*" In *Translation and Creation. Readings of Western Literature in Early Modern China, 1840–1918*, edited by David Pollard, 127–49. Amsterdam & Philadelphia: John Benjamins.

Clark, Herbert, and Richard Gerrig. 1990. "Quotations as Demonstrations." *Language* 66: 764–805.

De Bosch, Hieronymus, ed. 1795. *Anthologia Graeca cum versione Latina Hugonis Grotii.* Volume 1. Utrecht: B. Wild & J. Altheer.

Dudden, Alexis. 2004. "Japan's Engagement with International Terms." In *Tokens of Exchange. The Problem of Translation in Global Circulations*, edited by Lydia Liu, 165–91. Durham & London: Duke University Press.

Frank, Armin Paul. 1992. "Toward a Cultural History of Literary Translation: 'Histories,' 'Systems,' and Other Forms of Synthesizing Research." In *Geschichte, System, Literarische Übersetzung/Histories, Systems, Literary Translations*, edited by Harald Kittel, 369–87. Berlin: Erich Schmidt.

Hashimoto, Satoru. 2017. "Civilization in Transformation: Liang Qichao's Theory and Practice of Translation, 1890s–1920s." In *Translation and Modernization in East Asia in the Nineteenth and Twentieth Centuries*, edited by Lawrence Wong Wang-Chi, 219–52. Hong Kong: University of Hong Kong Press.

Hermans, Theo. 2007. *The Conference of the Tongues.* Manchester & Kinderhook (NY): St Jerome.

Hermans, Theo. 2014. "Positioning Translators. Voices, Views and Values in Translation." *Language and Literature* 23: 285–301.

Hill, Michael Gibbs. 2013. *Lin Shu, Inc. Translation and the Making of Modern Chinese Culture.* Oxford: Oxford University Press.

Jones, Ernest. 1924. *Glossary for the Use of Translators of Psycho-Analytical Works.* London: Baillière, Tindall & Cox for the Institute of Psycho-Analysis.

Liu, Lydia. 2004. *The Clash of Empires. The Invention of China in Modern World Making.* Cambridge (Mass.) & London: Harvard University Press.

Lung, Rachel. 2016. "The Jiangnan Arsenal. A Microcosm of Translation and Ideological Transformation in 19th-century China." *Meta* 61: 37–52.

Maitland, Sarah. 2017. *What Is Cultural Translation?* London: Bloomsbury Academic.

Martin, J.R., and Peter White. 2005. *The Language of Evaluation. Appraisal in English.* London: Palgrave.

Meintjes, Libby. 2009. "How Translation Feels." In *Translation Studies in Africa*, edited by Judith Inggs and Libby Meintjes, 64–87. London & New York: Continuum.

Mish, John. 1964. "Creating an Image of Europe for China: Aleni's Hsi-fang ta-wen. Introduction, translation and notes." *Monumenta serica* 23: 1–87.

Montgomery, Scott. 2000. *Science in Translation. Movements of Knowledge through Cultures and Time.* Chicago & London: University of Chicago Press.

Mungello, David. 1989. *Curious Land. Jesuit Accommodation and the Origins of Sinology.* Honolulu: University of Hawaii Press.

Nicolaisen, Peter, and Daniel Göske. 2008. "William Faulkner in Germany: A Survey." *The Faulkner Journal* 24: 63–81.

Pym, Anthony. 1998. *Method in Translation History.* Manchester: St Jerome.

Pym, Anthony. 2004. "Propositions on Cross-cultural Communication and Translation." *Target* 16: 1–28.

Ricoeur, Paul. 1976. *Interpretation Theory. Discourse and the Surplus of Meaning.* Fort Worth: Texas Christian University Press.

Ricoeur, Paul. 2013. *Hermeneutics.* Translated by David Pellauer. Cambridge: Polity.

Ricoeur, Paul. 2016. *Hermeneutics and the Human Sciences.* Edited and translated by John B. Thompson. Cambridge: Cambridge University Press.

Rozmyslowicz, Tomasz. 2019. "Die Geschichtlichkeit der Translation(swissenschaft). Zur paradigmatischen Relevanz der maschinellen Übersetzung." *Chronotopos* 1 (2): 17–41.

Smit, W.A.P. 1975. *Kalliope in de Nederlanden. Het renaissancistisch-klassicistische epos van 1550 tot 1850. Eerste deel. I. Prolegomena. II. Opkomend tij (1550–1700).* Assen: Van Gorcum.

Steiner, Riccardo. 1987. "A World Wide International Trade Mark of Genuineness? Some Observations on the History of the English Translation of the Works of Sigmund Freud, Focusing Mainly on his Technical Terms." *International Review of Psycho-Analysis* 14: 33–102.

Steiner, Riccardo. 1991. "To Explain Our Point of View to English Readers in English Words." *International Review of Psycho-Analysis* 18: 351–92.

Steiner, Riccardo. 1994. "'The Tower of Babel' or 'After Babel in Contemporary Psychoanalysis'? – and on its Relevance Today." *International Journal of Psychoanalysis* 75: 883–901.

Sturge, Kate. 2004. *"The Alien Within." Translation into German during the Nazi Regime.* Munich: Iudicium.

Van Dam, Harm-Jan. 2021. "Hugo Grotius vertaalt de Griekse Anthologie." In *Vertalen in de Nederlanden. Een cultuurgeschiedenis*, edited by Dirk Schoenaers, Theo Hermans, Inger Leemans, Cees Koster and Ton Naaijkens, 239–40. Amsterdam: Boom.

Venuti, Lawrence. 2004. "Retranslations: The Creation of Value." *Bucknell Review* 47: 25–38. Reprinted in Venuti, Lawrence. 2013. *Translation Changes Everything*, 96–108. London & New York: Routledge.

Wang, Hsien-Chun. 2010. "Discovering Steam Power in China, 1840s–1860s." *Technology and Culture* 51: 31–54.

Wong, Lawrence Wang-Chi. 1999. "An Act of Violence. Translation of Western Fiction in the Late Qing and Early Republican Period." In *The Literary Field of Twentieth-Century China*, edited by Michel Hockx, 21–42. Surrey: Curzon.

Wright, David. 1995. "Careers in Western Science in Nineteenth-Century China: Xu Shou and Xu Jianyin." *Journal of the Royal Asiatic Society*, 3rd series, 5: 49–90.

Conclusion

'The past is another country. They do things differently there'. The opening of L.P. Hartley's novel *The Go-Between* may be one of the most tired quotations about history, but it not only registers the foreignness of the past, its spatial metaphor also invites comparison with the kind of cross-border traffic that translation typically engages in.

There are other parallels between history and translation. Like historical research, translation provides access to something that, without the translator's or historian's active intervention, would have remained locked away in another tongue or in a forgotten past. And just as historians tend to emphasise the uniqueness of a given episode from the past, a translation that is perceived as a translation and circulates with this label attached reminds its recipient of the alien original of which it speaks – an original that remains there in its own language, changed only by the fact that it has now found a translation.

A historical account may seek to create the impression of being a transparent window on the past, giving us direct access to the reality of that past. But all it takes is a differently tuned account to make us realise that every historical account is a construct. An illusionist or domesticating translation asks to be read as if it were an original or even *the* original, but all it takes is another translation to reveal the illusionism of even the most illusionist translation. And both translations and historical accounts have to be consciously crafted in language.

A translation does not reproduce the original or coincide with it. Both the asymmetry between languages and the interpretive nature of translation make for omissions, additions and shifts in meaning. A historical account does not present the past 'as it was'. It adds to, omits from and interprets the archival record for the sake of the narrative it presents.

Both translations and histories are representations that embody interpretations of their object. As interpretations they open up prospects and, in so doing, draw attention to similar and contrasting interpretations and invite alternative approaches. That is why the past is inexhaustible and translation an open-ended series.

I don't want to stretch these parallels beyond their usefulness as a spur for thought. In practice, the historian's work contains an element of translation, as Koselleck, Skinner and others recognised. Historians translate the archival

DOI: 10.4324/9781315178134-7

record into their own conceptual apparatus. That does not mean historians are simply translators. Narrative is not an essential feature of translation as it is of historiography. Nor are translators simply historians, even though translation necessarily involves a temporal dimension and both translators and historians re-ignite the past in the present.

The interface between history and translation constitutes a rich seam, as the preceding chapter will hopefully have shown. Still, we have barely scratched the surface. A collection like *Debating New Approaches to History*, edited by Marek Tamm and Peter Burke (2019), features chapters on global, postcolonial, environmental, gender, digital, posthumanist and neurohistory, as well as on the history of memory, of knowledge, of emotions, of things and of visual culture. Some of these approaches have received attention from translation historians (notably postcolonial and gender history), others are dealt with in the present book (global history, history of memory), but that still leaves a good number that may be worth exploring with translation in mind (digital history and the history of knowledge and of emotions, for a start).

History is a large mansion with many rooms. It still accommodates a vast amount of research on what are – rightly or wrongly – assumed to be monolingual environments. But it is no longer true to say that all or even most historians neglect translation. In this respect, the shift of attention to the transnational and the transcultural has made a crucial difference, and one that students of translation should take a close interest in. Historians have integrated translations into much of their work. They have pointed out the dangers of blithely assuming semantic transparency across languages. They have argued that the translation of a given term may indicate no more than a fragile, contingent matching of sorts rather than a relation of conceptual equivalence. They have urged researchers to take historical translations as they come rather than as the researcher might have wanted them to be as judged by today's critical canons. They have been acutely aware of the difference made by different media in representing the past.

Above all, the engagement with phenomena that are trans- has created a fertile common ground between translation studies and historical research. Translation scholars can bring to it their sensitivity to the cross-lingual and the cross-cultural. Historians can remind them that translation is only ever a part of something much larger than translation.

Paradigmen der Kulturwissenschaften, edited by Andreas Gipper and Susanne Klengel, 141–60. Würzburg: Königshausen & Neumann.

Baddeley, Susan, and Anne Debrosse. 2015. "Dictionnaires, manuels, traités théoriques." In *Histoire des traductions en langue française. XVe et XVIe siècles 1470–1610*, edited by Véronique Duché, 291–354. Lagrasse: Verdier.

Baigorri-Jalón, Jesús. 2014. *From Paris to Nuremberg. The Birth of Conference Interpreting*. Amsterdam & Philadelphia: John Benjamins.

Baker, Mona. 2006. *Translation and Conflict. A Narrative Account*. London & New York: Routledge.

Baker, Mona. 2010. "Narratives of Terrorism and Security. Accurate Translations, Suspicious Frames." *Critical Studies on Terrorism* 3: 347–64.

Ball, Terence. 1998. "Conceptual History and the History of Political Thought." In *History of Concepts: Comparative Perspectives*, edited by Ian Hampsher-Monk, Karin Tilmans and Frank van Vree, 75–86. Amsterdam: Amsterdam University Press.

Ballantyne, James R. 1859. *Christianity Contrasted with Hindū Philosophy*. London: James Madden.

Bandia, Paul. 2005. "Esquisse d'une histoire de la traduction en Afrique." *Meta* 50: 957–71.

Bandia, Paul. 2009. "African Tradition." In *Routledge Encyclopedia of Translation Studies*, 2nd ed., edited by Mona Baker and Gabriela Saldanha, 313–20. London & New York: Routledge.

Barthes, Roland. 1981. "The Discourse of History." Translated by Stephen Bann. *Comparative Criticism* 3: 7–20. Original, French, 1967.

Bassi, Serena. 2015. "Italy's Salman Rushdie. The Renarration of 'Roberto Saviano' in English for the Post-9/11 Cultural Market." *Translation Studies* 8: 48–62.

Bastin, Georges. 2009. "Latin American Tradition." In *Routledge Encyclopedia of Translation Studies*, 2nd ed., edited by Mona Baker and Gabriela Saldanha, 486–92. London & New York: Routledge.

Bastin, Georges, and Paul Bandia, eds. 2006. *Charting the Future of Translation History*. Ottawa: University of Ottawa Press.

Batchelor, Kathryn. 2017. "Introduction: *histoire croisée*, Microhistory and Translation History." In *Translating Frantz Fanon across Continents and Languages*, edited by Kathryn Batchelor, 1–16. London: Routledge.

Batchelor, Kathryn. 2018. *Translation and Paratexts*. London & New York: Routledge.

Bell, David. 2002. "Total History and Microhistory: The French and Italian Paradigms." In *A Companion to Western Historical Thought*, edited by Lloyd Kramer and Sarah Maza, 262–76. London: Blackwell.

Belle, Marie-Alice, and Brenda Hosington. 2017. "Translation, History and Print. A Model for the Study of Printed Translations in Early Modern Britain." *Translation Studies* 10: 2–21.

Bennett, Adrian Arthur. 1967. *John Fryer. The Introduction of Western Science and Technology into Nineteenth-Century China*. Cambridge (Mass.): Harvard University Asia Center.

Bennett, Karen. 2007. "Epistemicide! The Tale of a Predatory Discourse." *The Translator* 13: 151–69.

Bennett, Karen. 2015. "Towards an Epistemological Monoculture: Mechanisms of Epistemicide in European Research Publication." In *English as a Scientific and Research Language, Volume 2*, edited by Ramón Plo Alastrué and Carmen Pérez-Llantada, 9–36. Berlin: De Gruyter.

Bentley, Jerry H. 1996. "Cross-Cultural Interaction and Periodization in World History." *The American Historical Review* 101: 749–70.

Bibliography

Adamo, Sergia. 2006. "Microhistory of Translation." In *Charting the Future of Translation History*, edited by Georges Bastin and Paul Bandia, 81–100. Ottawa: University of Ottawa Press.

Aeschylus. 2009. *Oresteia: Agamemnon. Libation-Bearers. Eumenides.* Edited and translated by Alan Sommerstein. Cambridge (Mass.): Harvard University Press.

Anderson, Clare. 2012. *Subaltern Lives. Biographies of Colonialism in the Indian Ocean World 1790–1920.* Cambridge: Cambridge University Press.

Andrade, Tonio. 2021. *The Last Embassy. The Dutch Mission of 1795 and the Forgotten History of Western Encounters with China.* Princeton & Oxford: Princeton University Press.

Ankersmit, Frank. 1983. *Narrative Logic. A Semantic Analysis of the Historian's Language.* The Hague: Martinus Nijhoff.

Ankersmit, Frank. 2017. "A Dialogue with Jouni-Matti Kuukkanen." *Journal of the Philosophy of History* 11: 38–58.

Appiah, Kwame Anthony. 2012. "Thick Translation" [1993]. In *The Translation Studies Reader*, 3rd ed., edited by Lawrence Venuti, 331–43. London & New York: Routledge.

Archetti, Cristina. 2019. "Mapping Transnational Journalism in the Age of Flows: Or How I Ditched 'Foreign Correspondence' and the 'Immigrant Press' and Started to Love *Histoire Croisée*." *Journalism Studies* 20: 2150–66.

Assmann, Aleida. 2008. "Canon and Archive." In *Cultural Memory Studies. An International and Interdisciplinary Handbook*, edited by Astrid Erll, Ansgar Nünning and Sarah Young, 97–108. Berlin & New York: Walter de Gruyter.

Assmann, Aleida. 2018. "One Land and Three Narratives: Palestinian Sites of Memory in Israel." *Memory Studies* 11: 287–300.

Assmann, Jan. 2008. "Communicative and Cultural Memory." In *Cultural Memory Studies. An International and Interdisciplinary Handbook*, edited by Astrid Erll, Ansgar Nünning and Sarah Young, 109–18. Berlin & New York: Walter de Gruyter.

Athanasius. 1567. *Den brief van die heilige bisschop van Alexandrien Athanasius.* Translated by Jacop vande Velde. Bruges: Pieter de Clerck.

Bachleitner, Norbert. 1989. "'Übersetzungsfabriken.' Das deutsche Übersetzungswesen in der ersten Hälfte des 19. Jahrhunderts." *Internationales Archiv für Sozialgeschichte der deutschen Literatur* 14: 1–49.

Bachleitner, Norbert. 2009. "A Proposal to Include Book History in Translation Studies. Illustrated with German Translations of Scott and Flaubert." *Arcadia* 44: 420–40.

Bachmann-Medick, Doris. 2008. "Übersetzung in der Weltgesellschaft. Impuls eines 'translational turn.'" In *Kultur, Übersetzung, Lebenswelten. Beiträge zu aktuellen*

Bentley, Jerry H, ed. 2011. *The Oxford Handbook of World History.* Oxford: Oxford University Press.

Berman, Antoine. 1990. "La retraduction comme espace de la traduction." *Palimpsestes* 4: 1–7.

Berman, Antoine. 2008. *L'âge de la traduction. 'La tâche du traducteur' de Walter Benjamin, un commentaire.* Saint-Denis: Presses universitaires de Vincennes.

Berman, Antoine. 2018. *The Age of Translation. A Commentary on Walter Benjamin's "The Task of the Translator."* Translated by Chantal Wright. London & New York: Routledge.

Bertrand, Romain, and Guillaume Calafat. 2018. "La microhistoire globale: affaire(s) à suivre". *Annales* 73: 3–18.

Binns, J.W. 1990. *Intellectual Culture in Elizabethan and Jacobean England. The Latin Writings of the Age.* Leeds: Francis Cairns.

Borges, Jorge Luis. 2012. "The Translators of *The Thousand and One Nights.*" Translated by Esther Allen. In *The Translation Studies Reader*, 3rd ed., edited by Lawrence Venuti, 92–106. London & New York: Routledge. Original, Spanish, 1935.

Braudel, Fernand. 1972. *The Mediterranean and the Mediterranean World in the Age of Philip II.* Translated by Siân Reynolds. London: Collins. Original, French, 1949.

Bridges, Lucas. 2019. *Uttermost Part of the Earth. Tierra del Fuego's Indians and Settlers. A Personal Story* [1947]. Ushuaia: Südpol.

Bridges, Thomas. 1866. "Manners and Customs of the Firelanders." *A Voice for South America* 13: 201–14.

Bridges, Thomas. 1869. "The Southern or Fuegian Mission." *The South American Missionary Magazine* 3: 10–4.

Bridges, Thomas. 1870a. "The Fuegian or Southern Mission." *The South American Missionary Magazine* 4: 39–43.

Bridges, Thomas. 1870b. "The Fuegian or Southern Mission." *The South American Missionary Magazine* 4: 127–37.

Bridges, Thomas. 1872. Letter, 11 March 1872. *The South American Missionary Magazine* 6: 98–101.

Bridges, Thomas. 1873. Undated letter. *The South American Missionary Magazine* 7: 27–30.

Bridges, Thomas. 1875. "Southern Mission. Ushuwia." *The South American Missionary Magazine* 9: 214–21.

Bridges, Thomas. 1879. Letter, 1 January 1979. *The South American Missionary Magazine* 13: 102–5.

Bridges, Thomas. 1881. *Gospl Lyc Ecamanāci. The Gospel of S. Luke Translated into the Yahgan Language.* London: British and Foreign Bible Society.

Bridges, Thomas. 1882. Letter, 5 January 1882. *The South American Missionary Magazine* 16: 101–5.

Bridges, Thomas. 1883. *Aposl'ndian Ūstāgy. The Acts of the Apostles Translated into the Yahgan Language.* London: British and Foreign Bible Society.

Bridges, Thomas. 1884a. Letter, 24 October 1883. *The South American Missionary Magazine* 18: 30–4.

Bridges, Thomas. 1884b. Letter, 20 June 1884. *The South American Missionary Magazine* 18: 222–4.

Bridges, Thomas. 1885. "The Yahgans of Tierra del Fuego." *The Journal of the Anthropological Institute of Great Britain and Ireland* 14: 288–9.

Bridges, Thomas. 1886. *Gospel Jon Ecamanāci. The Gospel of S. John Translated into the Yahgan Language.* London: British and Foreign Bible Society.

Bridges, Thomas. 1887. "Tierra del Fuego. Past, Present, and Future." *The South American Missionary Magazine* 21: 7–8.

Bridges, Thomas. 1987. *Yámana-English. A Dictionary of the Speech of Tierra del Fuego.* Edited by Ferdinand Hestermann and Martin Gusinde [1933]. Buenos Aires: Zagier y Urruty Publicaciones.

Brockey, Liam. 2007. *Journey to the East. The Jesuit Mission to China, 1579–1724.* Cambridge (Mass.) & London: Belknap Press of Harvard University Press.

Brodzki, Bella. 2007. *Can These Bones Live? Translation, Survival and Cultural Memory.* Stanford: Stanford University Press.

Brook, Timothy. 2008. *Vermeer's Hat. The Seventeenth Century and the Dawn of the Global World.* London: Profile Books.

Brower, Reuben. 1959. "Seven Agamemnons." In *On Translation,* edited by Reuben Brower, 173–95. Cambridge (Mass.): Harvard University Press. Reprinted in Brower, Reuben. 1974. *Mirror on Mirror: Translation, Imitation, Parody,* 159–80. Cambridge (Mass.): Harvard University Press.

Brownlie, Siobhan. 2016. *Mapping Memory in Translation.* Basingstoke & New York: Palgrave Macmillan.

Bruni Aretino, Leonardo. 1928. *Humanistisch-philosophische Schriften,* edited by Hans Baron. Leipzig & Berlin: B.G. Teubner.

Bull, Charles. 1867. "Journal of a visit […] to Keppel Island, by the colonial chaplain of the Falkland Islands, October, 1866." *The South American Missionary Magazine* 1: 47–49.

Burckhardt, Frederick, and James Secord, eds. 2015. *The Correspondence of Charles Darwin. Volume 22.* Cambridge: Cambridge University Press.

Burke, Martin, and Melvin Richter, eds. 2012. *Why Concepts Matter. Translating Social and Political Thought.* Leiden & Boston: Brill.

Burke, Peter. 2007. "Cultures of Translation in Early Modern Europe." In *Cultural Translation in Early Modern Europe,* edited by Peter Burke and Po-Chia Hsia, 7–38. Cambridge: Cambridge University Press.

Burton, Richard. 1885. *The Book of the Thousand Nights and a Night. Volume 1.* Printed by the Burton Club for Private Subscribers Only.

Buzelin, Hélène. 2006. "Independent Publisher in the Networks of Translation." *TTR* 19: 135–73.

Buzelin, Hélène. 2007. "Translations 'in the making.'" In *Constructing a Sociology of Translation,* edited by Michaela Wolf and Alexandra Fukari, 135–69. Amsterdam & Philadelphia: John Benjamins.

Carr, David. 2001. "Getting the Story Straight. Narrative and Historical Knowledge" [1949]. In *The History and Narrative Reader,* edited by Geoffrey Roberts, 197–208. London & New York: Routledge.

Carrier, Peter, and Kobi Kabalek. 2014. "Cultural Memory and Transcultural Memory – A Conceptual Analysis." In *The Transcultural Turn. Interrogating Memory Between and Beyond Borders,* edited by Lucy Bond and Jessica Rapson, 39–60. Berlin & Boston: De Gruyter.

Cassin, Barbara, ed. 2014. *Dictionary of Untranslatables. A Philosophical Lexicon.* Translated by Steven Rendall *et al.* Princeton & Oxford: Princeton University Press.

Chakrabarty, Dipesh. 2000. *Provincializing Europe. Postcolonial Thought and Historical Difference.* Princeton & Oxford: Princeton University Press.

Chalvin, Antoine. 2011. "Comment écrire une histoire aréale de la traduction?" In *Between Cultures and Texts. Itineraries in Translation History. Entre les cultures et les textes.*

Itinéraires en histoire de la traduction, edited by Antoine Chalvin, Anne Lange and Daniele Monticelli, 77–86. Frankfurt: Peter Lang.

Chalvin, Antoine, Jean-Léon Muller, Katre Talviste, and Marie Vrinat-Nikolov. 2019. *Histoire de la traduction littéraire en Europe médiane. Des origines à 1989.* Rennes: Presses universitaires de Rennes.

Chapman, Anne. 2010. *European Encounters with the Yámana People of Cape Horn, Before and After Darwin.* Cambridge: Cambridge University Press.

Chapman, Seymour. 1978. *Story and Discourse. Narrative Structure in Fiction and Film.* Ithaca & London: Cornell University Press.

Chen, Xin. 2019. "The Reception of Hayden White in China (1987–2018)" in "Globalizing Hayden White," edited by Ewa Domańska and María Inés La Greca, *Rethinking History* 23: 546–53.

Cheung, Martha. 1998. "The Discourse of Occidentalism? Wei Yi and Lin Shu's Treatment of Religious Material in their Translation of *Uncle Tom's Cabin.*" In *Translation and Creation. Readings of Western Literature in Early Modern China, 1840–1918*, edited by David Pollard, 127–49. Amsterdam & Philadelphia: John Benjamins.

Cheung, Martha, ed. 2006. *An Anthology of Chinese Discourse on Translation. Volume One. From Earliest Times to the Buddhist Project.* Manchester: St Jerome.

Cheung, Martha. 2012. "The Mediated Nature of Knowledge and the Pushing-Hands Approach to Research on Translation History." *Translation Studies* 5: 156–71.

Cheung, Martha, ed. 2017. *An Anthology of Chinese Discourse on Translation. Volume Two. From the Late Twelfth Century to 1800*, edited by Robert Neather. London & New York: Routledge.

Chevrel, Yves, and Jean-Yves Masson, gen. eds. 2012–9. *Histoire des traductions en langue française.* 4 vols. Paris: Verdier.

Clark, Herbert, and Richard Gerrig. 1990. "Quotations as Demonstrations." *Language* 66: 764–805.

Colombo, Alice. 2019. "Intersections between Translation and Book History: Reflections and New Directions." *Comparative Critical Studies* 16: 147–60.

Cooper, John. 1917. *Analytical and Critical Bibliography of the Tribes of Tierra del Fuego and Adjacent Territory.* Washington: Bureau of American Ethnology, Smithsonian Institution.

Copeland, Rita. 1989. "The Fortunes of *non verbum pro verbo*, or why Jerome is not a Ciceronian." In *The Medieval Translator. The Theory and Practice of Translation in the Middle Ages*, edited by Roger Ellis, 15–36. Cambridge: D.S. Brewer.

Darnton, Robert. 1984. *The Great Cat Massacre and Other Episodes in French Cultural History.* New York: Basic Books.

Darwin, Charles. 1989. *Voyage of the Beagle* [1839]. Edited by Janet Browne and Michael Neve. London: Penguin.

Davies, Peter. 2014. "Testimony and Translation." *Translation and Literature* 23: 170–84.

Davies, Peter. 2017. "Ethics and the Translation of Holocaust Lives." In *Translating Holocaust Lives*, edited by Jean Boase-Beier, Peter Davies, Andrea Hammel and Marion Winters, 23–43. London: Bloomsbury.

Davies, Peter. 2018. *Witness between Languages. The Translation of Holocaust Testimonies in Context.* Rochester: Camden House.

Davis, Natalie Zemon. 1983. *The Return of Martin Guerre.* Cambridge (Mass.): Harvard University Press.

Deane-Cox, Sharon. 2013. "The Translator as Secondary Witness. Mediating Memory in Antelme's *L'espèce humaine.*" *Translation Studies* 6: 309–23.

De Bosch, Hieronymus, ed. 1795. *Anthologia Graeca cum versione Latina Hugonis Grotii.* Volume 1. Utrecht: B. Wild & J. Altheer.

DeLater, James. 2002. *Translation Theory in the Age of Louis XIV. The 1683 De optimo genere interpretandi (On the best kind of translating) of Pierre-Daniel Huet (1630–1721).* Manchester: St Jerome.

Delisle, Jean. 2009. "Canadian Tradition." In *Routledge Encyclopedia of Translation Studies*, 2nd ed., edited by Mona Baker and Gabriela Saldanha, 362–9. London & New York: Routledge.

Delisle, Jean, and Judith Woodsworth, eds. 2012. *Translators Through History.* 2nd ed. Amsterdam & Philadelphia: John Benjamins.

Den Boer, Pim. 2001. "Vergelijkende begripsgeschiedenis." In *Beschaving. Een geschiedenis van de begrippen hoofsheid, heusheid, beschaving en cultuur*, edited by Pim den Boer, 15–78. Amsterdam: Amsterdam University Press.

Den Boer, Pim. 2007. "Towards a Comparative History of Concepts: Civilisation and beschaving." *Contributions to the History of Concepts* 3: 207–33.

De Vito, Christian. 2019. "History without Scale: The Micro-Spatial Perspective." *Past and Present* 242: 348–72.

D'hulst, Lieven. 2014. *Essais d'histoire de la traduction. Avatars de Janus.* Paris: Classiques Garnier.

Diamond, Jared. 1997. *Guns, Germs and Steel. A Short History of Everybody for the Last 13,000 Years.* London: Jonathan Cape.

Dodson, Michael. 2005. "Translating Science, Translating Empire. The Power of Language in Colonial India." *Comparative Studies in Society and History* 47: 809–35.

Dolet, Etienne. 1981. "The Way to Translate Well from One Language to Another." Translated by James Holmes. *Modern Poetry in Translation* no. 41–42: 54–56. Original, French, 1540.

Domańska, Ewa. 1998. *Encounters. Philosophy of History after Postmodernism.* Charlottesville & London: University Press of Virginia.

Dray, W. H. 1954. "Explanatory Narrative in History." *The Philosophical Quarterly* 4: 15–27.

Dudden, Alexis. 2004. "Japan's Engagement with International Terms." In *Tokens of Exchange. The Problem of Translation in Global Circulations*, edited by Lydia Liu, 165–91. Durham & London: Duke University Press.

Ellis, Alexander. 1884. "Eleventh Annual Address of the President to the Philological Society, Delivered at the Anniversary Meeting, Friday, 19th May, 1882." *Transactions of the Philological Society*, 1–148.

Erll, Astrid. 2009. "Remembering across Time, Space and Cultures: Premediation, Remediation and the 'Indian Mutiny.'" In *Mediation, Remediation and the Dynamics of Cultural Memory*, edited by Astrid Erll and Ann Rigney, 109–38. Berlin & New York: Walter de Gruyter.

Erll, Astrid. 2011. "Travelling Memory." *Parallax* 17 (4): 4–18.

Erll, Astrid. 2017. "Media and the Dynamics of Memory." In *Handbook of Culture and Memory*, edited by Brady Wagoner, 305–24. New York: Oxford University Press.

Erll, Astrid, and Ann Rigney. 2009. "Introduction. Cultural Memory and its Dynamics." In *Mediation, Remediation and the Dynamics of Cultural Memory*, edited by Astrid Erll and Ann Rigney, 1–11. Berlin & New York: Walter de Gruyter.

Even-Zohar, Itamar. 1990. "Polysystem Studies." Special issue of *Poetics Today* 11: 1.

Finkelstein, David, and Alistair McCleery, ed. 2006. *The Book History Reader.* London & New York: Routledge.

France, Peter, and Stuart Gillespie, gen. eds. 2005–. *The Oxford History of Literary Translation in English*. 5 vols. Oxford: Oxford University Press.

Frank, Armin Paul. 1992. "Toward a Cultural History of Literary Translation: 'Histories,' 'Systems,' and Other Forms of Synthesizing Research." In *Geschichte, System, Literarische Übersetzung / Histories, Systems, Literary Translations*, edited by Harald Kittel, 369–87. Berlin: Erich Schmidt.

Froeyman, Anton. 2009. "Concepts of Causation in Historiography." *Historical Methods* 42: 116–28.

Gallagher, Catherine, and Stephen Greenblatt. 2000. *Practicing New Historicism*. Chicago & London: University of Chicago Press.

Garson, J.G. 1886. "On the Inhabitants of Tierra del Fuego." *The Journal of the Anthropological Institute of Great Britain and Ireland* 15: 141–160.

Geertz, Clifford. 1973. *The Interpretation of Cultures. Selected Essays*. New York: BasicBooks.

Ghobrial, John-Paul. 2019. "Introduction: Seeing the World like a Microhistorian." *Past and Present* 242: 1–22.

Ginzburg, Carlo. 1980. *The Cheese and the Worms. The Cosmos of a Sixteenth-Century Miller*. Translated by John and Anne Tedeschi. London: Routledge & Kegan Paul. Original, Italian, 1976.

Ginzburg, Carlo. 1993. "Microhistory: Two or Three Things that I Know about It." Translated by John and Anne Tedeschi. *Critical Inquiry* 20: 10–35.

Guha, Ranajit. 2001. "Subaltern Studies: Projects for Our Time and Their Convergence." In *The Latin American Subaltern Studies Reader*, edited by Ileana Rodríguez and María Milagros López, 35–46. Durham (NC) & London: Duke University Press.

Guldi, Jo, and David Armitage. 2014. *The History Manifesto*. Cambridge: Cambridge University Press.

Ha, Young-Sun. 2011. "The Global Diffusion of the Western Concept of Civilisation to Nineteenth-Century Korea." In *Cultural Transfers in Dispute. Representations in Asia, Europe and the Arab World since the Middle Ages*, edited by Jörg Feuchter, Friedhelm Hoffmann and Bee Yun, 283–98. Frankfurt & New York: Campus.

Hankins, James. 1987. "The New Language." In *The Humanism of Leonardo Bruni. Selected Texts*, edited by Gordon Griffiths, James Hankins and David Thompson, 197–235. Binghamton: Medieval & Renaissance Texts & Studies/The Renaissance Society of America.

Harris, Steven. 1996. "Confession-Building, Long-Distance Networks, and the Organization of Jesuit Science." *Early Science and Medicine* 1: 287–318.

Hashimoto, Satoru. 2017. "Civilization in Transformation: Liang Qichao's Theory and Practice of Translation, 1890s–1920s." In *Translation and Modernization in East Asia in the Nineteenth and Twentieth Centuries*, edited by Lawrence Wong Wang-Chi, 219–52. Hong Kong: University of Hong Kong Press.

Heilbron, Johan. 1999. "Towards a Sociology of Translation. Book Translations as a Cultural World-System." *European Journal of Social Theory* 2: 429–44.

Hermans, Theo. 1985. "Images of Translation. Metaphor and Imagery in the Renaissance Discourse on Translation." In *The Manipulation of Literature. Studies in Literary Translation*, edited by Theo Hermans, 103–35. London & Sydney: Croom Helm.

Hermans, Theo. 1999. *Translation in Systems. Descriptive and Systemic Approaches Explained*. Manchester: St Jerome.

Hermans, Theo. 2007. *The Conference of the Tongues*. Manchester & Kinderhook (NY): St Jerome.

Hermans, Theo. 2014. "Positioning Translators. Voices, Views and Values in Translation." *Language and Literature* 23: 285–301.

Hermans, Theo. 2015. "Schleiermacher and Plato, Hermeneutics and Translation." In *Friedrich Schleiermacher and the Question of Translation*, edited by Larisa Cercel and Adriana Şerban, 77–106. Berlin & Boston: De Gruyter.

Hermans, Theo. 2019. "Schleiermacher." In *The Routledge Handbook of Translation and Philosophy*, edited by Piers Rawling and Philip Wilson, 17–33. London & New York: Routledge.

Heuser, Ryan, and Long Le-Khac. 2012. *A Quantitative Literary History of 2,958 Nineteenth-Century British Novels: The Semantic Cohort Method*. Stanford: Stanford Literary Lab.

Hill, Michael Gibbs. 2013. *Lin Shu, Inc. Translation and the Making of Modern Chinese Culture*. Oxford: Oxford University Press.

Howland, Douglas. 2002. *Translating the West. Language and Political Reason in Nineteenth-Century Japan*. Honolulu: University of Hawai'i Press.

Howland, Douglas. 2005. *Personal Liberty and Public Good. The Introduction of John Stuart Mill to Japan and China*. Toronto: Toronto University Press.

Howland, Douglas. 2012. "The Public Limits of Liberty: Nakamura Keiu's Translation of J.S. Mill." In *Why Concepts Matter. Translating Social and Political Thought*, edited by Martin Burke and Melvin Richter, 177–92. Leiden & Boston: Brill.

Humboldt, Wilhelm von. 1967. "On the Historian's Task" [1821; translator unknown]. *History and Theory* 6: 57–71.

Hyades, Paul. 1884. "Sur les Fuégiens." *Bulletins de la Société anthropologique de Paris* 7: 616–620.

Hyades, Paul. 1885a. "Sur l'état actuel des Fuégiens de l'archipel du cap Horn." *Bulletins de la Société anthropologique de Paris* 8: 200–9.

Hyades, Paul. 1885b. "La rougeole chez les Fuégiens." *Bulletins de la Société anthropologique de Paris* 8: 462–3.

Hyades, Paul. 1886. "Les épidémies chez les Fuégiens." *Bulletins de la Société anthropologique de Paris* (2nd series) 1: 202–5.

Ifversen, Jan. 2011. "About Key Concepts and How to Study Them." *Contributions to the History of Concepts* 6: 65–88.

Israel, Hephzibah, and Matthias Frenz. 2019. "Translation Traces in the Archive: Unfixing Documents, Destabilising Evidence." *The Translator* 25: 335–48.

Jay, Martin. 2011. "Historical Explanation and the Event. Reflections on the Limits of Contextualization." *New Literary History* 42: 557–71.

Jones, Ernest. 1924. *Glossary for the Use of Translators of Psycho-Analytical Works*. London: Baillière, Tindall & Cox for the Institute of Psycho-Analysis.

Jones, Henry. 2019. "Searching for Statesmanship. A Corpus-Based Analysis of Translated Political Discourse." *Polis* 36: 216–41.

Jones, Henry. 2020a. "Jowett's Thucydides. A Corpus-Based Analysis of Translation as Political Intervention." *Translation Studies* 13: 333–351.

Jones, Henry. 2020b. "Retranslating Thucydides as a Scientific Historian." *Target* 32: 59–82.

Kansteiner, W. 1993. "Hayden White's Critique of the Writing of History." *History and Theory* 32: 273–96.

Kittel, Harald. 1988. "Kontinuität und Diskrepanzen." In *Die literarische Übersetzung. Stand und Perspektiven ihrer Erforschung*, edited by Harald Kittel, 158–79. Berlin: Erich Schmidt.

Kleinman, Sylvie. 2012. "'Amidst Clamour and Confusion': Civilian and Military Linguists at War in the Franco-Irish Campaigns against Britain (1792–1804)." In *Languages and the Military. Alliances, Occupation and Peace Building*, edited by Hilary Footitt and Michael Kelly, 25–46. Basingstoke: Palgrave Macmillan.

Koselleck, Reinhart. 1985. *Futures Past. On the Semantics of Historical Time*. Translated by Keith Tribe. Cambridge (Mass.): MIT Press.

Koselleck, Reinhart. 1989. "Social History and Conceptual History." *International Journal of Politics, Culture and Society* 2: 308–25.

Koselleck, Reinhart. 2006. "Crisis." Translated by Michaela Richter. *Journal of the History of Ideas* 67: 357–400.

Koselleck, Reinhart. 2011. "Introduction and Prefaces to the *Geschichtliche Grundbegriffe*." Translated by Michaela Richter. *Contributions to the History of Concepts* 6: 1–37.

Krishnamurthy, Ramesh. 2009. "Indian Tradition." In *Routledge Encyclopedia of Translation Studies*, 2nd ed., edited by Mona Baker and Gabriela Saldanha, 449–58. London & New York: Routledge.

Kujamäki, Pekka, and Hilary Footitt. 2016. "Military History and Translation Studies. Shifting Territories, Uneasy Borders." In *Border Crossings. Translation Studies and Other Disciplines*, edited by Yves Gambier and Luc van Doorslaer, 49–71. Amsterdam & Philadelphia: John Benjamins.

Lafarga, Francisco, ed. 1996. *El discurso sobre la traducción en la historia. Antología bilingüe*. Barcelona: EUB.

Lafarga, Francisco, and Luis Pegenaute, eds. 2013. *Diccionario histórico de la traducción en Hispanomérica*. Madrid & Frankfurt: Iberoamericana & Vervuert.

Landsberg, Alison. 2004. *Prosthetic Memory. The Transformation of American Remembrance in the Age of Mass Culture*. New York: Columbia University Press.

Lane, Edward. 1839. *The Thousand and One Nights, Commonly Called, in England, the Arabian Nights' Entertainment*. London: Charles Knight.

Lässig, Simone. 2012. "Übersetzungen in der Geschichte – Geschichte als Übersetzung? Überlegungen zu einem analytischen Konzept und Forschungsgegenstand für die Geschichtswissenschaft." *Geschichte und Gesellschaft* 38: 189–216.

Latour, Bruno. 1987. *Science in Action. How to Follow Scientists and Engineers through Society*. Cambridge (Mass.): Harvard University Press.

Latour, Bruno. 2005. *Reassembling the Social. An Introduction to Actor-Network-Theory*. Oxford: Oxford University Press.

Law, John. 2012. "Technology and Heterogeneous Engineering. The Case of Portuguese Expansion." In *The Social Contruction of Technological Systems*, edited by Wiebe Bijker, Thomas Hughes and Trevor Pinch, 105–27. Cambridge (Mass.): MIT Press.

Lemon, M.C. 2001. "The Structure of Narrative" [1995]. In *The History and Narrative Reader*, edited by Geoffrey Roberts, 107–29. London & New York: Routledge.

León-Portilla, Miguel. 1962. *The Broken Spears. The Aztec Account of the Conquest of Mexico*. Translated by Lysander Kemp. Boston: Beacon Press.

Leonhard, Jörn. 2008. "Von der Wortimitation zur semantischen Integration. Übersetzung als Kulturtransfer." In *Über-setzen*, edited by Ulrike Gleixner, 45–63 Essen: Klartext.

Le Roy Ladurie, Emmanuel. 1980. *Montaillou. Cathars and Catholics in a French Village 1294–1324*. Translated by Barbara Bray. Harmondsworth: Penguin.

Levý, Jiří. 2011. *The Art of Translation* [1963]. Edited by Zuzana Jettmarová. Translated by Patrick Corness. Amsterdam & Philadelphia: John Benjamins.

Lewis, Nicholas. 2021. "Revisiting *De Christiana Expeditione* as an Artefact of Globalisation." *Itinerario* 45: 47–69.

Lewis, Oscar. 1961. *The Children of Sánchez. Autobiography of a Mexican Family.* New York: Random House.

Lianeri, Alexandra. 2002. "Translation and the Establishment of Liberal Democracy in Nineteenth-Century England: Constructing the Political as an Interpretive Act." In *Translation and Power*, edited by Maria Tymoczko and Edwin Gentzler, 1–24. Amherst & Boston: University of Massachusetts Press.

Lianeri, Alexandra. 2006. "Translation and the Language(s) of Historiography. Understanding Ancient Greek and Chinese Ideas of History." In *Translating Others*, edited by Theo Hermans, 67–86. Manchester: St Jerome.

Littau, Karin. 2016. "Translation and the Materialities of Communication." *Translation Studies* 9: 82–113.

Liu, Lydia. 1995. *Translingual Practice. Literature, National Culture and Translated Modernity. China 1900–1937.* Stanford: Stanford University Press.

Liu, Lydia. 1999. "Legislating the Universal. The Circulation of International Law in the Nineteenth Century." In *Tokens of Exchange. The Problem of Translation in Global Circulations*, edited by Lydia Liu, 127–64. Durham & London: Duke University Press.

Liu, Lydia. 2004. *The Clash of Empires. The Invention of China in Modern World Making.* Cambridge (Mass.) & London: Harvard University Press.

Lung, Rachel. 2015. "Sillan Interpreters in 9th-century East Asian Exchanges." *Meta* 60: 238–55.

Lung, Rachel. 2016. "The Jiangnan Arsenal. A Microcosm of Translation and Ideological Transformation in 19th-century China." *Meta* 61: 37–52.

Luo, Wenyan. 2020. *Translation as Actor-Networking. Actors, Agencies and Networks in the Making of Arthur Waley's Translation of the Chinese "Journey to the West."* London & New York: Routledge.

Magnússon, Sigurður Gylfi. 2003. "The Singularization of History. Social History and Microhistory within the Postmodern State of Knowledge." *Journal of Social History* 36: 701–35.

Magnússon, Sigurður Gylfi. 2017. "Far-reaching Microhistory. The Use of Microhistorical Perspective in a Globalized World." *Rethinking History* 21: 312–41.

Magnússon, Sigurður Gylfi, and István Szijártó. 2013. *What is Microhistory? Theory and Practice.* London & New York: Routledge.

Maitland, Sarah. 2017. *What Is Cultural Translation?* London: Bloomsbury Academic.

Mak, Kam Wah (George). 2015. "To add or not to add? The British and Foreign Bible Society's Defence of the 'Without Note or Comment' Principle in Late Qing China." *Journal of the Royal Asiatic Society* 25: 329–354.

Malena, Anne. 2011. "Where is the 'History' in Translation History?" *TTR* 24: 87–115.

Manouvrier, L. 1881. "Sur les Fuégiens du Jardin d'acclimatation." *Bulletins de la Société anthropologique de Paris* 4: 760–74.

Mardrus, J.C. 1903. *Le livre des mille nuits et une nuit.* Volume 1. Paris: E. Fasquelle.

Marsh, John William. 1883. *Narrative of the Origin and Progress of the South American Mission.* London: South American Missionary Society.

Martin, Alison. 2018. *Nature Translated. Alexander von Humboldt's Works in Nineteenth-Century Britain.* Edinburgh: Edinburgh University Press.

Martin, J.R., and Peter White. 2005. *The Language of Evaluation. Appraisal in English.* London: Palgrave.

Martin, W.A.P. 1900. *A Cycle of Cathay or China, North and South. With personal reminiscences.* 3rd ed. New York: Fleming H. Revell Company.

McElduff, Siobhán. 2013. *Roman Theories of Translation. Surpassing the Source.* London & New York: Routledge.

Meintjes, Libby. 2009. "How Translation Feels." In *Translation Studies in Africa*, edited by Judith Inggs and Libby Meintjes, 64–87. London & New York: Continuum.

Mink, Louis. 2001. "Narrative Form as a Cognitive Instrument" [1978]. In *The History and Narrative Reader*, edited by Geoffrey Roberts, 211–20. London & New York: Routledge.

Mish, John. 1964. "Creating an Image of Europe for China: Aleni's Hsi-fang ta-wen. Introduction, translation and notes." *Monumenta serica* 23: 1–87.

Monod, Gabriel. 1897. *Portraits et souvenirs.* Paris: Calmann Lévy.

Montgomery, Scott. 2000. *Science in Translation. Movements of Knowledge through Cultures and Time.* Chicago & London: University of Chicago Press.

Moretti, Franco. 1998. *Atlas of the European Novel 1800–1900.* London & New York: Verso.

Moretti, Franco. 2013. *Distant Reading.* London: Verso.

Moyn, Samuel, and Andrew Sartori. 2013. "Approaches to Global Intellectual History." In *Global Intellectual History*, edited by Samuel Moyn and Andrew Sartori, 3–20. New York: Columbia University Press.

Munday, Jeremy. 2014. "Using Primary Sources to Produce a Microhistory of Translation and Translators: Theoretical and Methodological Concerns." *The Translator* 20: 64–80.

Mungello, David. 1989. *Curious Land. Jesuit Accommodation and the Origins of Sinology.* Honolulu: University of Hawaii Press.

Munslow, Alun. 2017. "History, Skepticism and the Past." *Rethinking History* 21: 474–88.

Nama, Charles A. 1993. "Historical, Theoretical and Terminological Perspectives of Translation in Africa." *Meta* 38: 414–25.

Nicolaisen, Peter, and Daniel Göske. 2008. "William Faulkner in Germany: A Survey." *The Faulkner Journal* 24: 63–81.

Norton, Glyn. 1984. *The Ideology and Language of Translation in Renaissance France and their Humanist Antecedents.* Genève: Droz.

Paisley, Fiona, and Pamela Scully. 2019. *Writing Transnational History.* London: Bloomsbury.

Park, Myoung-Kyu. 2012. "Conceptual History in Korea. Its Development and Prospects." *Contributions to the History of Concepts* 7: 36–50.

Pernau, Margrit. 2018. "Einführung: Neue Wege der Begriffsgeschichte." *Geschichte und Gesellschaft* 44: 5–28.

Pernau, Margrit, and Dominic Sachsenmaier, eds. 2016. *Global Conceptual History. A Reader*, 1–27. London: Bloomsbury.

Perrot d'Ablancourt, Nicolas. 1972. *Lettres et préfaces critiques.* Edited by Roger Zuber. Paris: Didier.

Pocock, J.G.A. 2019. "On the Unglobality of Contexts. Cambridge Methods and the History of Political Thought." *Global Intellectual History* 4: 1–14.

Poupaud, Sandra, Anthony Pym, and Ester Torres Simón. 2009. "Finding Translations. On the Use of Bibliographical Databases in Translation History." *Meta* 54: 264–78.

Prakash, Gyan. 1990. "Writing Post-Orientalist Histories of the Third World: Perspectives from Indian Historiography." *Comparative Studies in Society and History* 32: 383–408.

Pratt, Mary Louise. 1987. "Linguistic Utopias." In *The Linguistics of Writing. Arguments between Language and Literature*, edited by N. Farb, D. Attridge, A. Durant and C. McCabe, 48–66. New York: Methuen.

Prunč, Erich. 2007. *Entwicklungslinien der Translationswissenschaft. Von den Asymmetrien der Sprachen zu den Asymmetrien der Macht*. Berlin: Frank & Timme.

Pym, Anthony. 1998. *Method in Translation History*. Manchester: St Jerome.

Pym, Anthony. 2000. *Negotiating the Frontier. Translators and Intercultures in Hispanic History*. Manchester: St Jerome.

Pym, Anthony. 2004. "Propositions on Cross-cultural Communication and Translation." *Target* 16: 1–28.

Rafael, Vicente. 2016. *Motherless Tongues. The Insurgency of Language amid Wars of Translation*. Durham: Duke University Press.

Richter, Julia. 2020. *Translationshistoriographie*. Wien: nap.

Richter, Melvin. 1987. "*Begriffsgeschichte* and the History of Ideas." *Journal of the History of Ideas* 48: 247–63.

Richter, Melvin. 1990. "Reconstructing the History of Political Languages: Pocock, Skinner and the *Geschichtliche Grundbegriffe*." *History and Theory* 29: 38–70.

Ricoeur, Paul. 1976. *Interpretation Theory. Discourse and the Surplus of Meaning*. Fort Worth: Texas Christian University Press.

Ricoeur, Paul. 2013. *Hermeneutics*. Translated by David Pellauer. Cambridge: Polity.

Ricoeur, Paul. 2016. *Hermeneutics and the Human Sciences*. Edited and translated by John B. Thompson. Cambridge: Cambridge University Press.

Ridge, Stanley. 2009. "Translating Against the Grain. Negotiation of Meaning in the Colonial Trial of Chief Langalibalele and its Aftermath." In *Decentering Translation Studies. India and Beyond*, edited by Judy Wakabayashi and Rita Kothari, 195–212. Amsterdam & Philadelphia: John Benjamins.

Rigney, Ann. 2005. "Plenitude, Scarcity and the Circulation of Cultural Memory." *Journal of European Studies* 35: 11–28.

Rigney, Ann. 2015. "Cultural Memory Studies." In *Routledge International Handbook of Memory Studies*, edited by Anna Lisa Tota and Trever Hagen, 65–76. London & New York: Routledge.

Rimmon-Kenan, Shlomith. 1983. *Narrative Fiction. Contemporary Poetics*. London & New York: Methuen.

Rizzi, Andrea, Birgit Lang, and Anthony Pym. 2019. *What is Translation History? A Trust-Based Approach*. Cham: Palgrave Macmillan.

Roberts, Geoffrey, ed. 2001. *The History and Narrative Reader*. London & New York: Routledge.

Robinson, Douglas, ed. 2002. *Western Translation Theory from Herodotus to Nietzsche*. 2nd ed. Manchester: St Jerome.

Robinson, Douglas, ed. 2016. *The Pushing-Hands of Translation and its Theory*. London & New York: Routledge.

Rodríguez, Ileana. 2001. "Reading Subalterns Across Texts, Disciplines and Theories: From Representation to Recognition." In *The Latin American Subaltern Studies Reader*, edited by Ileana Rodríguez and María Milagros López, 1–32. Durham (NC) & London: Duke University Press.

Roland, Ruth. 1999. *Interpreters as Diplomats. A Diplomatic History of the Role of Interpreters in World Politics*. Ottawa: University of Ottawa Press.

Rothberg, Michael. 2009. *Multidirectional Memory. Remembering the Holocaust in the Age of Decolonization*. Stanford: Stanford University Press.

Rozmyslowicz, Tomasz. 2019. "Die Geschichtlichkeit der Translation(swissenschaft). Zur paradigmatischen Relevanz der maschinellen Übersetzung." *Chronotopos* 1 (2): 17–41.

Rundle, Christopher. 2012. "Translation as an Approach to History." *Translation Studies* 5: 232–40.

Rundle, Christopher. 2014. "Introduction. Theories and Methodologies of Translation History: The Value of an Interdisciplinary Approach." *The Translator* 20: 2–8.

Rundle, Christopher, ed. 2022. *The Routledge Handbook of Translation History*. London & New York: Routledge.

Ryle, Gilbert. 1971. "The Thinking of Thoughts." In *Collected Papers. Volume II: Collected Essays 1929-1968*, 480–96. London: Hutchinson.

Said, Edward. 1993. *Culture and Imperialism*. London: Vintage.

Salama-Carr, Myriam. 1990. *La traduction à l'époque abbaside. L'école de Ḥunain ibn Isḥāq et son importance pour la traduction*. Paris: Didier.

Saldanha, Gabriela, and Sharon O'Brien. 2013. *Research Methodologies in Translation Studies*. Manchester: St Jerome.

SAMS (South American Missionary Society). 1884. "Christian Civilization and the South American Mission." *The South American Missionary Magazine* 18: 53–67.

Sartori, Edward. 2005. "The Resonance of 'Culture.' Framing a Problem in Global Concept-History." *Comparative Studies in Society and History* 47: 676–99.

Schacker-Mill, Jennifer. 2000. "Otherness and Other-Worldliness. Edward W. Lane's Ethnographic Treatment of the Arabian Nights." *Journal of American Folklore* 113: 164–84.

Seidman, Naomi. 2006. *Faithful Renderings: Jewish–Christian Difference and the Politics of Translation*. Chicago & London: University of Chicago Press.

Sensbach, Jon. 2005. *Rebecca's Revival. Creating Black Christianity in the Atlantic World*. Cambridge (Mass.) & London: Harvard University Press.

Skinner, Quentin. 1969. "Meaning and Understanding in the History of Ideas." *History and Theory* 8: 3–53.

Skinner, Quentin. 1970. "Conventions and the Understanding of Speech Acts." *The Philosophical Quarterly* 20: 118–38.

Skinner, Quentin. 1989. "Language and Political Change." In *Political Innovation and Conceptual Change*, edited by Terence Ball, James Farr and Russell Hanson, 6–23. Cambridge: Cambridge University Press.

Skinner, Quentin. 2002. *Visions of Politics. Volume 1: Regarding Method*. Cambridge: Cambridge University Press.

Skinner, Quentin. 2010. "The Sovereign State: A Genealogy." In *Sovereignty in Fragments. The Past, Present and Future of a Contested Concept*, edited by Hent Kalmo and Quentin Skinner, 26–46. Cambridge: Cambridge University Press.

Skinner, Quentin. 2016. "Rhetoric and Conceptual Change" [1999]. In *Global Conceptual History. A Reader*, edited by Margrit Pernau and Dominic Sachsenmaier, 135–48. London: Bloomsbury.

Smit, W.A.P. 1975. *Kalliope in de Nederlanden. Het renaissancistisch-klassicistische epos van 1550 tot 1850. Eerste deel. I. Prolegomena. II. Opkomend tij (1550–1700)*. Assen: Van Gorcum.

Soll, Jacob. 2016. "Intellectual History and History of the Book." In *A Companion to Intellectual History*, edited by Richard Whatmore and Brian Young, 72–82. Chichester: John Wiley & Sons.

Somers, Margaret. 1994. "The Narrative Constitution of Identity: A Relational and Network Approach." *Theory and Society* 23: 605–49.

Somers, Margaret. 2001. "Narrativity, Narrative Identity and Social Action: Rethinking English Working-Class Formation" [1992]. In *The History and Narrative Reader*, edited by Geoffrey Roberts, 354–74. London & New York: Routledge.

Spiessens, Anneleen. 2019. "Deep Memory during the Crimean Crisis. References to the Great Patriotic War in Russian News Translation." *Target* 31: 398–419.

Standaert, Nicolas. 2003. "The Transmission of Renaissance Culture in Seventeenth-Century China." *Renaissance Studies* 17: 367–91.

Steiner, George. 1975. *After Babel. Aspects of Language and Translation.* London: Oxford University Press.

Steiner, Riccardo. 1987. "A World Wide International Trade Mark of Genuineness? Some Observations on the History of the English Translation of the Works of Sigmund Freud, Focusing Mainly on his Technical Terms." *International Review of Psycho-Analysis* 14: 33–102.

Steiner, Riccardo. 1991. "'To Explain Our Point of View to English Readers in English Words.'" *International Review of Psycho-Analysis* 18: 351–92.

Steiner, Riccardo. 1994. "'The Tower of Babel' or 'After Babel in Contemporary Psychoanalysis'? – and on its Relevance Today." *International Journal of Psychoanalysis* 75: 883–901.

Steinmetz, Willibald. 2012. "Some Thoughts on a History of Twentieth-Century German Basic Concepts." *Contributions to the History of Concepts* 7: 87–100.

Sturge, Kate. 2004. *"The Alien Within." Translation into German during the Nazi Regime.* Munich: Iudicium.

Stuurman, Siep. 2013. "Common Humanity and Cultural Difference on the Sedentary-Nomadic Border. Herodotus, Sima Qian and Ibn Khaldun." In *Global Intellectual History*, edited by Samuel Moyn and Andrew Sartori, 33–58. New York: Columbia University Press.

Takeda, Kayoko, and Jesús Baigorri Jalón, eds. 2016. *New Insights in the History of Interpreting.* Amsterdam & Philadelphia: John Benjamins.

Tamm, Marek, and Peter Burke, eds. 2019. *Debating New Approaches to History.* London: Bloomsbury Academic.

Thornber, Karen. 2009. *Empire of Texts in Motion. Chinese, Korean, and Taiwanese Transculturation of Japanese Literature.* Cambridge (Mass.): Harvard University Asia Center.

Toury, Gideon. 1995. *Descriptive Translation Studies and Beyond.* Amsterdam & Philadelphia: John Benjamins.

Tribe, Keith. 2016. "Intellectual History as *Begriffsgeschichte*." In *A Companion to Intellectual History*, edited by Richard Whatmore and Brian Young, 61–71. Chichester: John Wiley & Sons.

Trivedi, Harish. 2006. "In Our Own Time, On Our Own Terms. 'Translation' in India." In *Translating Others*, edited by Theo Hermans, 102–19. Manchester: St Jerome.

Van Dam, Harm-Jan. 2021. "Hugo Grotius vertaalt de Griekse Anthologie." In *Vertalen in de Nederlanden. Een cultuurgeschiedenis*, edited by Dirk Schoenaers, Theo Hermans, Inger Leemans, Cees Koster and Ton Naaijkens, 239–40. Amsterdam: Boom.

Van Gelderen, Martin. 1998. "Between Cambridge and Heidelberg. Concepts, Languages and Images in Intellectual History." In *History of Concepts: Comparative Perspectives*, edited by Ian Hampsher-Monk, Karin Tilmans and Frank van Vree, 227–38. Amsterdam: Amsterdam University Press.

Veeser, H. Aram, ed. 1989. *The New Historicism.* London & New York: Routledge.

Venuti, Lawrence. 1995. *The Translator's Invisibility. A History of Translation.* London & New York: Routledge.

Venuti, Lawrence. 2004. "Retranslations: The Creation of Value." *Bucknell Review* 47: 25–38. Reprinted in Venuti, Lawrence. 2013. *Translation Changes Everything*, 96–108. London & New York: Routledge.

Venuti, Lawrence. 2005. "Translation, History, Narrative." *Meta* 50: 800–16.

Venuti, Lawrence. 2009. "American Tradition." In *Routledge Encyclopedia of Translation Studies*, 2nd ed., edited by Mona Baker and Gabriela Saldanha, 320–8. London & New York: Routledge.

Vidal Claramonte, Carmen África. 2018. *La traducción y la(s) historia(s). Nuevas vías para la investigación*. Granada: Gomares.

Von Ranke, Leopold. 1824. *Geschichten der romanischen und germanischen Völker*. Volume 1. Leipzig & Berlin: G. Reimer.

Wakabayashi, Judy. 2005. "Translation in the East Asian Cultural Sphere. Shared Roots, Divergent Paths?" In *Asian Translation Traditions*, edited by Eva Hung and Judy Wakabayashi, 17–65. Manchester: St Jerome.

Wakabayashi, Judy. 2012. "Japanese Translation Historiography: Origins, Strengths, Weaknesses and Lessons." *Translation Studies* 5: 172–88.

Wakabayashi, Judy. 2019a. "Time Matters: Conceptual and Methodological Considerations in Translation Timescapes." *Chronotopos* 1: 23–39.

Wakabayashi, Judy. 2019b. "Digital Approaches to Translation History." *Translation and Interpreting* 11: 132–45.

Wang, Hsien-Chun. 2010. "Discovering Steam Power in China, 1840s–1860s." *Technology and Culture* 51: 31–54.

Wells, Julia. 1998. "Eva's Men. Gender and Power in the Establishment of the Cape of Good Hope, 1652–74." *Journal of African History* 39: 417–37.

Werner, Michael, and Bénédicte Zimmermann. 2002. "Vergleich, Transfer, Verflechtung. Der Ansatz der *histoire croisée* under die Herausforderung des Transnationalen." *Geschichte und Gesellschaft* 28: 607–36.

Werner, Michael, and Bénédicte Zimmermann. 2006. "*Histoire croisée* and the Challenge of Reflexivity." *History and Theory* 45: 30–50.

Wertsch, James. 2002. *Voices of Collective Remembering*. Cambridge: Cambridge University Press.

Wertsch, James. 2008. "Blank Spots in Collective Memory. A Case Study of Russia." *Annals of the American Academy of Political and Social Science* 617: 58–71.

White, Hayden. 1973. *Metahistory. The Historical Imagination in Nineteenth-Century Europe*. Baltimore & London: Johns Hopkins University Press.

White, Hayden. 1978. *Tropics of Discourse. Essays in Cultural Criticism*. Baltimore & London: Johns Hopkins University Press.

White, Hayden. 1986. "Historical Pluralism." *Critical Inquiry* 12: 480–93.

White, Hayden. 1989. "'Figuring the nature of the times deceased': Literary Theory and Historical Writing." In *The Future of Literary Theory*, edited by Ralph Cohen, 19–43. London & New York: Routledge.

White, Hayden. 2005. "Introduction: Historical Fiction, Fictional History, and Historical Reality." *Rethinking History* 9: 147–57.

White, Hayden. 2013. "History as Fulfillment." In *Philosophy of History after Hayden White*, edited by Robert Doran, 35–46. London: Bloomsbury.

Wolf, Michaela. 2012. *Die vielsprachige Seele Kakaniens. Übersetzen und Dolmetschen in der Habsburgmonarchie 1848 bis 1918*. Vienna: Böhlau.

Wolf, Michaela. 2015a. "Histoire croisée." In *Researching Translation and Interpreting*, edited by Claudia Angelelli and Brian Baer, 229–35. London & New York: Routledge.

Wolf, Michaela. 2015b. *The Habsburg Monarchy's Many-Languaged Soul. Translating and Interpreting, 1848–1918*. Translated by Kate Sturge. Amsterdam & Philadelphia: John Benjamins.

Wong, Lawrence Wang-Chi. 1999. "An Act of Violence. Translation of Western Fiction in the Late Qing and Early Republican Period." In *The Literary Field of Twentieth-Century* China, edited by Michel Hockx, 21–42. Surrey: Curzon.

Wright, David. 1995. "Careers in Western Science in Nineteenth-Century China: Xu Shou and Xu Jianyin." *Journal of the Royal Asiatic Society*, 3rd series, 5: 49–90.

Yang, Haiyan. 2013. "Knowledge across Borders. The Early Communication of Evolution in China." In *The Circulation of Knowledge between Britain, India and China. The Early-Modern World to the Twentieth Century*, edited by Bernard Lightman, Gordon McOuat and Larry Stewart, 181–208. Leiden & Boston: Brill.

Zhou, Xiaoyan, and Sanjun Sun. 2017. "Bibliography-Based Quantitative Translation History." *Perspectives* 25: 98–119.

Zhu, Yifan, and Kyung Hye Kim. 2020. "The Individual on the Move. Redefining 'individualism' in China." *Translation and Interpreting Studies* 15: 161–82.

Zinn, Howard. 1980. *A People's History of the United States. 1492–Present.* London: Longman.

Index

actor-network theory ix, 66–8
Adamo, Sergia 29, 56, 59
Aeschylus 121, 122
Aesop 132
Aleni, Giulio 130
Anderson, Clare 60
Andrade, Tonio 58–9
Ankersmit, Frank 13, 15
anthologies 44–7
Appiah, Kwame Anthony 57
Archetti, Cristina 65–6
archives 29, 57–9, 73–4, 102
Aristotle 80
Armitage, David 71–2
Assmann, Aleida 102, 103
Assmann, Jan 101
Athanasius of Alexandria 118–19
Austin, J. L. 84

Bachleitner, Norbert 42, 43
Bachmann-Medick, Doris 66
Baddeley, Susan 45
Baigorri-Jalón, Jesús 71
Baker, Mona 17, 21, 111
Ball, Charles 106
Ball, Terence 81
Ballantyne, Robert 81–2
Bandia, Paul viii, 34, 36
Barthes, Roland 12–13, 15
Bassi, Serena 18
Bastin, Georges 34
Batchelor, Kathryn 65, 126
Beecher Stowe, Harriet 131
Bell, David 58
Belle, Marie-Alice 43
Benjamin, Walter 46
Bennett, Adrian Arthur 134
Bennett, Karen 71
Bentley, Jerry 61, 69–70

Berman, Antoine 16, 46
Bertrand, Romain 64
bibliographies 28–31, 72
Binns, J. W. 46
Blaeu, Willem 115
Boase-Beier, Jean 112
Boccaccio, Giovanni 123
Bodin, Jean 96
Bonaparte, Napoleon 111
book history x, 30, 43, 48, 58, 84
Borges, Jorge Luis 38–41
Bourdieu, Pierre 33
Braudel, Fernand 54, 70
Bridges, Lucas 5, 7, 11
Bridges, Thomas 1–12, 16, 124
Brockey, Liam 64
Brodzki, Bella 102, 104
Brook, Timothy 115
Brower, Reuben 121–3, 135
Browning, Robert 122
Brownlie, Siobhan 101, 108, 110, 112
Bruner, Jerome 17
Bruni, Leonardo 45, 46
Bull, Charles 2, 5
Burckhardt, Frederick 5, 6
Burke, Martin 96
Burke, Peter 28, 31, 140
Burton, Richard 38–41
Buzelin, Hélène 67–8

Calafat, Guillaume 64
Callon, Michel 66
Carr, David 17, 22
Carrier, Peter 103, 108
Cassin, Barbara 16, 89
causation 42–3
Chakrabarty, Dipesh 12, 14, 53, 54, 61–2, 86
Chalvin, Antoine 37–8

Chapman, Anne 5, 7, 8
Chapman, Seymour 9
Cheung, Martha 19, 20–1, 47–8, 130–2, 135
Chevrel, Yves 36
Christopherson, John 45–6
Cicero, Marcus Tullius 45
civilisation (concept of) 87
Clark, Herbert 125
collective memory 100, 107, 110, 111
Colombo, Alice 43
Colston, Edward 103
communicative memory 101, 107
comparative conceptual history 87–9
compliant reading 127
conceptual history ix, 79–96
connected history 60
Cooper, John 5
Copeland, Rita 46
Copernicus, Nicolaus 130
corpora, corpus tools 73–4, 80, 93
countermemory 103
cultural archive 81, 105
cultural memory 100–2
culture (concept of) 87, 96

Danto, Arthur 10
Darnton, Robert 54, 56–9
Darwin, Charles 4–6, 11, 60
databases 29–30, 74
Davies, Peter 108, 109, 112
Davis, Natalie Zemon 54
Deane-Cox, Sharon 108, 109
De Bosch, Hieronymus 118
Debrosse, Anne 45
deep memory 111
deictic shift 126–7
DeLater, James 46
Delbo, Charlotte 107
Delisle, Jean 34
Den Boer, Pim 87
Derrida, Jacques 91
De Vito, Christian 65
Dhondt, Jan 26
D'hulst, Lieven 31
Diamond, Jared 69
diasporic memory 105
digital humanities 72, 74
distant reading 73
Dodson, Michael 82
Dolet, Etienne 44–6
Domańska, Ewa 10, 13
Donne, John 40

Dray, W. H. 12
Dryden, John 101
Dudden, Alexis 133
Durkheim, Emile 96
Dutt, Shoshee Chunder 106

Eichmann, Adolf 106
Ellis, Alexander 3, 6, 10
emplotment 9, 15–16, 43
Ennin 57
entangled history ix, 60, 65–6
equivalence 62, 68, 84, 88, 91, 95, 124, 133, 140
Erasmus, Desiderius 119
Erll, Astrid 103, 104–6, 112
eurocentrism 61
Eva *see* Krotoa
Even-Zohar, Itamar 59

Faulkner, William 129
Finkelstein, David 48
Flaubert, Gustave 40
Footitt, Hilary 28, 29
Forster, E. M. 9
framing 18, 126, 127
France, Peter 36
Franco, Francisco 17
Frank, Armin Paul 123–4
Frenz, Matthias 29
Freud, Sigmund 124
Froeyman, Anton 31, 43
Fryer, John 134
Fustel de Coulanges, Numa Denis 12, 13

Galileo Galilei 130
Gallagher, Catherine 57
Galland, Antoine 38–40
Garson, J. G. 5, 8
Geertz, Clifford 57
geography 35–8, 60
Gerrig, Richard 125
Ghobrial, John-Paul 64
Gillespie, Stuart 36
Ginzburg, Carlo 54, 55, 57, 58
global history 38, 60, 62–3
globalisation ix, 60
global microhistory 64–5
global translation history 38
Gong (Prince) 133
Göske, Daniel 129
Greenblatt, Stephen 57
Grotius (De Groot), Hugo 118, 119, 123
Grossman, Vassily 112

Guha, Ranajit 54
Guldi, Jo 71–2

Ha Young-Sun 86
Halbwachs, Maurice 100
Hammel, Andrea 112
Hankins, James 45, 46
Harris, Steven 67
Hartley, L. P. 139
Hashimoto, Satoru 135
Heilbron, Johan 71
Hermans, Theo 44, 46, 90, 101, 107, 124, 125
Herodotus 88
Heuser, Ryan 72–3
Heyns, Michiel 123
Hill, Michael Gibbs 120, 124, 132–3, 135
histoire croisée ix, 60, 65
historicity of translations 123
history from below 53, 54
history of concepts ix, 79–96
history of ideas 82
Hitler, Adolf 111, 127
Hobbes, Thomas 80, 81, 96
Holocaust 108–10
Homer 118
Hosington, Brenda 43
Howland, Douglas 90–2
Huet, Pierre-Daniel 46
Humboldt, Alexander von 68, 120, 123
Humboldt, Wilhelm von 12, 14
Hume, David 62
Ḥunain ibn Isḥāq 70
Huxley, Thomas 132
Huygens, Christiaan 130
Hyades, Paul 4–6, 9

Ibn Khaldun 88
Ifversen, Jan 83
indirect translation 119–20
individualism (concept of) 92–4
intellectual history 82
intersection 65
intervention 89, 124–9, 131
Israel, Hephzibah 29

Jakobson, Roman 121
Jay, Martin 82
Jerome (Hieronymus, Eusebius Sophronius) 46
Jones, Ernest 124
Jones, Henry 79, 80

Kabalek, Kobi 103, 108
Kansteiner, Wulf 12
Kemp, Lysander 53
Kepler, Johannes 130
Khomeiny, Ruhollah 18
Kim, Kyung-Hye 92–3
Kittel, Harald 31
Kleinman, Sylvie 59
Koselleck, Reinhart ix, 19–20, 81–7, 92, 93, 96, 139
Krishnamurthy, Ramesh 34
Krotoa 57
Kujamäki, Pekka 29
Kuznetsov, Anatoli 112

Lafarga, Francisco 36, 46
La Fontaine, Jean de 40
Landsberg, Alison 107
Lane, Edward 38–41
Langalibalele 56, 58
Lang, Birgit viii
Lässig, Simone 66
Latour, Bruno 66, 67
Law, John 66, 67
Lemon, M. C. 9, 15
Leonhard, Jörn 87–8, 91, 96
León-Portilla, Miguel 53
Le Roy Ladurie, Emmanuel 54, 55, 57
Levý, Jiří 13, 125
Lewis, Nicholas 64
Lewis, Oscar 53, 54
Lianeri, Alexandra 79, 82, 88
Liang Qichao 96, 132–5
liberalism (concept of) 87–8, 96
liberty (concept of) 91–2
Lin Shu 130–3, 135
Lin Zexu 94
Littau, Karin 43
Littmann, Enno 39, 40
Liu, Lydia 28, 88, 89, 92, 94–5, 133
Long Le-Khac 72–3
longue durée 54, 70
Lung, Rachel 57, 58, 60, 134, 136
Luo Wenyan 74
Luther, Martin 123

Macartney, George 94
MacNeice, Louis 122
Madgett, Nicholas 59
Magnússon, Sigurður Gylfi 55, 57–9, 74
Maitland, Sarah 117
Mak Kam Wah (George) 3
Malena, Anne viii

Manouvrier, Léonce 7
Mantoux, Paul 70–1
Mardrus, J. C. 39, 40
Marsh, John William 3, 4
Martin, Alison 68
Martin, J. R. 127
Martin, W.A.P. 60
Masson, Jean-Yves 36
McElduff, Siobhán 44
McQueen, Steve 107
Meintjes, Libby 123
memory x, 100–12; *see also* collective
　　memory; communicative memory;
　　countermemory; cultural memory;
　　deep memory; diasporic memory;
　　multidirectional memory; personal
　　memory; prosthetic memory;
　　sites of memory; transcultural
　　(or transnational) memory
Menocchio 55, 58
methodological nationalism 61, 104
microhistory ix, 38, 54–60; *see also* global
　　microhistory
Mill, John Stuart 91–2
Milton, John 81
Mink, Louis 10, 22
minority history 53
Mish, John 130
Monod, Gabriel 12
Montgomery, Scott 41–2, 44, 70, 130
Moretti, Franco 72–3
Morhange-Bégué, Claude 104
Morin, Edgar 106
Morrison, Robert 94
motivation, motive 32, 33, 41
Moyn, Samuel 89–90
Müller, Filip 112
multidirectional memory 106–8
Munday, Jeremy 29, 96
Mungello, David 130
Munslow, Alun 18–19
Murray, Gilbert 122

Nabokov, Vladimir 16
Nakamura Keiu 91–2, 96
Nama, Charles Atangana 34, 36
narrative 7–11, 43, 53, 140; *see also*
　　socio-narrative
narrativism 11–21
national history 38
Neather, Robert 47
New Historicism 57
Newton, Isaac 130

Nicholls, Thomas 119
Nicolaisen, Peter 129
Nora, Pierre 102, 104, 108
Norton, Glyn 45

O'Brien, Sharon 58

Paisley, Fiona 60, 61, 63
Pammachius 46
Park Myoung-Kyu 86
Pegenaute, Luis 36
performative 84–5
Pericles 79
periodisation ix, 34–5, 69
Pernau, Margrit 84, 89, 94, 96
Perrot d'Ablancourt, Nicolas 13
personal memory 100–2, 107
Pirenne, Henri 12, 14
Planudes, Maximus 118
Plato 80
Pocock, J. G. A. 82, 83
polysystems theory 59
positioning 40, 133
Poupaud, Sandra 28
Prakash, Gyan 14
Pratt, Mary Louise 64
premediation 105–6, 108
prosthetic memory 107
Protten, Christian 63
Protten, Rebecca 63, 64
Prunč, Erich 44
pushing-hands 20–1
Pushkin, Alexander 16
Pym, Anthony viii, 16–17, 28, 31, 42, 96,
　　120, 126

Quine, Willard van Orman 121

Rafael, Vicente 28, 88–9
Ranke, Leopold von 14, 122
reality effect 12–13
referential illusion 12–13, 15
reflexivity 65
remediation 104–6
renarration 18, 127
research question 28
retranslation 16, 106, 110, 120
Richter, Julia viii, 28, 29, 32, 33, 41, 128
Richter, Melvin 83, 96
Ricci, Matteo 63, 64, 67
Ricoeur, Paul 116–17, 120, 127
Ridge, Stanley 56, 58
Rigney, Ann 102–4, 107

Rimmon-Kenan, Shlomith 9
Rizzi, Andrea viii
Roberts, Geoffrey 21
Robinson, Douglas 20, 46–7
Rodewald-Grebin, Vivian 128–9
Rodríguez, Ileana 54
Rodway, Stella 109
Roland, Ruth 71
Rothberg, Michael 106–7
Rouch, Jean 106
Roy, Rammohun 62
Rozmyslowicz, Tomasz 120
Rubens, Peter Paul 64
Rundle, Christopher viii, 27, 48, 128
Rushdie, Salman 18
Ryle, Gilbert 56–7

Sabine, Edward 68
Sabine, Elizabeth 68, 123
Sachsenmaier, Dominic 94, 96
Said, Edward 81
Salama-Carr, Myriam 70
Saldanha, Gabriela 58
Sartori, Edward 89–90, 96
Saviano, Roberto 18
Schacker-Mill, Jennifer 41
schematic narrative template 111
Schleiermacher, Friedrich 12, 46
Scott, Walter 110
Scully, Pamela 60, 61, 63
secondary witness 109
Secord, James 5, 6
Seidman, Naomi 108
semantic autonomy 116–17, 120,
    127, 131
semantic nominalism 91
semantic transparency 90–1
Seneca, Lucius Annaeus 121
Sensbach, Jon 63
Sesoienges (*or* Sisanianjiz) 6, 8
Seyssel, Claude de 119
Shakespeare, William 40
Sima Qian 88
Sisanianjiz *see* Sesoienges
sites of memory 102, 108
Skinner, Quentin x, 81, 83–6, 88, 90, 91,
    93, 94, 96, 117, 127, 139
Smiles, Samuel 92
Smit, W. A. P. 124
Smith, Adam 62
socio-narrative 17–18, 127
Soll, Jacob 84
Somers, Margaret 9, 17, 22

sovereignty (concept of) 88–9
speech act theory 84–5, 127
Sperry, Elmer 67
Spiessens, Anneleen 111–12
Standaert, Nicolas 64
Steiner, George 34
Steiner, Riccardo 124
Steinmetz, Willibald 87, 96
Stone, Lawrence 22
Strachey, James 124
Sturge, Kate 128–9, 135
Stuurman, Siep 88
Sullivan, Bartholomew 5, 6
Sullivan, John 59
Sun, Sanjun 28, 72
Swinburne, Algernon 40
Szijártó, István 55, 57–9, 74

tactical reading 127
Tamm, Marek 140
testimony 107–10, 112
thick description 56–7, 59
thick translation 57
Thornber, Karen 64
Thucydides 13, 79, 80
Tolstoy, Leo 11
Tone, Theobald Wolf 59
Torres Simón, Ester 28
total history 54
Tourneur, Cyril 40
Toury, Gideon 90
transcultural history 60, 62–3
transcultural (or transnational)
    memory 104–8
translation culture 44
translation factories 42–4, 120
translation memory 110
translator lexicon 30
transnational conceptual history
    86–90
transnational history ix, 38, 60, 62–3, 65
transparency effect 12
triangulation 117–18
Tribe, Keith 83
Trigault, Nicolas 63–4, 67
Trivedi, Harish 36, 62

Valla, Lorenzo 119
Vande Velde, Jacop 118–19
Van Dam, Harm-Jan 118
Van Gelderen, Martin 82
Van Mander, Karel 124
Van Niekerk, Marlene 123

Veeser, H. Aram 57
Venuti, Lawrence 13, 16–17, 34, 71, 72, 120, 125
Vermeer, Johannes 115
Victoria (Queen) 94
Vidal Claramonte, Carmen-África viii
Vidyasagar, Iswarchandra 62
Virgil (Publius Vergilius Maro) 33, 118
Vondel, Joost van den 33

Wainhouse, Austryn 104
Wakabayashi, Judy viii, 17, 19, 34–7, 48, 72, 74
Waley, Arthur 74
Walpole, Hugh 128
Wang Hsien-Chu 134
Warburg, Aby 100
Weber, Max 96
Weilu 132
Wei Yi 130, 131, 135
Wells, Julia 57–8
Werner, Michael 65, 68
Wertsch, James 103, 110–11
Wheaton, Henry 95, 96, 133
White, Hayden ix, 7, 10–20, 22, 53, 125
White, Peter 127

Wiesel, Elie 108–10, 112
Wiesel, Marion 110
Winters, Marion 112
Wolf, Michaela 30–1, 33, 36, 65
Wong Wang-Chi (Lawrence) 131
world history ix, 60, 69–70
Wright, Chantal 46
Wright, David 134

Xavier, Francis 64
Xin Chen 19
Xu Shou 133, 134
Xu Jianyin 133–4

Yan Fu 132–5
Yang Haiyan 60
yi (Chinese character) 94–6
Yu Sinŏn 57, 58

Zeng Guofan 134
Zeng Zonggong 131
Zhou Xiaoyan 28, 72
Zhu Yifan 92–3
Zimmermann, Bénédicte 65, 68
Zinn, Howard 53
Żywulska, Krystyna 112